MANUAL

tv technical operations

MANUAL

16MM FILM CUTTING
John Burder

BASIC BETACAM AND DVCPRO CAMERAWORK,
SECOND EDITION
Peter Ward

BASIC FILM TECHNIQUE
Ken Daley

BASIC STUDIO DIRECTING
Rod Fairweather

BASIC TV REPORTING, SECOND EDITION
Ivor Yorke

BASIC TV TECHNOLOGY, SECOND EDITION
Robert L. Hartwig

CONTINUITY HANDBOOK FOR SINGLE CAMERA
SHOOTING, THIRD EDITION
Avril Rowlands

FOR TV AND VIDEO, THIRD EDITION
Bernard Wilkie

DIGITAL VIDEO CAMERAWORK
Peter Ward

EFFECTIVE TV PRODUCTION, THIRD EDITION
Gerald Millerson

FILM TECHNOLOGY IN POST PRODUCTION
Dominic Case

GRAMMAR OF THE EDIT
Roy Thompson

GRAMMAR OF THE SHOT
Roy Thompson

LIGHTING FOR VIDEO, THIRD EDITION
Gerald Millerson

LOCAL RADIO JOURNALISM, SECOND EDITION
Paul Chantler and Sim Harris

MOTION PICTURE CAMERA AND LIGHTING
EQUIPMENT
David W. Samuelson

MOTION PICTURE CAMERA TECHNIQUES
David W. Samuelson

MULTI-CAMERA CAMERAWORK
Peter Ward

NONLINEAR EDITING
Patrick Morris

SINGLE CAMERA VIDEO PRODUCTION, SECOND
EDITION
Robert B. Musburger

SOUND RECORDING AND REPRODUCTION,
THIRD EDITION
Glyn Alkin

SOUND TECHNIQUES FOR VIDEO AND TV,
SECOND EDITION
Glyn Alkin

THE USE OF MICROPHONES, FOURTH EDITION
Alec Nisbett

VIDEO CAMERA TECHNIQUES, SECOND EDITION
Gerald Millerson

THE VIDEO STUDIO, THIRD EDITION
Alan Bermingham et al.

TV TECHNICAL OPERATIONS
Peter Ward

MANUAL

tv technical operations:

an introduction

peter ward

Focal Press

OXFORD AUCKLAND BOSTON JOHANNESBURG MELBOURNE NEW DELHI

Focal Press
An imprint of Butterworth-Heinemann
Linacre House, Jordan Hill, Oxford OX2 8DP
225 Wildwood Avenue, Woburn, MA 01801-2041
A division of Reed Educational and Professional Publishing Ltd

ℛ A member of the Reed Elsevier plc group

First published 2000

British Library Cataloguing in Publication Data

Ward, Peter, 1936–
  TV Technical operations: an introduction
  1. Television – Production and direction – Handbooks,
  manuals, etc. 2. Video recording – Handbooks, manuals, etc.
  3. Television – Production and direction – Terminology
  4. Television – Production and direction – Vocational guidance
  I. Title
  791.4'5'0232'023

Library of Congress Cataloging in Publication Data

Ward, Peter
  TV Technical operations: an introduction/Peter Ward.
  p. cm.
  Includes bibliographical references.
  ISBN 0–240–51568–4 (alk paper)
  1. Video recording 2. Television – Production and direction. I. Title

  TR850 W3723
  778.59–dc21
                                                                99–088823

ISBN 0 240 51568 4

Typeset by Florence Production Ltd, Stoodleigh, Devon
Printed and bound in Great Britain by Biddles Ltd, www.biddles.co.uk

PLANT A TREE

BTCV
British Trust for
Conservation Volunteers

FOR EVERY TITLE THAT WE PUBLISH, BUTTERWORTH-HEINEMANN
WILL PAY FOR BTCV TO PLANT AND CARE FOR A TREE.

Contents

ACKNOWLEDGEMENTS 7
INTRODUCTION 8

WORKING IN TELEVISION
THE BROADCAST INDUSTRY 10
OCCUPATIONAL SKILLS 12
STAFF AND FREELANCE
  WORK 14
TECHNOLOGY AND
  CONDUCT 16
TEAM WORK 18

TELEVISION PRODUCTION
PROGRAMME PRODUCTION 20
SHOT NUMBER SYSTEM 22
STUDIOS 24
TV PRODUCTION STAFF 26
LOCATION FACILITIES 28
REHEARSAL 30
TRANSMISSION 32

TELEVISION ENGINEERING
LIGHT INTO ELECTRICITY 34
COLOUR 36
THE DIGITAL SIGNAL 38
COMPRESSION 40
CHARGE COUPLED
  DEVICES 42
VISION CONTROL 44
GAMMA AND LINEAR
  MATRIX 46

**MULTI-CAMERA
CAMERAWORK**
INTRODUCTION TO TV
  CAMERAWORK 48
THE ZOOM LENS 50
FOCUS 52
CAMERA CONTROLS 54
CAMERA MOUNTINGS 56
CAMERA TECHNIQUE 58
OPERATIONAL SKILLS 60
CAMERA MOVEMENT 62
PICTURE MAKING SKILLS 64
COMPOSITION 66
INTERCUTTING 68

REHEARSAL 70
TRANSMISSION 1 72
TRANSMISSION 2 74
ROBOTIC CAMERAWORK 76

**AUDIO TECHNICAL
OPERATIONS**
INTRODUCTION TO TV
  SOUND 78
MICROPHONES 80
AUDIO MONITORING 82
AUDIO CONTROL 84
AUDIO RIG 86
RECORDING SOUND 88
AUDIO AND PROGRAMME
  PRODUCTION 90
DIGITAL AUDIO 92
STEREO 94

WORKING ON LOCATION
PREPARATION FOR
  LOCATION 96
OPERATIONAL CHECKS AT
  BASE 98
ROAD CRAFT 100
SAFETY 102
VIDEO RECORDING
  FORMATS 104
WHITE BALANCE 106
EXPOSURE 108
TIME CODE 110
STRUCTURE 112
SHOOTING FOR EDITING 114
INTERVIEWS 116

TELEVISION LIGHTING
THE NATURE OF LIGHT 118
VISUAL PERCEPTION 120
LIGHTING A FACE 122
LIGHTING LEVELS 124
LUMINAIRES 126
CONTROLLING LIGHT 128
STUDIO LIGHTING 130
VISION CONTROL 132
LOCATION LIGHTING 134
LIGHTING AN INTERVIEW 136

EDITING
INTRODUCTION TO EDITING 138
THE TECHNOLOGY OF NEWS
  EDITING 140
INSERT AND ASSEMBLY
  EDITING 142
TIME CODE 144
PERENNIAL EDITING
  TECHNIQUES 146
PERCEPTION AND SHOT
  TRANSITION 148
MATCHING SHOTS 150
BASIC EDITING PRINCIPLES 152
TYPES OF EDIT 154
FACT OR FICTION? 156
TELLING A STORY 158
STRUCTURING A SEQUENCE 160
FACTUAL EDITING 162
INTERVIEWS 164
CUTTING ON MOVEMENT 166
DOCUMENTARY 168

VISION MIXING
INTRODUCTION TO VISION
  MIXING 170
VISION MIXING
  TECHNOLOGY 172
VISUAL TRANSITIONS 174
VISION MIXING
  TECHNIQUES 176

INTERVIEWS 178
PRODUCTION METHODS 180
OPENING AND CLOSING 182
MAGAZINE FORMAT 184
TV DEMONSTRATION 186
MUSIC COVERAGE 188
CHROMA KEY 190
MIXER FACILITIES 192
FRAME STORE 194
CHARACTER GENERATORS 196
IN REHEARSAL 198
WORKING WITH THE
  DIRECTOR 200
TRANSMISSION 202

**NEWS AND MAGAZINE
ITEMS**
TV JOURNALISM 204
OBJECTIVITY 206
MAGAZINE ITEMS 208
CONDENSING TIME 210
STRUCTURE 212
ENGAGING THE AUDIENCE 214
INTERVIEWS 216
SNG 218

FURTHER READING 220

GLOSSARY ???

Acknowledgements

The author wishes to acknowledge the help and assistance in compiling this manual from many television colleagues and equipment manufacturers. In particular, Alan Bermingham for his help on the section on lighting, Chris Wherry for photographs and his help on the section on sound, Allison Chapman, Anton/Bauer Inc., Avid Technology, Cannon (UK) Ltd, JVC, OpTex, Panasonic, Sony Corporation, Thomson Broadcast Systems, Vinten Broadcast Ltd. Diagrams reprinted from Focal Press manuals include *The Video Studio*, A. Bermingham, M. Talbot-Smith, Ken Angola-Stephens and Ed Boyce; *Sound and Recording: An Introduction* Francis Rumsey and Tim McCormick; *The Gaffer's Handbook*, Harry C. Box, edited by Brian Fitt. My thanks for their help and co-operation, especially to Arthur Attenborough for his close interest in the project.

Introduction

Although the broadcasting industry covers a wide range of video productions, they all share certain basic techniques and require similar craft skills. This Media Manual on television technical operations is written as an introduction for young people entering the broadcast industry. The aim of the manual is to prepare them for working in mainstream television by discussing work attitudes as well as technique and technology, outlining:

- the need to develop a professional approach
- the need to develop the occupational skills needed to meet deadlines, work under pressure, and within budget
- the importance of understanding the potential of broadcast equipment in programme making, and the need to keep up-to-date with technique and technology
- the individual responsibility to ensure continuity of experience and training in all craft skills that technical operators are required to work in
- the need to maintain a critical appraisal of what and who influences their working practices, and how these influences affect production and viewers
- an introduction to the basic skills needed to work as a technical operator in television
- an introduction to broadcast equipment in general production use.

Broadcasting is always in the process of change. New technology, new production techniques, new methods of delivering the programme to the viewer are constantly introduced. Innovation and change have been the lifeblood of an industry created less than seventy years ago. To an understanding of technique and of how technology influences technique must be added the knowledge of programme making formats. A production team will expect each member of the unit to be fully familiar with the customary techniques of the programme format in production. Nobody, for example, will have the time to explain the rules of a sport that is being transmitted live. They will assume that the technical operator knows the standard TV response to different phases of the event.

This manual will concentrate on techniques associated with news and magazine programme production where most technical operators are usually employed, but most techniques are shared across the whole spectrum of television and film making.

There is a great deal of specialized jargon and technical terms used in programme production. Many of these terms are explained at the appropriate point in the text or definitions will be found in the Glossary at the back of the manual. For detailed explanation and more complex description of different aspects of programme production, see *Further reading*, pages 220 and 221.

Note: Through the manual I use terms such as 'cameraman' without wishing to imply that any production craft is restricted to one gender.

'Cameraman' for example is the customary title to describe a job practised by both men and women, and 'he' where it occurs, should be read
as 'he/she'.

The broadcast industry

The term broadcasting is colloquially applied to many types of video production and distribution such as:

■ terrestrial, satellite and cable networks
■ video production
■ corporate
■ education and training
■ video support units for organizations such as the police, fire, military and search and rescue services, etc.

With such a wide diversity of production objectives, there is obviously a wide range of techniques, yet they all share certain common techniques.

One essential shared characteristic is the need to communicate with word and picture. Whether the aim of a video is to sell a product, explain a technique or to entertain, the basic requirement is to find the appropriate method of presentation to suit the aim of the production. Telling a story through word and picture has a long history and the basis of any video communication can be simplified to the formula – what does the audience need to know, in what order and at what point in the production should they be told, and are the production methods employed adequate to fulfil these objectives.

A new entrant to the industry will be required to understand a range of customary techniques, to work to a set professional practices and develop a range of skills. Learning the ropes of a complex and diverse industry takes time. The first requirement is to recognize the need for training and to avoid trying to bluff your way through unfamiliar production methods without advice or instruction.

Industrial process – an industry
The audio/visual industry has a huge international turnover. For many millions of people, television is the prime means, and often the only choice of entertainment. Such a potentially profitable product requires tight budgetary control and efficient methods of production. Looking at the complexity of constructing a high rise building, it is self-evident that a number of specialist skills are required to complete the building on time, to a budget, and provide a structure that is safe, durable and fit for its intended purpose. Programme production has the same objectives with the need for a similar wide range of skills and expertise. It is easy to make the mistake of imagining that a long familiarity with television viewing provides adequate training to construct programmes. Frequently the mechanics of broadcast television are hidden or disguised by techniques invisible to the viewer. The usual reaction from viewers on observing a programme in production is to be amazed at the complexity and detail that is required. Television production is an industrial process that requires as much study and training as any other manufacturing process.

Rigging an outside broadcast camera.

Occupational skills

There are many separate craft skills that are required in video production. Each craft has a number of specialist abilities but all of the core skills of programme production share a knowledge of general programme making.

It is essential to be acquainted with the customary technique of different programme genres as well as having technical expertise and operational competence.

This shared body of expertise includes:

- The ability to work under pressure to a tight schedule leading to a recording or transmission. The ability to prepare, anticipate and concentrate as an individual whilst working as part of a coordinated team effort.
- The need to develop and expand craft skills and a complete understanding of the technology utilized for that craft.
- The ability to work in a team. Many people are under the misapprehension that being difficult is an expression of artistic and creative temperament. By all means strive to achieve excellence but not at the expense of causing everyone around you difficulties by your tantrums. Enthusiasm and friendliness will get repeat work – develop your 'people skills'. In television production you will always need the cooperation and support of your colleagues. Avoid copying role models who display cynicism and contempt for their colleagues and their job.
- As well as being skilled at your chosen craft, personal qualities such as being resourceful and persistent, self-motivated, self-reliant with quick reactions, maintaining enthusiasm even for routine familiar programmes, displaying patience and tact in stressful situations (there are many in television), and keeping in good health, are equally important.
- Multi-skilling is being flexible in approach, but more importantly, having a wide range of techniques and a knowledge of a variety of production skills. Television often works to a tight timetable and budget. Each member of the production team is expected to be competent and capable in the job they are undertaking.

Most television crafts involve making quick decisions, coordinating hand and eye and being aware of other craft activity around you. With such a practical profession, the four golden virtues most practised are preparation, anticipation, concentration and objectivity.

■ **Preparation** is essential for any operational activity controlled by time. Everyone in a production team must know what their role is, whether in a single twenty-five second shot or in a twenty-five minute continuous programme.

■ **Anticipation** avoids being surprised by events and therefore allows time to be created in order to deal with the unrehearsed or the unexpected.

■ **Concentration** on the job in hand focuses the mind and allows clarity of action.

■ **Objectivity** is necessary to avoid passing value judgements on the programme in production. The highest obtainable standards of technique should be applied whether you, individually, think the content is good, bad or indifferent.

Staff and freelance work

Advantages and disadvantages
If you start you career as a staff member of a large broadcasting organization you will probably receive support in training and instruction plus the advantage of continuity of employment and work experience. With a really large company you will probably be working with top-of-the-line equipment and have engineering support and spares when things go wrong. There is usually transport and overnight allowances for location work and free insurance, paid holidays, paid sick leave and a pension. Some of these advantages may have little appeal to someone who is metaphorically breaking-a-leg just to get behind a camera and work in the wonderful world of television. As a freelance, if do you actually break a leg, paid sick leave and a job to come back to when you are fit begins to have practical significance.

The downside of staff working is you may be stuck with a narrow range of routine programmes with little or no chance to develop creative abilities. The organization's priority is for efficient allocation of staff which usually means long and irregular hours with little or no choice of programme content, or control of social arrangements. A 'company' man hands over the management of his/her time to the needs of the organization.

A halfway stage between staff and freelance status is the contract, or a retainer guaranteeing so many days work. Some of the staff advantages are shared but there is the opportunity to move on to more fulfilling work (if it is available), at the time of your choice. Unfortunately, only a small percentage of freelancers can be selective in their choice of work. It is almost an eleventh commandment that a freelance never turns down work if he/she is available. Networking, having a broad range of contacts and being known to as many independent production companies as possible is one way of ensuring continuity of work; but it is no guarantee, and freelance working can be just as restrictive and routine as some types of staff work. Working in the television industry is enormously attractive to many people leaving college or school. Competition is intense for the very few companies that offer training. Failure to gain access to a trainee job leaves many people no alternative but to seek work as freelancers.

The business requirements for a freelance
A freelancer is a one man/woman self-employed business. To succeed it requires the business ability to organize work, tax, insurance, purchase of equipment as in other one-man businesses. In addition, television freelancers need a broad range of skills and the ability to sell themselves. With thousands upon thousands of young hopefuls attempting to get a toe-hold in the broadcast industry, it is definitely a buyer's market and a freelancer must have a wide range of skills and qualities to attract a buyer – and to get repeat orders.

When contemplating working as a freelancer, points to consider are:

- **Equipment:** There are as many types of freelance work as there are methods of video production. A very rough classification is freelance work using an employee's equipment and freelancers using their own equipment or hired-in equipment.

- **Owning equipment:** The main reason for owning your own equipment is control. It may take about three months to come to terms with a new format camera, for example, in order to fully exploit its potential. During that time, your own equipment can be customized to suit your particular area of work. Equipment hired for the day requires a wide range of experience of TV technology in order to quickly provide a competent service. Many programmes cannot budget for 'familiarization' time or tolerate incompetence with unknown equipment. In freelancing, your reputation is as good as your last job. It is essential that you are fast, efficient and reliable.

- **Leasing equipment:** Owning your own equipment is expensive and there is always the problem of when to re-equip with new technology and how to finance the purchase. This cost must be passed on to your 'clients' but it could make your daily rates uncompetitive. Leasing equipment or long term hire is another option. This allows you to pay for the use but not the ownership of the equipment. This avoids the expense of replacing redundant equipment but consistent employment will be needed to service a large monthly payment. Bear in mind that if you purchase or lease equipment, the cost of ownership is not just the lease payments, but the cost of service and maintenance

- **Suitable equipment:** Buy or lease the equipment that is suitable for your intended area of work. Decide where your market is and what equipment is required, e.g. do not buy a top-of-the-range camera for competitively priced wedding videos.

- **New or secondhand:** Decide if you need to buy new or is there second-hand stock that will be suitable for your intended use. If you buy secondhand get it checked by someone other than the seller.

- **Maintenance:** When you have bought the gear, look after it. Keep it clean, and serviceable. Use a qualified maintenance engineer if routine servicing is beyond your competence (e.g. head replacement in a camera). Just like a car, a camera will have an hourly running cost which needs to be taken into account when costing invoices.

- **Insurance:** Similar to car insurance, 'all risks' policies can include electrical or mechanical breakdown which can take effect once the manufacturer's guarantee has expired. Other insurable assets to consider are normal office contents, computers, mobile telephone, lap tops, and of course, cars. There are also earnings protection insurance policies against equipment failure, illness or accident, and public liability policies protecting your liability to third parties for bodily injury or damage to their property arising out of the work that you do. Employer's liability is obviously your liability to persons whom you employ and in the UK, that is a compulsory requirement under the terms of the Employers Liability Compulsory Insurance Act. Finally, you may also be liable for covering hired equipment.

- **Finding work:** Freelancers sell themselves, their skills and their approach to the job. To get employment opportunities you have to go and see people. Who do you contact? Asking other freelancers for an introduction may not produce results. Most freelancers will not recommend another technician unless they have previously worked with them. For a commission, agencies may find you work or act as an answering service for a monthly fee, but the reputable ones will need to establish your competence before recommending you to a client. It is unfortunate fact of life that you need experience to get work, but you need work to get experience.

- **Accountants:** An accountant can help you with the Inland Revenue and working as a freelancer. In the UK you may need to register for VAT and the Department of Social Security for self-employed stamps.

Technology and conduct

Technology and technique intertwine. How you do something in broadcasting depends on what equipment you are using. It is not simply a question of being told which button to press in order to get a professional result. In television camerawork, for example, an understanding of camera technology plus the ability to exploit and take into consideration the attributes of the camera and the lens characteristics are the basis of practical programme production. Although television and film production can only be created with technology, there seems to be a growing trend to ignore the mechanics and simply trust auto-technique features. Most equipment is now wrapped up with auto features in the hope of being user-friendly to technophobic customers, but technical operators must aim to understand what is happening when they are operating equipment rather than passively pressing a button and hoping the equipment 'will do the rest'.

Keeping up to date
One of the enduring characteristics of television broadcasting is that it is in a continuous state of change. New equipment, new techniques, new broadcasting outlets are introduced almost annually. Each change in technology requires evaluation in order to understand how it can be exploited in production. Keeping up with change is a crucial requirement, otherwise your skills will be as redundant as old equipment.

Working in a mass medium
Television is the most popular form of mass entertainment world wide and can exert an enormous influence on its audience. Everyone working in programme production has to take this into account when considering how their particular contribution can affect the audience.

On 11 May 1985, an outside broadcast unit was covering a football match in the north of England when a crowded stand caught fire. The match was abandoned as thousands of people struggled to leave the stadium. One cameraman close to the blaze managed to escape, other cameramen on the opposite side of the pitch turned their cameras on to the stand and became instantly 'news' cameramen. At first, no one knew the full horror of the situation but it became apparent as bodies were carried on to the pitch that many people had been killed. On realizing what was happening, some football fans turned their anger onto the TV cameraman and pelted them with missiles shouting 'ghouls – turn the cameras off'. The pictures the cameramen produced were seen world wide and alerted many people to the dangers of stadium fires and provoked changes in stadium design. Television is not the glitzy, glamourous business many newcomers to the industry imagine it to be and many people in their working career will face just as hard an ethical and professional decision as the cameraman covering that particular football match.

Professional conduct

As well as the qualities already discussed, there are many important aspects of being a television professional that are sometimes overlooked.

Timekeeping

The transmission of television programmes are timed to the second. A train can be delayed for five minutes and affect hundreds. A television programme delayed for five minutes can affect millions and have a knock-on effect for the rest of an evening's schedule. Every member of the cast and crew is vital to the success of the production and their timekeeping should be as precise as the running time of the programme.

Make certain, as a courtesy to your colleagues and to the efficiency of the production, that you are always ready to begin rehearsal, recording or transmission at the required time. There are often large numbers of cast and crew involved in a production and your arrival two minutes late can keep every one of them waiting.

Chatting to the artistes

Most front-of-camera people appreciate a friendly crew to modify a working atmosphere that often appears cold, technical and high pressure. Before a recording or transmission a presenter may be mentally running through his or her lines and moves and preparing for their performance. Avoid trying to engage them in informal talk which may distract and disturb their concentration at this crucial time.

Transmission lights

Check the warning lights above doors leading to operational areas and *do not enter* if a red or amber light is flashing or is on. This means the area is engaged in a transmission or recording. Wait for a blue light signifying the area is in rehearsal or line-up before entering. Check with the appropriate person (floor manager or stage manager, etc.) that your presence will not disrupt the rehearsal/recording.

Working in front of an audience

Wear appropriate clothing for the programme format. For example, a church service is a solemn act of worship and people may easily be offended if a technician appears to show disrespect for their beliefs by lounging around the church in jeans and sweat shirt. At formal events you may be required by the production company to wear formal clothes. At pop shoots and concerts you may appear conspicuous if you are not wearing informal clothes.

As well as appropriate dress, remember that the audience is there to watch the performance. If their attention is distracted by your behaviour their reaction and response to the programme will be diminished. As well as practising an invisible visual technique, try to be inconspicuous when working in front of an audience and, whenever it is possible, move out of their sightline to the performers.

Team work

Working as a team

The individual skills of many crafts combine to work together under the guidance of the director to transmit or record a programme. In live television, once a transmission (and sometimes a recording) has started there is no opportunity to stop and sort out production problems or make substantial alterations to the camera coverage of the programme. The basic requirement of live television is to get it right first time – there are no retakes.

With single camera location production, the priorities are different, but the same need for collaborative team work exists. The pressures of budget, time and distance require speed of application and the tight discipline of a close-knit unit. Without the back-up and facilities of base staff, and often working with hired-in, unfamiliar equipment, a small location crew need all the mutual assistance and support each member of the unit can offer.

Production team

Live and recorded 'as live' production methods rely on every member of the production team perfecting their input into the programme at the moment of transmission. All the different skills employed – performance, lighting, sound, vision control, vision mixing – interact, and the quality of the production is only as good as the weakest contribution. If one member of the team is badly prepared or lacks sufficient experience to resolve production problems, their incompetence will eventually affect the rest of the production team. The speed of multi-camera productions relies on everyone getting it right, first time.

Everyone wants to work and achieve the highest possible standards in their particular craft area, but television production is a group effort and good television techniques are working practices that enable other crafts to achieve a high standard of performance as well as the individual.

Perfect sound may be provided by a boom position that inhibits camera movement or a microphone position that casts shadows and intrudes into the shot. This may be perfect sound but it is bad television production sound. A shot that is composed with so much headroom that there is no space for the boom microphone to get close to the performers may be a great shot in isolation but it is also bad television production practice.

An awareness of the day-to-day problems of the other skills within the production team and a willingness to reach a compromise on one's own production demands will improve the quality of the whole programme. Monopolizing rehearsal time to get your particular problems sorted out may possibly prevent someone else resolving their difficulties.

Your contribution to the team effort is by:

- Being competent in your own job. This helps other craft skills to do theirs because they are not wrong footed by your operational errors and misjudgements.
- Being consistent in operational technique and reproducing accurately on transmission any part of the programme that was pre-rehearsed.
- Having an understanding and a respect for other people's skills and being willing to adjust your work to help resolve their production problems.
- Having a willingness to compromise from the ideal coupled with the judgement to assess the minimum standards that are acceptable.

Programme production

A video camera produces an electronic picture which can be transmitted and displayed on a TV set instantaneously; it requires no 'processing'. This is called live television. As an event happens, so it can be seen. Multi-camera production technique uses a number of cameras which are switched to in turn to show different viewpoints of an event. This production method allows the material to be transmitted as it occurs or to be recorded for future transmission. If it is recorded then the material can be edited before transmission. Single-camera coverage is usually recorded and the material receives extensive editing before transmission. This is similar to the film technique where one shot is recorded and then the single camera moved to another position or location to record another shot. The shots can be recorded out of sequence from their subsequent edited order. This type of production method is very flexible but does require more time in acquiring the material and in editing.

Pictures are nearly always accompanied by audio, either actual speech, music, or effects of the subject in shot, or sound is added in post-production. The old cliché that television is a visual medium is a half truth. In nearly every circumstance, the viewer wants to hear, as well as see, what is transmitted. Pictures may have a greater initial impact, but sound frequently adds atmosphere, emotion, and space to the image.

Planning a production

Every programme involves some type of advance planning. A two-minute news bulletin, broadcast four or five times a day, with a news reader reading straight to camera, will need scheduling of resources and people. It will require the news to be collected and scripted, for the presenter to have access to make-up, the studio facility to be booked and toohnicians to be scheduled to control the studio facilities. More complex programmes require a longer planning period, and a standard procedure to inform and involve all the diverse crafts and skills needed to mount the programme.

Two types of programming

Programmes can be roughly divided into those that have a content that has been conceived and devised for television and those programmes with a content that cannot be preplanned, or are events that take place independent of television coverage. Many programmes have a mixture of both types of content. If it is scripted for television, then the production is under the direct control of the production team who can arrange the content as they wish. The time scale of what happens on the screen is under their supervision and can be started and stopped as required. If it is an event that would happen independent of TV such as a sports event, then the production team will have to make arrangements to cover the event as it unfolds in its own time scale.

Programme planning – flow chart

- programme idea
- idea is commissioned/budget agreed
- research and script
- contract technical staff/performers
- detailed planning/design/rehearsals
- camera script/running order
- planning meetings/recces
- book facilities
- schedules and call sheets
- set and light studio or location
- rehearsal
- record or transmit
- post production
- transmission
- audience research and feedback

Planning for the unpredictable

There are many events covered by TV that contain unpredictable action which cannot be rehearsed such as sport, discussion programmes and other ad lib activities. No one knows when a goal is going to be scored in a football match or how the run of play will develop, but the TV camera deployment must provide for any of the normal eventualities in a match to be covered. Planning for this requires predicting potential incidents and having cameras assigned to capture such eventualities.

From the initial commissioned idea some form of script or, possibly to begin with, a rough 'running order' of the contents of the programme will be structured. The running order identifies individual sequences in the programme, what the sequences will contain, the vision and sound sources utilized and the duration of each item.

The next stage of the planning involves preparing a script and deciding on design requirements. The flow chart of decisions to be made before recording or transmission day depends on the programme format. Scenery needs to be built, scripts written, artistes contracted or programme guests contacted, technical facilities booked and pre-recorded inserts arranged and edited prior to the recording/transmission day. A regular weekly series will have a production planning formula which fits the turnaround time between each programme. It will also have some future projects in production.

Depending on the complexity of the programme, there will be planning meetings and/or recces if it is a location production with engineering managers, lighting directors, camera supervisors, sound supervisors and all other members of the production team who need advance information in order to plan for the programme.

Shot number system

For many programmes, a camera script will be prepared which breaks down the programme into sections or scenes, and then further subdivides any significant action into separately numbered shots which are assigned to specific cameras. This camera script is usually modified in rehearsal, but allows a reference point for all concerned in the production. The production assistant calls each shot number as they are taken during rehearsal and transmission/recording, and the director reminds everyone on talkback of any significant action/event that will occur. The shot number system binds together a whole range of different production activities from lighting changes, to equipment repositioning, scenery changes and vision mixing. It is not simply a structure for cameramen.

The shot number system provides for the most detailed planning and production precision in, for example, the camera coverage of an orchestral concert where the shots are directly linked to the orchestral score. The score is followed by the director, vision mixer and production assistant and each shot is cut to at a predetermined point in the score. But multi-camera coverage can use a mixture of other techniques including:

■ Some sequences of the production are shot numbered but other sequences are 'as-directed' (i.e. they are not pre-rehearsed). In this method of camera coverage, the director will identify what shots are required on each camera during the transmission or recording.

■ Cameras are assigned a role in a structured sequence of shots. For example, a game show where each sequence of the quiz or game will have a defined structure, but the order of the shots will depend on the progress of the game, e.g. if 'A' answers Camera 2 will be used. If 'B' answers then Camera 3 will be used, etc. This is the most common technique in covering group discussions.

■ Cameras are assigned a role (e.g. football coverage – one camera holds a wide shot, one camera is close, one camera picks up 'personality' shots, one camera for slo-mo replay, etc.). With this system, cameras stick to their 'role' and do not attempt to offer additional shots unless directed.

■ Cameras are assigned a role for part of the event. For example, a state occasion where a camera position allows unique coverage of a location – a section of a street through which the procession will pass – but is subsequently available to pick up other shots to reflect the atmosphere of the event.

■ An as-directed shoot such as a pop concert, where some cameras concentrate on lead singers, instrumentalist, etc., and other cameras are on wide shots and audience.

■ All cameras are isoed (i.e. they are individually recorded) and then edited together in post production. This technique is more likely to occur using PSC (portable single cameras).

371	1 A _____	Oh ah. /
	MS DEREK	

```
371   1 A_____   Oh ah.  /
      MS DEREK
                                     DEREK:
      ┌─────────────────┐
      │ 3 TIGHTEN FAST  │           I can't see 'em issuing every
      └─────────────────┘
                                     householder with a gun, Michael.

                                     MIKE:
372   3_____     It's coming, I tell you./ That's how
      MS MIKE
                                     they're going to save money on the
      ┌──────────────────┐
      │ 1A LOOSEN FAST   │           Police.  Just give everybody a gun,
      └──────────────────┘
                                     say look after yourself.  Twenty

373   2 A_____     years from now./ Mark my words.
      2/S MAUD/MAUREEN (REACTION)
374   3_____/     Burglar?  Never mind nine nine nine.
      MS MIKE
375   1 A_____      Big Bang/and have done.  I'm up for
      2/S DEREK/MAVIS (REACTION)
376   3_____      it./ And...And I'd have a law where
      MS MIKE
                                     the burglar's family'd have to pay

377   2 A_____      for cleaning the carpet./
      2/S A/B
      HOLD MAUREEN'S RISE ROF
                                     MAUREEN IS SITTING WITH MAUD AT A
      CLEAR 1 TO POS B               TABLE WITHIN EARSHOT.  SUDDENLY SHE
                                     INTERRUPTS THEM.
```

Shot numbers

Normally a script is divided into segments and itemized as shots. Any other change of visual source including VTR and electronic graphics is also assigned a shot number. The shot numbers are continuous and if during rehearsal an extra shot is added then it is given the previous shot number with an alphabet suffix (32 then new shot 32a followed by a second new shot 32b and so forth). This avoids renumbering the whole script.

If the programme contains 'as-directed' sequences such as a discussion then each camera will be given an indication on their individual cards such as 2 shot, MS, MCU, etc., followed by 'intercut' or 'as directed'.

Shot description

Shot descriptions are abbreviated as much as possible so that the information can be quickly scanned. In a complex show with many shot changes in a fast cutting sequence, the cameraman may have the briefest time to look away from the viewfinder to check the next shot and camera position.

Studios

A television studio equipped to mount live and recorded multi-camera productions usually contains three main areas: the studio floor area, the control rooms and a series of production rooms.

The studio floor area

The studio floor surface needs to be absolutely level and free from bumps, cracks or unevenness. One of the basic needs of multi-camera work is to move the camera 'on-shot' smoothly and quietly without the use of tracks or boards. If the floor surface cannot accommodate camera movement 'on-shot' then it is unsuitable for the production of continuous multi-camera programme making.

Access for scenery is through large double doors. There must be sufficient grid height overhead to accommodate a cyclorama, a 16ft+ cloth that is stretched taut in an arc around one, two or three sides of the studio to provide a lit backing. Suspended from the grid are lighting hoists that can be lowered for rigging lamps and individually routed to a numbered input into the lighting console. Access to the grid area is often required for rigging lamps, monitors, speakers and suspended scenery. Electrical driven hoists are used to suspend scenery and for flying in scenery pieces. Other hoists may be available for audience monitors and speakers or simply to liberate more floor space.

The studio walls are usually acoustically treated to improve the sound handling qualities. Installed at strategic positions along the studio walls are the technical facilities commonly called wall boxes. Monitors, microphones, foldback-loudspeakers, technical mains, and talkback can be plugged into these boxes to provide flexibility in technical rigging depending on the production layout. Positioned on the studio wall may be outlets for water, gas, etc. for production purposes. Studios require air-conditioning to extract the heat generated by the lamps and a 'house' lighting system, (plus emergency lights), when studio lamps are not switched on for rigging and de-rigging. Fire alarms and fire lanes are required to provide an unimpeded route for audiences and production staff to the fire exits.

Control rooms

Away from the studio floor area are the production control rooms. If they are sited above the floor level, there is often quick access via stairs straight on to the studio floor. The main studio production control room contains a vision mixing panel, a talkback system and communications to other technical areas, possibly a caption generator for in-vision text and possibly the control system of the prompter device. All the equipment is housed in a long customized desk facing a bank of preview picture monitors displaying each video source used in the production.

Control room monitor stack

Some of the preview monitors may be switchable depending on the number of video sources used in the production. These will include each camera's output, VTR, telecine and frame store outputs, any input from an outside broadcast that may be used or other studio inserts, caption generator and electronic graphics output, electronic VTR clock, a special effects output and a 'studio out' monitor displaying the visual source that is selected at the vision mixing panel. Other monitors may provide feeds of programmes currently being transmitted. Prominent on the monitor bank wall will be a large clock plus an indication of the studio status (e.g. blue light 'rehearsal', red light 'transmission').

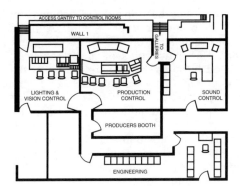

Sound, lighting and vision control

Adjacent to the production control room (commonly called the 'gallery') is the sound control room where the audio inputs to a programme are mixed. Opposite a bank of preview picture monitors and monitoring loudspeakers is a sound desk used to control the level and quality of the audio output. There will also be audio record and replay equipment.

Lighting and vision control usually share the same room and are equipped with preview monitors, a lighting console to control lamp intensity and for grouping lamps for coordinated lighting changes. A diagram of the lamps in use (mimic board), helps the console operator during rehearsal and transmission. Alongside the lighting area is the vision control panel which houses the controls for altering the exposure, black level, colour balance, gain and the gamma of each camera. From this position, the vision control engineer matches each camera's output so that, for example, the skin tones of a face that is in shot on several cameras is the same. If the studio is equipped with robotic cameras, the remote controls may be located on the vision control panel.

Each studio camera has its associated bay of equipment housed in the vision control room or in a technical area adjacent to the control rooms. Vision control also needs communications to other technical areas. Other production facilities used in multi-camera programming are a graphics area which feeds electronic graphics, animations and electronic text to the studio, a technical area where video frame store machines are centrally available and allocated according to production requirements. Half inch VTRs are often located in the production control area.

Two other rooms connected with programme making are the production office, which is the base for the planning and preparation of a programme, and a green room or hospitality room which is used for the reception of programme guests before and after the programme.

Television production staff

On the studio floor the floor manager (FM) relays information from the director during rehearsal and recording/transmission to the front-of-camera artistes, and liaises and coordinates all other technicians working on the studio floor. The FM may have an assistant floor manager (AFM) and/or a floor assistant (FA) working alongside, depending on the nature and complexity of the programme. Camera operators wear headsets to hear the director's instructions. There may be sound technicians on booms positioning a microphone in relation to artiste movement and the lighting design, or they may be rigging and adjusting personal microphones worn by the programme presenters. A prompter operator controls the script text displayed on a television screen attached to the front of the camera. This allows presenters to look straight at the lens while reading scripted links via a mirror reflection of the text monitor. Depending on the studio, the prompt may be controlled from the control room, the studio floor, or another production area. Scene-hands may be needed to reposition furniture and/or scenery during rehearsal and recording/transmission. Electricians working with the lighting director pre-rig and adjust lamps and electrical equipment according to the lighting plot. Other members of the production team such as the designer, make-up supervisor, costume design and wardrobe may be on the studio floor, in the control rooms or working in their own specific areas (e.g., make-up). Additional crafts will augment the basic production team depending on the demands of the programme (e.g., a special effects designer).

Post production
Planning and acquiring the video and audio material is the first stage of programme production. There is often a second stage of post production when the material is edited and audio dubbed (see Editing, pages 138–169).

Other production areas include graphics area where graphic designers provide electronically generated visual material for the programme as well as two dimensional graphics. Usually a central technical area where engineers operate video machines to provide prerecorded inserts into the programme (although VTRs may be run by control room staff), and also to record the programme if required. Often a studio or maintenance engineer will be responsible for the serviceability and line-up of all studio equipment.

In addition to the control room staff (see opposite), these are the basic crafts involved with everyday programme making. Depending on the type of programme, there may be many other specialist staff on the production team such as property master, special effects, unit managers, painters, carpenters, etc. On OB units, riggers drive the OB vehicles, rig cables, lay tracks and track cameras. There is often an overlap of job functions, and a multi-skiller may be required to work in any of these production skills.

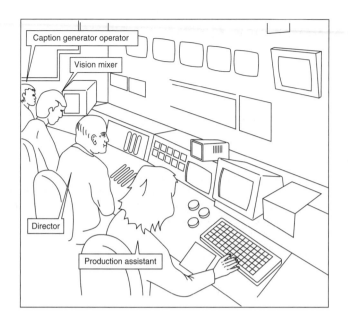

Caption generator operator

Vision mixer

Director

Production assistant

Control room staff

Walk into a control room which is engaged in making a programme and there will usually be a programme director with a script or running order on the desk, talking into a microphone to a number of other production personnel. Talkback – the information from the director and the responses from other members of the crew – is the lifeblood of any multi-camera production. On one side of the director sits the production assistant who works with the director in the preparation of the programme. She times the show, calls the shot numbers and in some broadcast organizations, will cue video machines to replay pre-recorded inserts. On the other side of the director is the vision mixer working from a script and under direction, operating the vision mixing panel switching between cameras and all other vision sources.

Also in the control room there may be a technical coordinator who deals with planning and communications, a producer or editor who, depending on programme formats, will oversee content and running order of items. There may also be a caption generator operator who adds text to the pictures (e.g. name superimpositions abbreviated to 'super').

In the sound control room, the sound supervisor controls the audio and can talk to sound assistants on the studio floor. Possibly there is also a sound assistant playing-in music and effects. In the lighting and vision control room, the lighting director sits with his lighting plot and a console operator at the lighting console and balances the intensity of each lamp in the studio according to the shot and the requirements of the production, and groups the lamps for lighting changes and effects if needed.

A vision control operator, responsible for the exposure and matching the cameras, sits alongside, and may also control robotic cameras. There are usually four adjustable presets on a robotic camera. The variable lens angle can be selected and the pan and tilt head adjusted to frame up a specific shot. These positions, plus an elevation unit on the camera mount to adjust camera height, are stored in a memory bank to be recalled when that specific shot is required.

Location facilities

Outside broadcasting

An outside broadcast (OB) is any multi-camera video format programme or programme insert that is transmitted or recorded outside the studio complex. Most of the equipment permanently installed in a studio complex is required for an outside broadcast. Production, sound, engineering and recording facilities are usually housed in customized vehicles (often referred to as 'scanners'), or as a travelling kit of lightweight, portable vision mixing panels, video tape recorders and associated engineering equipment, sound mixers, etc., housed in cases and reassembled in a suitable area at the location. In general terms, studio productions have more control of setting, staging, programme content than an OB. There is a logistic difficulty in duplicating all these facilities outside the studio, but location recording offers the advantage of complex and actual settings plus the ability to cover a huge range of events that are not specifically staged for television.

OB vehicles

The main OB vehicle houses the control room which serves the same function as a studio control but the equipment and operating areas are designed and compressed to fit a much smaller space. Technical support vehicles are used for transporting cable, sound and camera equipment, monitors, lighting gear, and other production facilities that may be required. In addition there may be a separate VTR vehicle equipped with recording and slow motion machines, etc. For a live transmission, there will be a radio links vehicle or portable equipment which may be a terrestrial or a satellite link or alternatively, a land line that carries the programme back to a base station or transmitter. The number of vehicles on site will increase with the complexity of the programme and the rig. There may be props, scenery, furniture to be delivered to the site. Dressing rooms, make-up and catering may be required.

PSC units

Lightweight cameras combined with a video recorder allow the same flexibility in location production previously enjoyed by film cameras. The techniques developed with this type of video camera and recorder are a mixture of TV and film method. The material can be edited or it can be used live. It uses the technology of video but can use the discontinuous recording methods of film. Whereas live multi-camera television broadcasts often require the separation of operational responsibility, the one-piece camera and recorder can be controlled by one person. To competently employ this video/film hybrid technique, a basic knowledge of video recording, sound, lighting, video editing and TV journalism needs to be developed (see Working on location, pages 96–117).

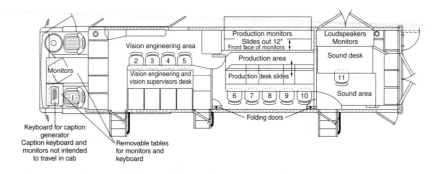

Layout – outside broadcast control room

1 Caption generator operator
2 Vision engineer
3 Vision supervisor
4 Vision engineer
5 Vision engineer
6 Engineering manager
7 Editor/producer
8 Vision mixer
9 Director
10 Production assistant
11 Sound supervisor

Rehearsal

The rehearsal period is structured in a variety of ways depending on the programme.

Blocking or looking at shots allows the whole production team to make the necessary adjustments section by section. The programme is rehearsed shot by shot, stopping each time there is a problem (e.g. unsatisfactory framing, unacceptable sound, unflattering lighting, etc.). During this phase of the rehearsal, shots are established, lighting and sound adjusted. A solution is found or will be found before continuing with the rehearsal. This may be followed by a **run-through** of a particular sequence adding pre-recorded inserts and this gives an indication of the time needed for camera moves, pace of movement and change of shot. Finally, depending on the programme, there may be a full **dress run-through** from opening titles to end credits. This final rehearsal is an attempt to run the programme exactly as it will be transmitted or recorded with no stoppages. The dress run may reveal logistical problems of moving cameras, presenters, scenery, etc. between sequences and all the other craft adjustments that need to be made in continuous camera coverage. Any significant alterations to the production as the result of this rehearsal may be rehearsed again (time permitting) or the production crew will be made aware of any unrehearsed material or shots before the recording or transmission. The rehearsal period should be used to check the production requirements for the *whole* programme. There is no point in having a perfectly rehearsed third of a programme if the remaining two-thirds could not be rehearsed because of lack of time.

Rehearse/record

There are two main methods for recording a programme using multi-cameras:

1 Rehearse a section of the programme and record that section.
2 Rehearse the whole of the programme and then record or transmit the programme 'live'.

To some extent the first method of rehearse/record is efficient in that only small sections are rehearsed and remembered, but it does require a high level of concentration throughout the shooting day because the production is periodically in 'transmission' conditions and sometimes allows insufficient time for all disciplines to get it right.

The second method requires extended rehearsal unless production content is so flexible that coverage is arranged by assigning a role for each camera during the programme (e.g. 'Camera One on a wide shot', 'Camera Two on close-ups', etc.). If content is precisely known (e.g. drama serials/soaps, sitcoms, etc.) then the camera rehearsal will involve working through the programme shot by shot so that everyone associated with the production is aware of what is required.

Invisible technique

There are a number of basic visual conventions used in television production. Many of these standard visual techniques were developed in the early part of the twentieth century when the first film makers had to experiment and invent the grammar of editing, shot-size and the variety of camera movements that are now standard. The ability to find ways of shooting subjects and then editing the shots together without distracting the audience was learnt by the commercial cinema over a number of years. The guiding concept was the need to persuade the audience that they were watching continuous action in 'real' time. This required the mechanics of film-making to be hidden from the audience; that is to be invisible. Invisible technique places the emphasis on the content of the shot rather than production technique in order to achieve a seamless flow of images directing the viewers' attention to the narrative. It allows shot change to be unobtrusive and directs attention to what is contained within the frame and to smoothly move the camera to a new viewpoint without distracting the audience.

'Invisible' technique

- Shots are structured to enable the audience to understand the space, time and logic of the action.
- Each shot follows the line of action to maintain consistent screen direction so that the geography of the action is completely intelligible (e.g. camera positions on a football match). This directs the audience to the content of the production rather than the mechanics of television production.
- Invisible technique creates the illusion that distinct, separate shots (possibly recorded out of sequence and at different times), form part of a *continuous* event witnessed by the audience.

Customary technique

The nature of many programmes (e.g. sport, discussion programmes) does not allow precise information about shots either to be rehearsed or confirmed. Multi-camera production technique relies on the assumption that every member of the production crew is equipped with a knowledge of the conventions of the specific programme format and has a thorough mastery of the basic skills in their particular craft. Information about shots will be supplied during rehearsal and/or during transmission/recording, but it will be assumed by the director that the production staff will respond with customary technique to the specific programme requirements (e.g. matched shots for interviews, see Interviews, p. 116).

Transmission

Pre-transmission checks

On most programmes there is period prior to transmission or recording for a facilities check, an engineering line-up and to establish communications, make-up and costume check for presenters, a 'confidence' brief or running order check by the director to the cast and crew. This period is also used by all crew members to review their individual role in the production and a last chance for staff to query any point on which they are uncertain.

Although it is the director's role to provide all relevant information, it is easy for someone who has worked closely with the programme content for several weeks to assume that other people will know the material as well as themselves. It is up to each member of the production crew to extract the information they require to do their job. If, to solve a problem, you require a production change after the rehearsal has ended, always make the alteration through the director so that everyone in the production team is aware of the change even if you imagine it will have no knock-on effect.

There is often a point in rehearsal where confusion arises and a problem appears insoluble. If you have a bright idea to clear this logjam then make your suggestion, but the production crew should avoid bombarding the director with numerous conflicting ideas. A production that is 'directed from the floor' soon loses coherence and efficiency.

Prior to transmission and recording

The usual procedure is that all the crew and cast will be in position at least five minutes before transmission or recording time or longer if additional rehearsal or briefing is required before transmission/recording. The floor manager checks that everyone is present and that the studio doors are closed or the location is ready. Recording/transmission lights are switched on over any door leading into the studio or production area.

Silence is established and the director will check that each section is standing by before the final thirty seconds is counted to transmission or recording. A VTR identification clock may be run before a recording.

If there has been adequate rehearsal, the recording should provide no problems with the director cueing action and prompting everyone of upcoming events (e.g. 'X is now going to stand up', 'Y is going to move over to the demonstration table'). Any engineering breakdowns or equipment failures will require the director to state clear alternatives to the rehearsed programme. An experienced crew will also mentally anticipate how the breakdown will affect their individual operation. It is usually advisable to be positive in an emergency and stick with the decision.

Light into electricity

The (non) standard TV signal

Converting a three-dimensional moving image into a video signal requires a method of accurately translating light into electricity and then back into an image viewed on a TV monitor. This translation involves adopting a standard signal with a method of synchronization of line and frame repetition at the point of production, transmission and reception/video replay. There are many variables in the way this translation is accomplished:

- The number of lines in the picture and the number of pictures per second in monochrome television broadcasting were historically chosen to be compatible with the frequency of the AC power supply. There were 50 Hz countries and 60 Hz countries and so there arose over time two major scanning standards of 625 line/50 frames per second and 525 line/59.94 frames per second.
- A further division was established with the introduction of colour when different regions of the world chose different colour encoding systems such as NTSC, PAL and SECAM.
- The colour signal can be passed through the production chain either as a composite signal or as a component signal.
- The aspect ratio of the broadcast image (the ratio of the width of the image to its height) added another variable with ratios varying between 4:3, 16:9 and 14:9. Also methods of transmitting film images with other aspect ratios were evolved.
- The conversion of an analogue signal into a digital signal introduced other variables depending on the sampling rate and the degree of compression employed.

There are therefore not one but many 'standard signals' depending on region, production requirements and recording format. Fortunately, a programme originating in one standard can usually be converted into another standard with minimum loss of quality. Conversion between aspect ratios, however, often requires either a compromise on ideal picture framing or viewing conditions or special provision when originating the image.

Subjectivity

Number of lines, interlace and frame rate, transmission system, design of the camera, compression and sampling all affect how accurately the viewer sees the original event. The TV monitor imposes its own restraints. All these factors including resolution, contrast range, colour rendering, etc. are dependent on engineering decisions, budget restraints and statuary control and regulation. The translation between light and electricity is therefore influenced by choice and at each stage of the process, subjective decisions are made. In one sense electronic engineering 'standards' are no more objective than programme production. Most of this manual is concerned with the subjective choices available in video acquisition.

The television scanning system

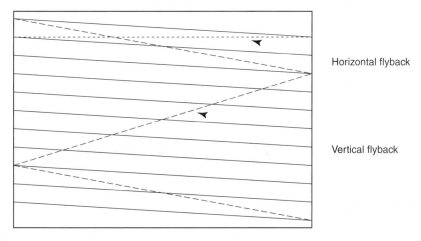

Horizontal flyback

Vertical flyback

The television picture is made up of a series of lines which are transmitted with synchronizing pulses to ensure that the display monitor scans the same area of the image as the camera. In the PAL 625 line system, each of the 25 frames per second is made up of two sets of lines (fields) that interlace and cover different parts of the display. The picture is scanned a line at a time and at the end of each line a new line is started at the left-hand side until the bottom of the picture is reached. In the first field the odd lines are scanned after which the beam returns to scan the even lines. The first field (odd lines) begins with a full line and ends on a half line. The second field (even lines) begins with a half line and ends on a full line.

The television waveform

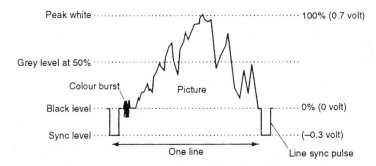

The waveform of the one-volt television signal divides into two parts at black level. Above black, the signal varies depending on the tones in the picture from black (0 V) to peak white (0.7 V). Below black, the signal (which is never seen) is used for synchronizing the start of each line and frame. A colour burst provides the receiver with information to allow colour signal processing.

Colour

How the eye sees colour

There are three colour sensitive receptors in the eye which respond respectively to the primary colours of red, green and blue. All colours are seen by a mixture of signals from the three systems.

Colour television adopts the same principle by using a prism behind the lens to split the light from a scene into three separate channels (see figure opposite). The amplitude of these individual colour signals depends on the actual colour in the televised scene. Colours which are composed of two or more of these primary colours produce proportional signals in each channel. A fourth signal, called the luminance signal, is obtained by combining proportions of the red, green and blue signals. It is this signal which allows compatibility with a monochrome display. The amplitude of the signal at any moment is proportional to the brightness of the particular picture element being scanned.

White balance

In colorimetry it is convenient to think of white being obtained from equal amounts of red, green and blue light. This concept is continued in colour cameras. When exposed to a white surface (neutral scene), the three signals are matched to the green signal to give equal amounts of red, green and blue. This is known as white balance. The actual amounts of red, green and blue light when white is displayed on a colour tube are in the proportion of 30% red lumens, 59% green lumens and 11% blue lumens. Although the eye adapts if the colour temperature illuminating a white subject alters (see topic White balance, page 106), there is no adaption by the camera and the three video amplifiers have to be adjusted to ensure they have unity output.

Colour difference signals

To avoid transmitting three separate red, green and blue signals and therefore trebling the bandwidth required for each TV channel, a method was devised to combine (encode) the colour signals with the luminance signal.

The ability of the eye to see fine detail depends for the most part on differences in luminance in the image and only, to a much smaller extent, on colour contrast. This allows the luminance (Y) information to be transmitted at high definition and the colour information at a lower definition resulting in another saving on bandwidth. Two colour difference signals are obtained, Er (red) – Ey (luminance) and Eb (blue) – Ey (luminance), by electronically subtracting the luminance signal from the output of the red and blue amplifiers. These two colour signals are coded into the luminance signal (Ey) and transmitted as a single, bandwidth-saving signal. Different solutions on how to modulate the colour information has resulted in each country choosing between one of three systems – NTSC, PAL and SECAM.

At the receiver, the signal can be decoded to produce separate red, green, blue and luminance signals necessary for a colour picture.

Light into electricity

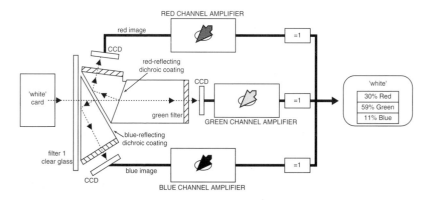

Additive colour

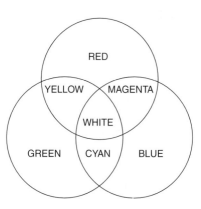

A *composite video signal* is an encoded combined colour signal using one of the coding standards – NTSC, PAL or SECAM. This can be achieved using the luminance (Y) signal and the colour difference signals or red minus luminance ($E_r - E_y$) and blue minus luminance ($E_b - E_y$). The signals are derived from the original red, green and blue sources and are a form of analogue compression.

A *component video signal* is one in which the luminance and the chrominance remain as separate components, i.e. separate Y, R–Y and B–Y signals.

The digital signal

Limitation of analogue signal

The analogue signal can suffer degradation during processing through the signal chain, particularly in multi-generation editing where impairment to the signal is cumulative. By coding the video signal into a digital form, a stream of numbers is produced which change sufficiently often to mimic the analogue continuous signal (see figure opposite).

The digital signal

Whereas an analogue signal is an unbroken voltage variation, a pulse coded modulated (PCM) digital signal is a series of numbers each representing the analogue signal voltage at a specific moment in time. The number of times the analogue signal is measured is called the *sampling rate* or sampling frequency. The value of each measured voltage is converted to a whole number by a process called *quantizing.* These series of whole numbers are recorded or transmitted rather than the waveform itself. The advantage of using whole numbers is they are not prone to drift and the original information in whole numbers is better able to resist unwanted change. The method of quantizing to whole numbers will have an effect on the accuracy of the conversion of the analogue signal to digital. Any sampling rate which is high enough could be used for video, but it is common to make the sampling rate a whole number of the line rate allowing samples to be taken in the same place on every line.

A monochrome digital image would consist of a rectangular array of sampled points of brightness stored as a number. These points are known as picture cells, or more usually abbreviated to *pixels.* The closer the pixels are together, the greater the resolution and the more continuous the image will appear. The greater the number of pixels, the greater the amount of data that will need to be stored, with a corresponding increase in cost. A typical 625/50 frame consists of over a third of a million pixels. A colour image will require three separate values for each pixel representing brightness, hue and saturation for each individual sampled point of the image. These three values can represent red, green and blue elements or colour difference values of luminance, red minus luminance and blue minus luminance. A moving image will require the three values of each pixel to be updated continuously.

Advantages of the digital signal

When a digital recording is copied, the same numbers appear on the copy. It is not a dub, it is a clone. As the copy is indistinguishable from the original there is no generation loss. Digital TV allows an easy interface with computers and becomes a branch of data processing.

Binary counting

8 bit number = byte (contraction of 'by eight')

Binary counting	1	1	1	1	1	1	1	1	=	255_{10}
Decimal counting	128	64	32	16	8	4	2	1	=	255_{10}
Binary number	1	0	0	0	0	0	1	0	=	$128+2 = 130_{10}$
Binary number	1	0	0	0	0	0	1	1	=	$128+2+1 = 131_{10}$
Binary number	1	0	0	0	0	1	0	0	=	?

10 bit number

Binary counting	1	1	1	1	1	1	1	1	1	1	$= 1023_{10}$
Decimal counting	512	256	128	64	32	16	8	4	2	1	$= 1023_{10}$

Analogue to digital

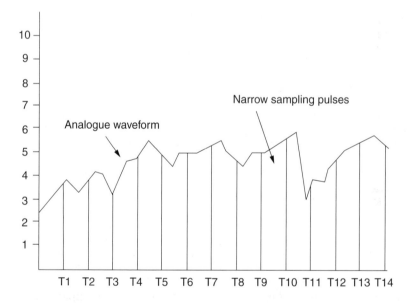

The continuously varying voltage of the TV signal (the analogue signal) is measured (or sampled) at a set number of positions per television line and converted into a stream of numbers (the digital signal) which alters in magnitude in proportion to the original signal.

Storing the signal as binary numbers (ones and zeros) has two advantages. It provides a robust signal that is resistant to noise and distortion and can be restored to its original condition whenever required. Secondly, it enables computer techniques to be applied to the video signal creating numerous opportunities for picture manipulation and to re-order the digital samples for standards conversion.

Compression

Why compression is needed

Compression, data reduction or bit-rate reduction, is the technique of filtering out some of the information that is contained in a digital video signal. By eliminating selected data, the signal can be passed through a channel that has a lower bit rate. The ratio between the source and the channel bit rates is called the compression factor. At the receiving end of the channel a decoder will attempt to restore the compressed signal to near its original range of values. A compressor is designed to recognize and pass on the useful part of the input signal known as the *entropy*. The remaining part of the input signal is called the *redundancy*. It is redundant because the filtered-out information can be predicted from what has already been received by the decoder. If the decoder cannot reconstruct the withheld data, then the signal is incomplete and the compression has degraded the original signal. This may or may not be acceptable when viewing the received image.

What is redundant?

Portions of an image may contain elements that are unchanging from frame to frame (e.g. the background set behind a newsreader). Considerable saving in the amount of data transmitted can be achieved if, on a shot change, all of the image is transmitted and then with each successive frame only that which alters from frame to frame is transmitted. The image can then be reconstructed by the decoder by adding the changing elements of the image to the static or unvarying parts of the image. The degree of compression cannot be so severe that information is lost. For example, even if the newsreader background set is static in the frame, a shadow of the newsreader moving on the background must be preserved even if the shadow is undesirable.

Motion compensation

Passing on only the difference between one picture and the next means that at any instant in time, an image can only be reconstructed by reference to a previous 'complete' picture. Editing such compressed pictures can only occur on a complete frame. If there is significant movement in the frame there will be very little redundancy and therefore very little compression possible. To overcome this problem, motion compensation compression attempts to make even movement information 'redundant' by measuring successive areas of pictures which contain movement and producing motion vectors. These are applied to the object and its predicted new position reconstructed. Any errors are eliminated by comparing the reconstructed movement with the actual movement of the original image. The coder sends the motion vectors and the discrepancies along the channel to the decoder which shifts the previous picture by the vectors and adds the discrepancies to reproduce the next picture. This allows a saving in the amount of data that needs to be transmitted along a channel even with movement.

Ideal compression

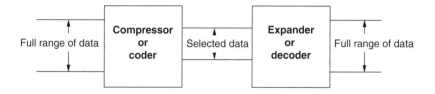

Quantizing

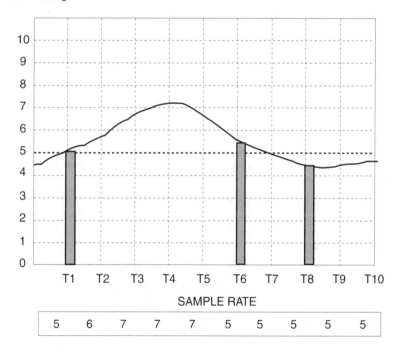

The data stored is transmitted as whole numbers. In the above diagram sample T1 = 5. T6 (although peaking at 5.5) would be stored as 5 and T8 (peaking at 4.5) would also be stored as 5.

■ **Aliasing**: This is caused by the sampling frequency being too low to faithfully reproduce image detail.

■ **Quantizing**: In 8-bit video conversion there are 256 quantizing intervals because that is the number of codes available from an 8-bit number. With 10-bit conversion there are 1024 codes available.

A full frame of digital television sampled according to CCIR 601 requires just under 1 Mbyte of storage (829 kbytes for 625 lines, 701 kbytes for 525 lines).

Charge coupled devices

MOS capacitors

A MOS capacitor (see figure opposite) is a sandwich of a metal electrode insulated by a film of silicon dioxide from a layer of P-type silicon. If a positive voltage is applied to the metal electrode, a low energy well is created close to the interface between the silicon dioxide and the silicon. Any free electrons will be attracted to this well and stored. They can then be moved on to an adjacent cell if a deeper depletion region is created there.

The ability to store a charge is fundamental to the operation of the charge coupled device plus a method of transferring the charge.

Charge coupled device

If a photosensor replaces the top metal electrode, and each picture element (abbreviated to pixel) is grouped to form a large array as the imaging device behind a prism block and lens, we have the basic structure of a CCD camera. Each pixel (between 500 and 800 per picture line) will develop a charge in proportion to the brightness of that part of the image focused onto it. A method is then required to read out the different charges of each of the half a million or so pixels in a scanning order matching the line and frame structure of the originating TV picture. Currently there are three types of sensors in use, differing in the position of their storage area and the method of transfer.

- **Frame transfer:** The first method of transfer developed was the frame transfer (FT) structure. The silicon chip containing the imaging area of pixels is split into two parts. One half is the array of photosensors exposed to the image produced by the lens and a duplicate set of sensors (for charge storage) is masked so that no light (and therefore no build up of charge) can affect it. A charge pattern is created in each picture field which is then rapidly passed vertically to the storage area during vertical blanking. Because the individual pixel charges are passed through other pixels a mechanical shutter is required to cut the light off from the lens during the transfer.

- An important requirement for all types of CCDs is that the noise produced by each sensor must be equivalent, otherwise patterns of noise may be discernible in the darker areas of the picture.

- **Interline transfer:** To eliminate the need for a mechanical shutter, interline transfer (IT) was developed. With this method, the storage cell was placed adjacent to the pick-up pixel, so that during field blanking the charge generated in the photosensor is shifted sideways into the corresponding storage element. The performance of the two types of cell (photosensor and storage) can be optimized for their specific function although there is a reduction in sensitivity because a proportion of the pick-up area forms part of the storage area.

- **Frame interline transfer:** This type of CCD, as its name suggests, incorporates features of both the FT and the IT structures.

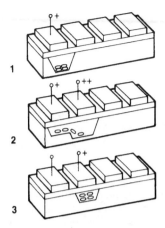

1: After a positive voltage (e.g. 5 V) is applied to the electrode, a low-energy well is created below the oxide/semiconductor surface, attracting free electrons.

2: If 10 V is applied to the adjacent electrode, a deeper low-energy well is created, attracting free electrons which now flow into this deeper bucket.

3: If the voltage on the first electrode is removed and the second electrode voltage is reduced to 5 V, the process can be repeated with the third cell. The charge can be moved along a line of capacitors by a chain of pulses (called a transfer clock) applied to the electrodes.

By replacing the electrode with a light-sensitive substance called a 'photosensor', a charge proportional to the incident light is transferred using the above technique.

The Hyper HAD

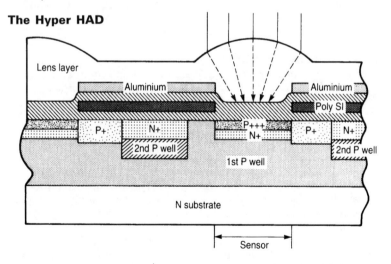

The Hyper HAD has a microlens positioned on each pixel which increases the light-capturing ability of each photosensor area, doubling the camera sensitivity.

Vision control

Camera matching
A basic requirement in multi-camera productions is that there are no mismatches of exposure or colour rendition when cameras are intercut. This is achieved by remotely controlling the aperture (affecting exposure) and colour adjustment of each camera by vision control where the output of each camera is compared, adjusted and matched. Built in ND (neutral density) filters and colour correction filters between lens and CCDs can also be switched in when required.

Iris
The remote control of the lens aperture (iris) on each camera is essential for correct exposure and to match cameras. Although it is possible on many studio programmes to balance lighting levels and therefore work with almost the same aperture on the majority of shots, there are many situations where large variations in lighting levels require constant adjustment of aperture to maintain correct exposure.

Gain (master gain)
The gain of the head amplifiers can be increased if insufficient light is available to adequately expose the picture. The amount of additional gain is calibrated in dBs, (see Glossary for definition of dBs). For example, switching in +6 dB of gain is the equivalent of opening one stop of the lens, which would double the amount of light available to the sensors. The extra gain in amplification is achieved by a corresponding decrease in the signal-to-noise ratio and therefore will increase the noise in the picture.

Black-level adjustment (lift)
The black level in a picture can be adjusted to expand or crush the dark tones in an image. Its 'correct' setting is when black is reproduced as black rather than a dark shade of grey or dark grey is reproduced as black, but adjusting the level of what is reproduced as black can be a decision based on production requirements.

Detail enhancement and skin tone detail
In most video cameras, image enhancement is used to improve picture quality. One technique is to raise the contrast at the dark-to-light and light-to-dark transitions, to make the edges of objects appear sharper, both horizontally and vertically. This is done electronically by overshooting the signal at the transition between different tones to improve the rendering of detail. The degree of electronic manipulation of edge detail is variable but one limiting factor in the amount of enhancement that can be used is the adverse effect on faces. When pictures are 'over-contoured' skin detail can appear intrusive and unnatural; every imperfection is enhanced and becomes noticeable.

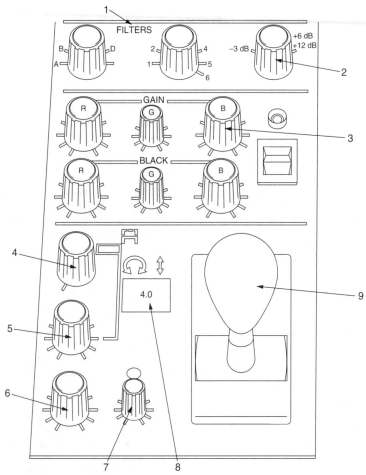

Vision control

This is a typical operational control panel (OCP) for a full-facilities camera.

1. Remote control of filter wheels located between lens and light-splitting system (colour correction, neutral density and effects filters).
2. Master gain control; extra gain is used when operating in low light.
3. Gain and black trims, used for minor adjustment of colour gain and black level when matching pictures.
4. Auto/manual iris control.
5. Detail enhancement.
6. Contrast control, used to modify the 'law', i.e. to stretch/crush appropriate parts of the grey scale.
7. Range control, adjusts the range over which the joystick will operate, and selects the mean aperture.
8. Readout of lens aperture.
9. Joystick, the main operational control, has three functions.
Twist to adjust master black level.
Forward/back to open/close iris.
Depress to switch channel to preview monitor.

Gamma and linear matrix

Gamma

Although there can be considerable image manipulation during production, the picture the viewer will finally see is dependent on the characteristics of their TV set. The cathode ray display tube, however, has certain limitations. The television image is created by a stream of electrons bombarding a phosphor coating on the inside face of the display tube. The rate of change of this beam and therefore the change in picture brightness does not rise linearly, in-step with changes in the signal level corresponding to the changes in the original image brightness variations.

As shown in the Figure 1(a) graph opposite, the beam current, when plotted against the input voltage, rises in an exponential curve. This means that dark parts of the signal will appear on the tube face much darker than they actually are, and bright parts of the signal will appear much brighter than they should be. The overall aim of the television system is to reproduce accurately the original image and therefore some type of correction needs to be introduced to compensate for the non-linear effect of the cathode ray tube beam. The relationship between the input brightness ratios and the output brightness ratios is termed the gamma of the overall system. To achieve a gamma of 1 (i.e. a linear relationship between the original and the displayed image – a straight line in Figure 1b graph) a correcting signal in the camera must be applied to compensate for the distortion created at the display tube. Uncorrected, the gamma exponent of the TV system caused by the display tube characteristics is about 2.4. Thus the camera's gamma to compensate for the non-linearity of the TV system is about 0.44/0.45. This brings an overall gamma of approximately 1.1 (2.4 × 0.45) slightly above a linear relationship to compensate for the effect of the ambient light falling on the viewer's display tube. There is the facility to alter the amount of gamma correction in the camera for production purposes. The application of gamma correction to the signal in the camera also helps to reduce noise in the blacks.

Linear matrix

As detailed in 'Colour' (page 36), all hues in the visible spectrum can be matched by the mixture of the three primary colours, red, green and blue. In the ideal spectrum characteristics of the three primary colours, blue contains a small proportion of red and a small negative proportion of green. Green contains a spectral response of negative proportions of both blue and red. It is not optically possible to produce negative light in the camera but these negative light values cannot be ignored if faithful colour reproduction is to be achieved. The linear matrix circuit in the camera compensates for these values by electronically generating and adding signals corresponding to the negative spectral response to the R, G and B video signals. This circuit is placed before the gamma correction so that compensation does not vary due to the amount of gamma correction.

Gamma correction

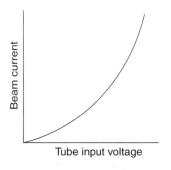

Figure 1a Gamma due to tube characteristic

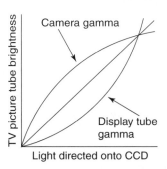

Figure 1b Gamma correction

Linear matrix

		EBU				SKIN	
	RED	GREEN	BLUE		RED	GREEN	BLUE
RED	1.22	−0.18	−0.04		1.1	−0.07	−0.03
GREEN	−0.05	1.11	−0.06		−0.04	1.15	−0.11
BLUE	0	−0.33	1.33		0	−0.2	1.2
		BBC				RAI	
RED	0.89	0.04	−0.15		1.22	−0.18	−0.04
GREEN	−0.1	0.99	0.11		−0.05	1.14	−0.09
BLUE	−0.01	−0.21	1.22		0	−0.18	1

The values chosen for the linear matrix determine the colour relationships and opinions of what the mix of RBG should be varies depending on which images need to be optimally presented by the broadcaster. Usually the broadcast organization chooses the skin tones of presenters as the basis for the choice of matrix values. As the exact value of skin tones differ from country to country, each region has its own preferred rendering of skin-tone values, resulting in large variations among broadcast organizations. Digital cameras have a range of user-selectable possible matrices.

The table show the different colour matrices chosen by the European Broadcast Union, the BBC (UK), RAI (Italy) and a standard camera matrix. The reds in the RAI choice are more brilliantly rendered than those of the others. The BBC matrix tends to produce softer colour rendition, while the EBU matrix is constructed to minimize the objective colour differences between a broad range of colours.

Introduction to TV camerawork

The basic principles of camerawork

There are a number of basic visual conventions used by the majority of cameramen operating broadcast cameras. Many of these standard camera techniques were developed in the early part of the twentieth century when the first film makers had to experiment and invent the grammar of editing, shot-size and the variety of camera movements that are now standard. The guiding concept was the need to persuade the audience that they were watching continuous action in 'real' time. This required the mechanics of film-making to be hidden from the audience; that is to be invisible. Invisible technique places the emphasis on the content of the shot rather than production technique in order to achieve a seamless flow of images directing the viewer's attention to the narrative. It aims for unobtrusive shot change without any visual distraction or discontinuity of image.

A coherent technique

The point of this brief history of visual storytelling is rather than simply committing to memory a list of do's and don'ts about TV camerawork, it is better for you to understand *why* these visual conventions exist. There is a coherent technique behind most TV camerawork. The way a shot is framed up, the way a zoom is carried out, the amount of headroom given to a certain size of shot is not simply a matter of personal taste, although that often affects shot composition; it is also a product of ninety odd years of telling a story in pictures. The development of invisible technique created the majority of these visual conventions. Knowing why a camerawork convention exists is preferable to simply committing to memory a string of instructions. You can then apply the principles of invisible technique whenever you meet up with a new production requirement.

Basic skills

This section of the manual identifies the following skills needed by a cameraman working on a multi-camera production in addition to a knowledge of production methods (see page 20, Programme production):

- **Technology:** an understanding of camera technology, lens characteristics and studio/OB arrangements.
- **Basic skills:** anticipation, preparation and concentration.
- **Operational skills:** basic camera and pedestal operational skills.
- **Picture making skills:** positioning the camera and lens.
- **Intercutting:** matching shots and edit point...
- **Composition:** an understanding of shot composition.
- **Recording and transmission:** rehearsal and transmission procedure.

Basic shot size conventions

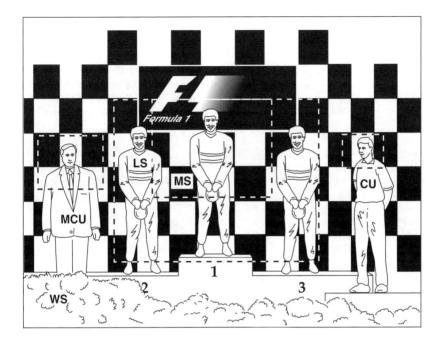

Because so much of television programming involves people talking, a number of standard shot sizes have evolved centred on the human body. In general, these shot sizes avoid cutting people at natural joints of the body such as neck, elbows, knees. Normal interview shots include:

- **CU (close up)** Bottom of frame cuts where the knot of tie would be.
- **MCU (medium close up)** Bottom of the frame cuts where the top of a breast pocket of a jacket would be.
- **MS (medium shot)** Bottom of frame cuts at the waist.

Other standard shot descriptions are:

- **BCU (big close up)** The whole face fills the screen. Top of frame cuts the forehead. Bottom of the frame cuts the edge of chin avoiding any part of the mouth going out of frame (rarely used in interviews).
- **LS (long shot)** The long shot includes the whole figure.
- **WS (wide shot)** A wide shot includes the figure in a landscape or setting.
- **O/S 2s (over-the-shoulder 2 shot)** Looking over the shoulder of a foreground figure framing part of the head and shoulders to another participant.
- **2 shot, 3 shots, etc.,** identifies the number of people in frame composed in different configurations.

Note: Precise framing conventions for these standard shot descriptions vary with directors and cameramen. One person's MCU is another's MS. Check that your understanding of the position of the bottom frame line on any of these shots shares the same size convention for each description as the director with whom you are working.

The zoom lens

Focal length

When parallel rays of light pass through a convex lens, they will converge to one point on the optical axis. This point is called the focal point of the lens. The focal length of the lens is indicated by the distance from the centre of the lens or the principal point of a compound lens (e.g. a zoom lens) to the focal point. The longer the focal length of a lens, the smaller its angle of view will be; and the shorter the focal length of a lens, the wider its angle of view.

Angle of view

The approximate horizontal angle of view of a fixed focal length lens can be calculated by using its focal length and the size of the pick-up sensors of the camera.

Although there are prime lenses (fixed focal length) available, the majority of broadcast video cameras are fitted with a zoom lens which can alter its focal length and therefore the angle of view over a certain range. This is achieved by moving one part of the lens system (the variator) to change the size of the image and by automatically gearing another part of the lens system (the compensator) to simultaneously move and maintain focus. This alters the image size and therefore the effective focal length of the lens.

Zoom ratio

A zoom lens can vary its focal length. The ratio of the longest focal length a zoom lens can achieve (the telephoto end), with the shortest focal length obtainable (its wide-angle end), is its zoom ratio. Lenses with ratios in excess of 50:1 can be obtained but the exact choice of ratio and the focal length at the wide end of the zoom will depend very much on what you want to do with the lens. Large zoom ratios are heavy, often require a great deal of power to operate the servo controls and have a reduced f-number (see below).

Extender

A zoom lens can be fitted with an internal extender lens system which allows the zoom to be used on a different set of focal lengths. For example, a 2× extender on a 14 × 8.5 mm zoom would transform the range from 8.5–119 mm to 17–238 mm, but it may also lose more than a stop at maximum aperture.

F-number

The f-number of a lens is a method of indicating how much light can pass through the lens. It is inversely proportional to the focal length of the lens and directly proportional to the diameter of the effective aperture of the lens. For a given focal length, the larger the aperture of the lens, the smaller its f-number and the brighter the image it produces.

Focal length

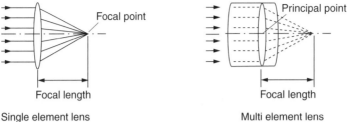

Focal point

Focal length

Single element lens

Principal point

Focal length

Multi element lens

Horizontal angle of view

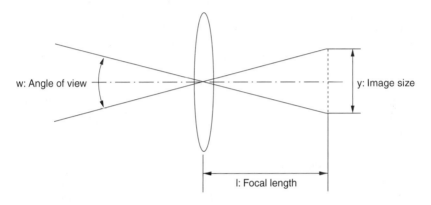

w: Angle of view

y: Image size

l: Focal length

For a camera fitted with 2/3" CCDs the formula would be:

$$\text{Angle of view} = \frac{2 \tan^{-1} 8.8 \text{ mm (width of CCD)}}{2 \times \text{focal length (mm)}}$$

F-number range

F-numbers are arranged in a scale where each increment is multiplied by $\sqrt{2}$ (1.414). Each time the f-number is increased by one stop, the exposure is decreased by half:

| 1.4 | 2 | 2.8 | 4 | 5.6 | 8 | 11 | 16 | 22 |

The effective aperture of a zoom is not its actual diameter, but the diameter of the image of the diaphragm seen from in front of the lens. This is called the entrance pupil of the lens. When the lens is zoomed (i.e. the focal length is altered) the diameter of the lens which is proportional to focal length alters and also its entrance pupil. The f-number is small at the wide angle end of the zoom and larger at the narrowest angle. This may cause f-number drop or ramping at the telephoto end on an OB when the entrance pupil diameter equals the diameter of the focusing lens group and cannot become any larger.

Focus

Focusing is the act of adjusting the lens elements to achieve a sharp image at the focal plane. Objects either side of this focus zone may still look reasonably sharp depending on their distance from the lens, the lens aperture, and the lens angle. The area covering the objects that are in acceptable focus is called the depth of field. The depth of field can be considerable if the widest angle of the zoom is selected and, whilst working with a small aperture, a subject is selected for focus at some distance from the lens. When zooming into this subject, the depth of field or zone of acceptable sharpness will decrease.

Follow focus
Television is often a 'talking head' medium and the eyes need to be in sharp focus. Sharpest focus can be checked 'off-shot' by rocking the focus zone behind and then in front of the eyes. Detecting 'on-shot' which plane of the picture is in focus is more difficult. You, as the cameraman, must be the first to detect loss of focus, but this can only be achieved if the viewfinder definition is better than the definition of the viewer's display and the plane of sharpest focus can be seen without rocking focus.

As camera or subject moves there will be a loss of focus which needs to be corrected. The art of focusing is to know which way to focus and not to overshoot. Practise following focus as someone walks towards the lens (UK convention – turn the capstan clockwise). Turn capstan anti-clockwise as the subject moves away from camera. Practise throwing focus from one subject to another.

Zoom lens and focus
A zoom lens is designed to keep the same focal plane throughout the whole of its range (provided the back focus has been correctly adjusted). To zoom into a subject, the lens must first be fully zoomed in on the subject and focused. Then zoom out to the wider angle. The zoom will now stay in focus for the whole range of its travel. If possible, always pre-focus before zooming in. Even if a zoom has not been rehearsed, always pre-focus whenever possible on the tightest shot of the subject. This is the best way of checking focus and it also prepares for a zoom-in if required. When zooming into a subject on which the focus has not been predetermined (blind zooming), it is best to be focused slightly back behind the subject so that you know where your zone of focus is. As focusing becomes more critical at the end of the zoom range, focus can be pulled forward. This helps to correct focus the right way.

Within a composition, visual attention is directed to the subject in sharpest focus. Attention can be transferred to another part of the frame by throwing focus onto that subject. Use the principle of invisible technique and match the speed of the focus pull to the motivating action.

Dual format cameras

The transition between 4:3 aspect ratio television and the conversion to 16:9 has produced an interim generation of dual format cameras. Different techniques are employed to use the same CCD for both formats.

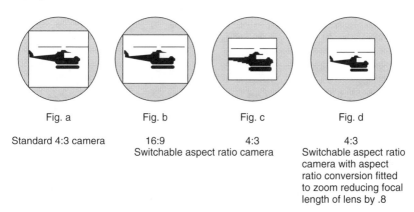

Fig. a	Fig. b	Fig. c	Fig. d
Standard 4:3 camera	16:9	4:3	4:3
	Switchable aspect ratio camera		Switchable aspect ratio camera with aspect ratio conversion fitted to zoom reducing focal length of lens by .8

The horizontal angle of view is related to the focal length of the lens and the width of the CCD image. In a dual format camera, if the CCD is optimized for 16:9 format, the angle of view will be smaller working in the 4:3 format compared to working in 16:9 using the same focal length of the lens. At the shortest focal length the loss is about 20%. When switched to 4:3 working, there will be a 9 mm diameter image (c) compared to the 11mm diagonal image when working in 16:9 or the 11 mm diameter image of the conventional 4:3 format camera (a). This change in horizontal lens angle when switching formats can be remedied by employing an optical unit in the zoom (similar to an extender but producing negative magnification) which shortens the focal length when working in the 4:3 mode (d). This 0.8 reduction of focal length produces the same range of angles of view as a conventional 4:3 camera using the equivalent zoom lens. It is not essential when working in 16:9/4:3 dual aspect ratio camera to fit a lens with a 0.8 convertor, only an awareness that the lens angle will be narrower than its equivalent use with a standard 4:3 camera.

Depth of field

Changing the f-number alters the depth of field – the portion of the field of view which appears sharply in focus. This zone extends in front and behind the subject on which the lens is focused and will increase as the f-number increases. The greater the distance of the subject from the camera, the greater the depth of field. The depth of field is greater behind the subject than in front and is dependent on the focal length of the lens. F-number and therefore depth of field can be adjusted by altering light level or by the use of neutral density filters.

Minimum object distance

The distance from the front of the lens to the nearest subject that can be kept in focus is called the minimum object distance (MOD). Many zooms are fitted with a macro mechanism which allows objects closer than the lens MOD to be held in focus. The macro shifts several lens groups inside the lens to allow close focus, but this prevents the lens being used as a constant focus zoom. Close focusing (inside the MOD) can sometimes be achieved by using the flange-back adjustment.

Camera controls

The professional broadcast video camera consists of a zoom lens (some-times servo controlled from behind the camera), attached to a camera body containing three or four light sensors (CCD or charge coupled device), electronic circuits to process the signal, an electronic viewfinder, and various production facilities such as talkback, filter controls, mixed viewfinder, switches, etc.

The three vital facilities that keep the camera operator in touch with programme production when working in a multi-camera mode are viewfinder, talkback and cue lights. Without a good quality viewfinder he/she is unable to frame-up and focus the shot. Without talkback and cue lights, he/she is unaware when the shot will be taken.

Operational controls which have a significant influence on the opera-tion of the camera and transform it from an electronic device into a programme production tool are:

- servo controls of the zoom lens which allow a smooth take-off, precise control of speed of zoom and positive focus
- a pan/tilt head to enable the fluid control of camera movement. The pan/tilt head should be adjustable to achieve precise balance in order to cater for a wide range of camera/lens combinations and additional attachments such as prompters. It should also have the facility to accommodate the varying centres of gravity (C of G) of different lens/camera/viewfinder combinations
- a camera mounting which allows the camera operator to position the camera and lens quickly, smoothly and with precision for the desired shot and for the camera to remain at that setting until it is reposi-tioned.

In addition to the operational controls there is obviously a requirement that cameras produce a high quality electronic picture. This will depend on the design characteristics of the camera's performance such as its sensitivity, resolution, contrast range, colour matrix, etc.

The technical quality of the image produced by the camera has an important influence on how the viewer responds to the production. However, the priorities for a cameraman are often centred on the handling ability of the camera, lens and mounting, plus the need to work with a reasonable depth-of-field in an ad lib situation, coupled with the necessity of seeing the focus zone in the viewfinder. In addition, good communications are essential, whether in a crowded studio or operating in a remote location. If the operators cannot hear or talk to the control room, then their contribution is severely impaired.

Facilities found on a multi-camera production camera

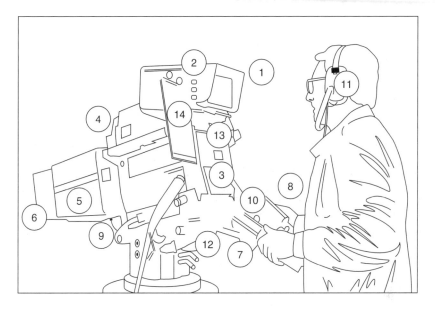

1 *An electronic viewfinder* which is usually monochrome although some cameras have the choice of colour or mono. Focusing of a broadcast video camera is through the viewfinder. The definition of the electronic picture therefore must allow the cameraman to be the *first* person in the production chain to see loss of optical focus.

2 *Viewfinder controls* – brightness, contrast, peaking (to accentuate edge definition as an aid to focusing); may also have controls for viewfinder image size.

3 *Mixed viewfinder* controls to enable the viewfinder picture to be switched to other video combinations.

4 *Cue lights* in the viewfinder, on the front of camera and on the front of lens are lit when the camera output is selected at the vision mixing panel. Cue lights outside the viewfinder (on the camera body and lens) can be switched out of circuit if required.

5 *Zoom lens* – available in a range of zoom ratios.

6 *Lens hood* – to help control flare and degradation and as partial protection against rain.

7 *Zoom thumb control* on adjustable pan bar.

8 *Zoom focus capstan* wheel on pan bar.

9 *Range extender* for zoom lens.

10 *Shot box* – to pre-set a range of zoom angles of views.

11 *Headset* and headset jack points for talkback from and to the control room staff.

12 *Talkback volume* – controlling production and engineering talkback and programme sound level to the headset.

13 *Filter wheel* – fitted with a range of colour correction filters, neutral density and effects filters.

14 *Crib card holder* and sometimes crib card illumination.

55

Camera mountings

There are a wide range of camera mountings available to cover the diverse requirements of multi-camera programme making in the studio and on location. No one camera mounting will necessarily embrace all styles of camerawork and all weights of equipment. Which mounting to use will depend on:

■ Is the mounting to be transported to its operating position (i.e. at a location rather than operated daily in a studio)? Equipment that may have to be carried up stairs or rigged in difficult locations will need to be lighter and easily rigged and de-rigged compared to equipment used permanently in a studio.

■ Is the mounting to be used to reposition the camera 'on-shot' or is simply to have the ability to reposition 'off-shot'? A tripod on wheels (if the ground surface is suitable) can be repositioned to a new camera position but is unsuitable for development shots. A pedestal mounting with steerable wheels and smooth adjustment of height will allow a development on shot if operated on a level floor.

■ What all-up weight will the mounting need to support (e.g. camera, lens and possibly a camera operator)?

The simplest way of moving a lightweight camera is to carry it on the shoulder (on or off-shot) although this will not give such a smooth movement as using a harness around the torso to steady the camera. There are a range of lightweight tripods, portable pedestals and jib-arms that can be used with a lightweight camera. There is also the facility to rig a lightweight camera on the end of a boom arm and to remotely control its movement on a servo-driven pan/tilt head and to remotely control the lens. At the other end of the scale there are cranes capable of elevating a full facility camera and camera operator to a lens height of over twenty feet.

Pan/tilt heads

A good pan and tilt head will have adjustment for the centre of gravity (C of G) of the combination of camera/recorder, lens and viewfinder in use. If the C of G is not adjusted, the camera will either be difficult to move from the horizontal or it will tilt forwards or backwards. Adjustment of the C of G balance should not be confused with mid-point balance, which involves positioning the camera and lens to find the point of balance on the head.

The setting of the friction or drag control of the head depends on the shot and personal preference. Using a very narrow lens for an extreme close shot (e.g. a bird nesting), may require much more friction than that needed to pan the camera smoothly when following rapid impromptu movement (e.g. skating). Some cameramen prefer a heavy drag or 'feel' on the head so that there is weight to push against while others remove all friction allowing the head to be panned at the slightest touch.

Continuous adjustment

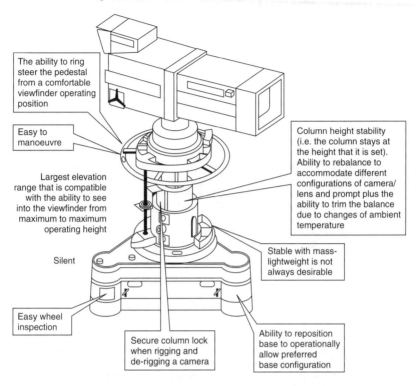

The ability to ring steer the pedestal from a comfortable viewfinder operating position

Easy to manoeuvre

Largest elevation range that is compatible with the ability to see into the viewfinder from maximum to maximum operating height

Silent

Easy wheel inspection

Column height stability (i.e. the column stays at the height that it is set). Ability to rebalance to accommodate different configurations of camera/lens and prompt plus the ability to trim the balance due to changes of ambient temperature

Stable with mass-lightweight is not always desirable

Secure column lock when rigging and de-rigging a camera

Ability to reposition base to operationally allow preferred base configuration

Live or 'recorded as live' television production requires a camera mounting that can be quickly and silently repositioned 'off' shot and have the flexibility to be smoothly positioned 'on' shot to accomplish pre-rehearsed camera movements. It must also be capable of instant small adjustments in track or crab mode to compensate for masking by artistes or wrong positioning. A usable shot must always be provided in a continuous programme even though the position of the artistes is not as rehearsed. In a studio these requirements are best served by a pedestal camera mounting controlled by the cameraman who can instantly compensate without misunderstanding or delay between tracker and cameraman.

The cameraman, whilst operating the camera, can also move the camera forwards, backwards or sideways by means of the ring steering wheel which alters the direction of the double wheel positioned at each corner of the base and he can alter the camera height. This must be accomplished silently, smoothly and with minimum effort. Continuous adjustment of the pedestal requires a smooth floor and complete mastery in the use of a pedestal. Smoothly positioning the camera 'on' and 'off' shot requires learning skills in the use of the mounting.

Camera technique

The six basic principles of multi-camera camerawork are:

1 preparation
2 anticipation
3 concentration
4 invisible technique
5 silent operation
6 teamwork.

Preparation
Look at the script to find out how the show is broken down into sections, recording periods, etc. Try to get an overall picture of the working day. Check that your camera cable is 'eighted' with no obstruction and carry out a pre-rehearsal on your camera and mounting (see page 71, Pre-rehearsal check list).

Preparation and anticipation
The rehearsal period is the time to discover what the contribution from each craft group will be. Each member of the camera crew has to establish what their role in the production is via a two-way exchange of information with the director and by talking to the other cameramen. In many rehearsals, all the information may be supplied on preplanned camera cards and a floor plan marked with camera positions. The feasibility of the planning is then tested by a rehearsal of every shot.

With other programme formats, the barest information on a running order is supplied and the camera operator has to seek details of the camera coverage that may affect him. Experience enables the right questions to be asked as this is the only opportunity to discover what is required before a camera operator is faced with a 'live' performance. Each member of the crew has to work in the real time of the programme and all decisions are governed by the time-scale of the event. Whilst the planning may have taken months or weeks, and the rehearsal days or hours, transmission is governed by the time-scale of the event covered. Shot decisions have to be made in seconds with no time-out to consider the best way of tackling a particular situation. Preparation and anticipation are essential in order to create the time for fast camerawork.

Concentration
Do not let your attention drift towards the content of the show unless it is linked with cues for camera movement you are involved with. A basic rule in any simple activity such as repositioning a monitor is applicable all the way through multi-camera production practice – if possible, never do something on recording or transmission that was not done on rehearsal. There are many exceptions to this injunction but until you have sufficient production experience, stick to the rule.

Language of camera movement

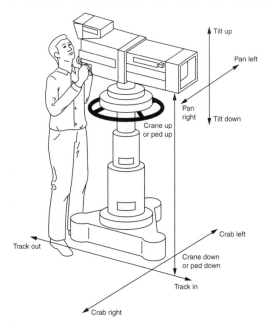

The pan

The simplest camera movement is the pan. It is often used to give visual variety amongst a number of static shots but usually the main use of a pan, apart from keeping a moving subject in frame, is to show relationships.

Essential operational points when panning:

- motivate the pan by action, to show relationships or to reveal new information
- ensure that the end frame has significance
- match speed of movement to mood and content
- synchronize all reframing with the action
- use dominant lines or movement to bridge first and end frame
- use the appropriate lens angle
- accelerate and decelerate the pan in the correct ratio
- correct friction (and cams)
- anticipation
- correct body posture
- correct choice of lens angle

Condition of the pan/tilt head

Controlled smooth camera movement cannot be achieved unless the correct friction has been selected for the programme format. The amount of friction constraining vertical and horizontal movement is often a personal choice. Each cameraman needs to balance out the need for easy flexible movement against the operational difficulties of holding the camera steady when tracking, crabbing and panning the camera without friction.

A compromise amount of friction is therefore selected which suits the programme requirements and weather conditions. Using a long lens continuously at its narrow end in a high wind may require more friction than the same operation in a flat calm.

Operational skills

Eye, hand and body co-ordination
Invisible camera technique requires camera movement to be unobtrusive and matched to content. Panning and tilting the camera is a basic skill that requires considerable practice until there is complete coordination between the eye and hand. A requirement of good camerawork is the ability to move the camera smoothly and to be able to accelerate/decelerate movement.

Control of pedestal
At each corner of the base of the pedestal are a pair of wheels. Their direction is controlled by the large steering ring positioned under the trim weight storage tray. The direction of the alignment of the wheels is communicated to the hand by a raised red indicator attached to the steering ring so that without looking away from the viewfinder, information is always available as to the direction the pedestal will move when pushed. The alignment of the base of the pedestal can be adjusted to avoid constantly working with a corner of the base directly behind the camera.

Variable lens angle
A zoom lens has a continuously variable lens angle and is therefore useful in multi-camera TV production for adjusting the image size without moving the camera position. When operating from behind the camera, the adjustment is controlled on most television cameras via the thumb on a two-way rocker switch which alters the direction and speed of the zoom. A good servo zoom should allow a smooth imperceptible take-up of the movement of the zoom which can then be accelerated by the thumb control to match the requirements of the shot. There is usually provision to alter the response of the thumb control so that a very slow zoom rate can be selected or a very fast zoom speed for the same movement of the thumb control.

Zoom and composition
The zoom lens allows the desired framing of a shot to be quickly achieved. Shot size can be quickly altered out of vision to provide a range shots. Each shot can have the required size and framing to match other cameras (see page 68, Intercutting). Extended zoom ranges (30:1–40:1–70:1) allow a wide range of shots to be obtained from a fixed position (e.g. on an OB scaffold tower/hoist), and provides for visual movement across terrain where tracking would not be possible.

Readjustment on shot
The zoom is often used to adjust the shot to improve the composition when the content of the shot changes. Trimming the shot 'in vision' may be unavoidable in the coverage of spontaneous or unknown content, but it quickly becomes an irritant if repeatedly used. Fidgeting with the framing by altering the zoom angle 'on-shot' should be avoided.

Pivot points

A common mistake with users of domestic camcorders is to centre the subject of interest in the frame and then to zoom towards them keeping the subject the same distance from all four sides of the frame. The visual effect is as if the frame implodes in on them from all sides. A more pleasing visual movement is to keep two sides of the frame at the same distance from the subject for the whole of the movement.

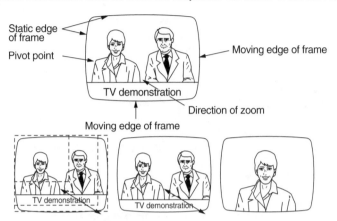

Static edge of frame

Pivot point

Moving edge of frame

TV demonstration

Direction of zoom

Moving edge of frame

TV demonstration

TV demonstration

Preselect one or two adjacent sides of the frame to the main subject of the zoom and whilst maintaining their position at a set distance from the main subject of the zoom allow the other two sides of the frame to change their relative position to the subject. Keep the same relationship of the two adjacent frame edges to the selected subject during the whole of the zoom movement.

The point that is chosen to be held stationary in the frame is called the pivot point. Using a pivot point allows the subject image to grow progressively larger (or smaller) within the frame whilst avoiding the impression of the frame contracting in towards them.

Marking up a pedestal position

The marks made with a floor crayon are quickly erased by pedestal and cable movement across them. They will need re-marking as there is a great deal of activity across the floor between rehearsal and transmission/recording. 'Lo-tack' tape (designed to be easily removed on de-rig) is more permanent but there is a risk, if there are too many marks on the studio floor, of bumping over the tape when moving on shot and causing a jump in the framing.

Repositioning the camera at speed

When repositioning the camera at speed across the studio floor, turn the camera in the direction of travel as it is easier to push a camera than to run backwards. Make certain that you walk around the pedestal in a direction that provides suffi-cient slack cable between camera and cable clamp on the pedestal base rather than winding the cable loop around the column. Pushing the camera onto a new set also allows you to start composing the shot before you come to rest and speeds up the move.

Camera movement

There is the paradox of creating camera movement to provide visual excitement or visual change whilst attempting to make the movement 'invisible'. Invisible in the sense that the aim of the technique is to avoid the audience's attention switching from the programme content to the camerawork. This is achieved when camera movement matches the movement of the action and good composition is maintained throughout the move. The intention is to emphasize subject – picture content, rather than technique.

From bad to better
A good rule of thumb for any camera movement which involves at some point a bad body posture for operating or a bad sightline to the viewfinder, is to start from the worst operating condition, and, during the camera development, unwind to a good operating position. This allows framing and focus at the end of the shot to be adjusted when working in the best operating position.

Camera cable
More pedestal movements 'on' shot have suffered from cables being fouled, snagged or stood on than possibly for any other reason. If there is no-one on the crew cable clearing, make certain that there is a sufficient length of unimpeded cable available for the intended movement.

Viewfinder
If there is a change of height of the camera or, during a crabbing movement, it is necessary to position the body away from the centre of the viewfinder, provision must be made to alter the viewfinder hood in order to see the whole of the viewfinder image.

Two types of camera movement
There are broadly two types of camera movement: **functional**, the camera is moved to keep the subject in frame, and **decorative**, the camera is moved to provide variety and interest or to explain an idea.

When to re-frame
A common dilemma is when to re-frame a subject who is swaying in and out of reasonable framing. The shot may be too tight for someone who can only talk when they move or they may make big hand movements to emphasize a point. The solution is loosen off the shot. It is seldom a good idea to constantly pan to keep someone in frame as inevitably you will be 'wrong-footed' and compensate for an anticipated movement that does not happen. If the shot cannot be contained without continuous re-framing then the incessant moving background will eventually become a distraction from the main subject of the shot.

Basic advice for movement

■ Try to disguise camera movement by synchronizing with subject movement. Start and stop the movement at the same time as the subject.

■ When zooming, hold one side of the frame static as a 'pivot point' rather than zooming in to the centre of the frame.

■ Try to find a reason to motivate the zoom and to disguise the zoom. Use a combination of pan and zoom.

■ Panning and zooming are done to show relationships. If the beginning of the shot and the end of the shot are interesting but the middle section is not, it is better to cut between the start of the shot and the end frame rather than to pan or to zoom. Begin and end on a point of interest when panning. If the end of the shot is uninteresting why pan to it? Have a reason for drawing attention to the final image of a pan.

■ Pace the pan so that the viewer can see what the camera is panning over. Hold the frame at the beginning and end of the pan.

■ Use dominant lines or contours to pan across or along. Find some subject movement to motivate the pan.

■ When panning movement, leave space in the frame in the direction the subject is moving.

Perspective of mass

The composition of a shot is affected by the distance of the camera from the subject and the lens angle that is used. This will make a difference to the size relationships within the frame. The size relationship of objects in a field of view is known as the perspective of mass. Put simply, the closer an object is to us the larger it will appear and vice versa. The image of an object doubles in size whenever its distance is halved. This is a simple fact of geometric optics and it applies to a camera as it does to the eye. Adjusting the camera distance and the lens angle can provide the size relationships required for a composition.

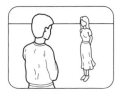

(a) Camera –
medium distance

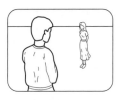

(b) Camera –
very close

(c) Long distance
from subjects

Working with the camera close to the subject (b) produces an increase in the size ratio between foreground and background figures. The foreground object appears unnaturally large and the background appears unnaturally small. It is a perspective of mass relationship we are not usually aware of. A wide-angle lens allows more of the foreground subject to be in frame and it is this combination that produces distortion when used too close to the face (a 'Pinnochio' nose).

A part of our perception of depth depends on judging size relationships. The smaller we perceive a known object, the further we judge it to be from us. The size relationships produced by a very narrow-angle lens at a distance from the subject (c), produces the illusion of squeezing the space between equal size figures. The camera distance from the subject produces the size relationships whilst the long focal length lens provides the magnification of the foreground and background. The space between the subjects in frame appears to be condensed.

63

Picture making skills

Central to the craft of camerawork are the skills required to create arresting and informative images. There is usually a reason why a shot is recorded on tape or film. The purpose may be simply to record an event or the image may play an important part in expressing a complex idea. Whatever the reasons that initiate the shot, the camera operator should have a clear understanding of the purpose behind the shot. After establishing why the shot is required, and usually this will be deduced purely from experience of the shot structure of the programme format, the cameraman will position the camera, adjust the lens angle, framing and focus. All four activities (including knowledge of programme formats) rely on an understanding of the visual design elements available to compose a shot within the standard television framing conventions. Effective picture making is the ability to manipulate the lens position and the lens angle within a particular programme context. The seven primary decisions which effects the image to be made when setting up a shot are:

1 camera angle (the position of the camera relative to the subject)
2 lens angle
3 camera distance from the subject
4 camera/lens height
5 frame
6 subject in focus
7 depth of field.

Camera position/lens angle
The composition of a shot is affected by the distance of the camera from the subject and the lens angle that is used. This will make a difference to the size relationships within the frame – the perspective of mass.

The subjective influence of camera height
Lens height will also control the way the audience identifies with the subject. Moving the horizon down below a person makes them more dominant because the viewer is forced to adopt a lower eyeline viewpoint. We are in the size relationship of children looking up to adults. A low lens height may also de-emphasize floor or ground level detail because we are looking along at ground level and reducing or eliminating indications of ground space between objects. This concentrates the viewer's interest on the vertical subjects. A high position lens height has the reverse effect. The many planes of the scene are emphasized like a scale model. Usually it is better to divide the frame into unequal parts by positioning the horizon line above or below the mid-point of the frame. Many cameramen intuitively use the rule of thirds (see page 67), to position the horizon. A composition can evoke space by panning up and placing the line low in frame. Placing a high horizon in the frame can balance a darker foreground land mass or subject with the more attention grabbing detail of a high key sky.

Lens height

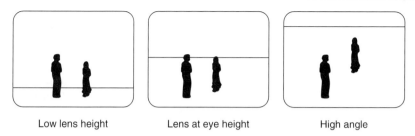

Low lens height   Lens at eye height   High angle

Lens height and tilt will control the perspective of line. Shooting low with a level camera will produce one type of line perspective; shooting from a high vantage point tilted down will produce another set of line relationships in the frame. On a flat surface, the horizon line cuts similar size figures at the same point. The height of that point is the height of the lens.

Form and content

The structural skeleton of the shot is only partially formed by content. For example, every cameraman knows that a shot of an object can be made more interesting if the camera is moved from a square-on, symmetrical viewpoint to an angle of view favouring more than one side or surface and/or the height of the lens is varied. Repositioning the camera is altering the structural skeleton, for while the content of the shot remains and is recognizable as a 'building', converging lines of rooftop, windows, doors, etc., have been altered and restructured to provide a more pleasing 'front surface' design.

Composition

Composition is commonly defined as arranging all the visual elements in the frame in a way that makes the image a satisfactory and complete whole. Integration of the image is obtained by the positioning of line, mass, colour and light in the most pleasing arrangement.

Many television cameramen know, through many years of experience, exactly how to position the lens in space or choose a different lens angle in order to improve the appearance of the shot. They are either working to inherited craft values of what is 'good' composition or they are repositioning and juggling with the camera until they intuitively feel that they have solved that particular visual problem. Frequently there is no time to analyse a situation and the only thing to fall back on is experience. Compositional experience is the result of many years of solving visual problems. Good visual communication is not a gift from heaven but is learnt from finding out in practice what does and does not work.

Controlling size relationships

As well as the standard methods of shot size and positioning the frame, composition can also be controlled by manipulating the perspective of mass. To increase the size of a background figure to a foreground figure it is common practice to reposition the camera back and zoom in to return to the original framing. The size relationships have now altered. It is not the narrower angle that produced this effect but the increased distance from the camera.

Moving the camera towards or away from the subject alters the size relationships between foreground and background objects. The perspective of mass changes in a similar way to our own perceptual experience when we move towards or away from an object. Tracking the camera therefore not only conforms to our normal visual expectations but sets up interesting rearrangements of all the visual elements in the camera's field of view.

Tracking into a scene extends the involvement of the viewer in that they are being allowed visually to move into the two-dimensional screen space. If depth is to be indicated it must be self-evident and contained in the composition of the image. A tracking shot provides a change in viewpoint and allows the viewer greater opportunity to experience the depth of the space pictured compared to either a zoom or a static shot. The important point to remember is that subject size relationship is a product of camera distance. How the subject fills the frame is a product of lens angle. This, of course, is the crucial distinction between tracking and zooming. Tracking the camera towards or away from the subject alters size relationships – the perspective of mass. Zooming the lens preserves the existing relative size relationships and magnifies or diminishes a portion of the shot.

Rule of thirds

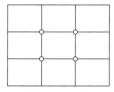 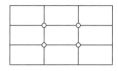

4:3 aspect ratio   16:9 aspect ratio

The rule of thirds proposes that an attractive balance can be achieved by placing the main subject on one of the intersections of two equally spaced lines horizontally in the frame and two lines equally spaced in the vertical.

Composition summary

Composition is the principal way of making clear the priorities of a shot. It emphasizes the main subject and eliminates or subdues competing elements of visual interest. There must be a reason for framing up any shot; good composition enables that reason to be transmitted to the viewer. Good visual communication is achieved by good composition. Here is a partial checklist of the do's and don'ts of composition:

■ The camera converts three dimensions into two dimensions. Try to compensate for the loss of the third dimension by looking for ways to represent depth in the composition.

■ Avoid dividing the frame into separated areas by strong vertical and horizontal elements unless this is a specific required effect.

■ Check the overall image, particularly background details (e.g. no chimneys/posts growing out of foreground subjects' heads).

■ Keep important action away from the edge of the frame but avoid repeating square-on, symmetrical eye-level, centre-of-frame shots.

■ Offset the dominant interest and balance this with a less important element.

■ Fill the frame if possible with interest and avoid large plain areas that are there simply because of the aspect ratio of the screen. If necessary, mask off part of the frame with a feature in the shot to give a more interesting composition.

■ Emphasize the most important element in the frame by its position using control of background, lens-angle, height, focus, shot size, movement, etc. Make certain that the eye is attracted to the part of the frame that is significant and avoid conflict with other elements in the frame.

■ Selective focus can control the composition. Pulling focus from one plane to another directs attention without reframing.

■ Attempt some visual mystery or surprise but the stronger the visual impact the more sparingly it should be used. Repeated zooming results in loss of impact and interest.

■ With profile shots, where people are looking out of frame, give additional space in the direction of their gaze for 'looking room'. Similarly when someone is walking across frame, give more space in front of them than behind.

■ Give consistent headroom for the same sized shots decreasing the amount with CUs and BCUs. Always cut the top of the head rather than the chin in extreme close up.

■ The eyes are the centre of attention in shots of faces. A good rule-of-thumb is to place them one third from the top of frame.

67

Intercutting

What makes a shot change invisible?

Continuous camera coverage of an event using a number of cameras relies on a stream of invisible shot changes. Invisible in the sense that the transition between each shot does not distract the audience. Although individual camera operators frame up their own shots, the pictures they produce must fit the context of the programme and match what other cameramen are providing. No shot can be composed in isolation – its effect on the viewer will be related to the preceding and succeeding shot.

Interviews

Multi-camera coverage of an interview is about the most widespread format on television after the straight-to-camera shot of a presenter. The staging of an interview usually involves placing the chairs for good camera angles, lighting, sound and for the ease and comfort of the guests and the anchor person. The space between people should be a comfortable talking distance.

Editing conventions sometimes rely on everyone involved in the production having a knowledge of well known shot patterns (see shot sizes, page 49), such as singles, two-shots, o/s two-shots, etc., in the customary camera coverage of an interview. This speeds up programme production when matching shots of people in a discussion and allows fast and flexible team working because everyone is aware of the conventions.

Matching to other cameras

In addition to setting up the optimum position for singles, two-shots, etc., camera operators need to match their shots with the other cameras. The medium close-ups (MCUs), etc., should be the same size with the same amount of headroom, looking room, the same height, and if possible, roughly the same lens angle (therefore the same distance from their respective subjects), especially when intercutting on over-the-shoulder two-shots. This avoids a mismatch of the perspective of mass. The best method of matching shots is to use the mixed viewfinder facility or to check with a monitor displaying studio out.

Eyeline

Eyeline is an imaginary line between an observer and the subject of their observation. In a discussion, the participants are usually reacting to each other and will switch their eyeline to whoever is speaking. The audience, in a sense, is a silent participant and they will have a greater involvement in the discussion if they feel that the speaker is including them in the conversation. This is achieved if cameras take up positions in and around the set to achieve good eyeline shots of all the participants. That is, both eyes of each speaker, when talking, can be seen on camera rather than profile or semi-profile shots.

Crossing the line diagram

There may be a number of variations in shots available depending on the number of participants and the method of staging the discussion/interview. All of these shot variations need to be one side of an imaginary line drawn between the participants.

To intercut between people to create the appearance of a normal conversation between them, every shot of a sequence should stay the same side of an imaginary line drawn between the speakers *unless* a shot is taken exactly on this imaginary line or a camera move crosses the line and allows a reorientation (and a repositioning of all cameras) on the opposite side of the old 'line'.

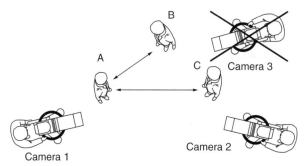

Cameras 1 and 2 can be intercut on subjects A, B, and C, but camera 3 (apart from being in camera 1's shot) cannot be intercut with 1 or 2 except if 1 is on subject B and 3 is on subject A.

Cross shooting

A standard cross shooting arrangement is for the participants to be seated facing each other and for cameras to take up positions close to the shoulders of the participants.

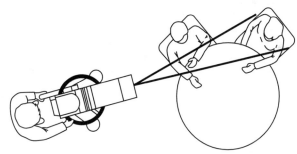

MCU position with good eyeline can be quickly zoomed out and reframed to provide a tight over-the-shoulder 2 shot without repositioning the pedestal.

The usual method of finding the optimum camera position is to position the camera to provide a well composed over-the-shoulder two-shot then zoom in to check that a clean single can be obtained of the participant facing camera. A tight over-the-shoulder two-shot always risks masking or a poorly composed shot if the foreground figure should lean left or right. To instantly compensate, if this should occur, set the pedestal steering wheel in a position to allow crabbing left or right for rapid repositioning on or off shot (see page 75, headroom and looking room diagrams).

69

Rehearsal

If you are inexperienced in operating a camera, try to keep the following points in mind during rehearsal:

- Use the rehearsal period to establish what your specific contribution will be. Ask questions if you are unsure.
- Make notes on your camera card or running order and mark up camera position if a precisely framed shot is required (e.g. a chroma key shot with an inset graphic).
- Make yourself aware of the role of other cameras and their repositions.
- Plan for the unexpected and have contingency plans for any eventuality.
- Do not over commit yourself with numerous camera repositions if you are unsure of the time available to implement them.
- Check the cable routeing of the camera and any potential object on which it could get snagged (e.g. rostrum corners, stage weights, boom wheels).
- Remember that you must provide exactly the same compositions on transmission/recording as was agreed in rehearsal unless the programme is an 'as-directed' format.

When to offer shots

One of the hardest techniques for camera operators to master in multi-camera camerawork on a fast moving show is when to offer shots or when to wait for direction. A camera operator, for example, will often spot during a discussion a participant not on camera bursting to get their word in and may be tempted to offer up a shot of them. Many directors appreciate this contribution and providing there is the trust and experience developed in a long working relationship between camera crew, vision mixer and director, a variety of reaction shots can be offered and taken whilst still keeping up with the flow of the discussion. Alternatively, many directors dislike being left without a cover shot and prefer to decide on all camera movement. In these circumstances the camera operator must stick on the last directed shot until directed to do otherwise.

What shots are required?

Variation in camera angle and shot size are needed in most 'as-directed' situations to give variety and pace to the presentation. The director will ask for a string of requirements and coordinate each camera, but by listening to talkback and with the occasional use of the mixed viewfinder facility to see what shot has been selected, a camera operator will often be able to find an appropriate shot that matches the needs of the programme at that point. The judgement and the ability to assess what shot is relevant is part of the skill needed to be developed by a camera operator.

Pre-rehearsal check list

The following basic preparations should be followed when new to operating a camera:

■ Check over camera, mount, release pan/tilt locks and unlock pan/tilt head.
■ Check that the cable is 'eighted' and free to follow any camera movement.
■ Look through the camera cards if supplied and check opening position on floor plan if available.
■ Check that you can clearly hear production and engineering talkback on your headset and that all cue lights are functioning.
■ Set up the viewfinder (see page 99).
■ Get the feel of the camera movement and adjust friction.
■ Adjust pan bar and position of the zoom demand unit according to personal preference. Position of pan bar may need to be altered to accommodate very high or low shots during rehearsal.
■ Check focus and the varying zone of focus depending on zoom angle and check that the zoom holds focus over its whole range (i.e. check back-focus, see page 97).
■ Reduce the headset cable loop to the minimum operational requirements and tie off to the camera. A long loop can easily get snagged.

Camera position and key light

Key lights are positioned to produce the desired modelling on the presenter and are typically set to between 10 and 40 degrees either side of the eyeline position to the planned lens position (A). If the camera is crabbed beyond this point (B) and the presenter turns to face the lens then the modelling on the face becomes either non-existent (camera under key light) or 'over modelled' which results in an ugly nose shadow that spreads across the face.

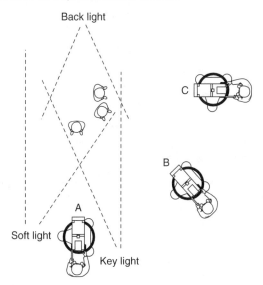

If the camera continues to crab away from the key light (C) then possibly the back light will start to illuminate the face with a key light acting as back light and there is no fill.

71

Transmission 1

Talkback discipline

With nearly all communication channelled through the control room, it is obviously important to choose the right time to talk to the director or control room. Do not interrupt an existing discussion or a briefing that will be addressed to the whole crew. Wait for a pause – and close to transmission or recording this never seems to occur – before opening your microphone and calling the control room. Keep the conversation brief and if questions from the director can be answered with a simple yes or no, nod the camera in the vertical direction for 'yes' and pan the camera in the horizontal direction for 'no'.

'As-directed' procedures

'As-directed' procedures require fast reflexes and an awareness of the development in programme content. Sometimes a programme will have sections which have a rehearsed shot structure interspersed with 'as-directed' sequences. For a camera operator, the danger point is the junction between the two. It is easy to be caught in the 'as-directed' mode of operation and therefore out of position for the scripted, numbered shot sequence.

Problems during the show

No live or 'record as live' programme will be without its problems or unexpected emergencies. Artistes missing their marks or prevented from getting to a prearranged position will need instant adjustment from the camera operator. Compensation will be needed for unexpected masking by people or structures. If a shot is missed, forget about it and make certain the next shot is there. Too often, a number of operational errors snowball because people spend time agonizing over their mistakes. If something is preventing you getting to a shot and you are unable to speak to the director, show on camera what the problem is. Help communicate other people's problems by showing on camera their circumstances (e.g. a stage manager who has lost talkback, equipment failure, etc.). If there is a production mistake on transmission, never spend time deciding on the cause. Get on with the next item and leave the post mortems until after the programme has finished. Remember to follow up operational incidents (equipment malfunction, the wrong equipment, communication failures, operational procedures, etc.) that affected your work and check that they will not occur next time.

Coping with change

If there is a major change during the programme, anticipate how it will affect your shots and be prepared to adjust to a new and unrehearsed situation. Never underestimate the importance of anticipation in making time for yourself. Do not allow the excitement and confusion of a situation to get in the way of thinking clearly in order to act decisively.

Visual memory and cue cards

The ability to remember the precise framing of a shot comes with practice and experience. There are no visual memory rules or procedures to be learnt as visual memory appears to operate at the instinctive level. At the speed at which some shots are required, the reflex selection of lens angle and framing are completed in an instant. In general, however, it is always a good idea to make notes on the camera card as a reminder of a shot.

Marking up

Most camera operators prefer to scribble a few words against a complex shot description as additional information noted at rehearsal. These abbreviated reminders (which may be incomprehensible to any one else) replace the typed shot description. The aim of any alteration to the card by the camera operator is to make instantly legible any essential camera movement and to link it to the action that cues it. During rehearsal, the camera operator will be marking up his card and marking the camera position, if necessary.

For example, a camera card may have the scribble *'2 lean fwd stands'* which translated by the camera operator means *'when she leans forward for the second time she will stand and I will need to crane up and focus fwd'*. A well laid out camera card will always have plenty of space for this type of rehearsal note. It is also important that the changeover between two cards occurs during a sequence of slow shot change to avoid hastily scrabbling to get the top card flipped over while looking for the next shot.

Working to cue lights

All television cameras designed for multi-camera working are fitted with red lamps on the camera and in the viewfinder called cue lights or tally lamps. The tempo of intercutting between cameras requires the camera operator to develop the ability to work at two speeds. Off-shot, there is often the need to find the required shot almost instantaneously. Once settled on the framing, and the camera is cut to, there may be the need to develop the shot (zoom in or out, pan, track, etc.) at a tempo controlled by the subject matter. Frequently this will be a slow, unobtrusive movement. When the cue light goes off, the camera operator is again released to find the next shot in the fastest possible time.

A mixed viewfinder

The camera operator can usually switch his/her viewfinder feed from the camera output to a mixed feed of camera output and a designated source (e.g. another camera).

VTR clearance

After a recording there will be a pause whilst VTR establish if they have a recording without fault or whilst the director decides if any section of the programme requires a retake. When the final clearance has been given the de-rig can begin.

Transmission 2

Often the most unpredictable factor in an outside broadcast is the weather. The positions of the cameras are usually controlled by the nature of the event but they are often sited to avoid looking into the sun. Extreme weather changes may be experienced during the period of rig, rehearse and transmit and therefore adequate precautions must be made to protect equipment against adverse weather, and to protect personnel against adverse weather.

Personal weather protection
Large scale events (e.g. golf) involve cameras being scattered a long way from the scanner. They also involve long transmissions. A camera operator setting out for the day therefore needs to equip himself with a choice of clothing to match any changing weather conditions. The standard advice in weather protection for equipment or people is to prepare for the worst. Those who work regularly out of doors must make themselves aware of the risks involved and how to protect themselves against sunburn, skin cancer, etc.

New to talkback
A camera operator new to wearing a headset and working with talkback might be overwhelmed by the amount of information received. With experience it is possible to ignore all but the information that affects camerawork. This is not simply camera direction. Any information that may affect future shots or shots that will be needed should be remembered by the camera operator and used when required.

Programme sound
It is often important to listen to programme sound. During a discussion, sports commentary, etc., the camera shots offered will be directly related to the information supplied by programme sound. Many camera operators prefer to work with one of the headset earpieces on one ear and the other earpiece off the ear. Programme sound can then be heard directly and the uncovered ear is available in case of solti-voce messages from other people such as floor mangers, etc., during transmission.

Silence
Reducing the amount of noise on recording/transmission can be achieved by:

■ reducing cable noise – correctly wrapping other cables (e.g. lights, prompt, etc.) around the camera cable reduces the surface area of the cable dragging on the floor if no cable clearer is present and a well maintained pedestal or other mounting to eliminate loose or rattly fixtures.
■ wearing soft soled shoes.

There is a trade off-between a fast move to achieve a specific shot against the amount of noise the move produces. If the noise is prohibitive then other ways must be found to achieve the shot.

Headroom

✗	✗	✓
Subject appears to be falling out of frame	Top of frame is crushing the subject	Match similar size shots with the same size headroom

Looking room

Eyes positioned at approx. half frame

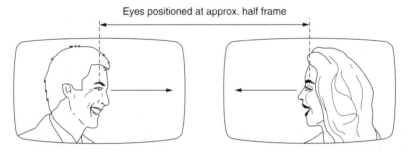

One of the compositional conventions of camerawork with profile shots, where people are looking out of frame, is to give additional space in the direction of their gaze for 'looking room'. Similarly when someone is walking across frame, to give more space in front of them than behind.

Robotic camerawork

Remote control

There are a number of camera remote control systems which attempt to mimic how a camera is manually operated. At the remote operating position the facilities include:

- the control of camera functions through a joystick, and/or rotating switch which allows control of pan, tilt, zoom and focus discreetly on shot
- the ability to remotely control the above functions on a number of cameras and to precisely set the time of a specific camera movement (e.g. zooming)
- the facility to set-up a number of shots on each camera, to label and store each set-up and the capability of rapidly recalling a specific shot. Sometimes this memorized data is recorded on a computer floppy disk which can be removed from the memory system for future programmes
- the stored parameters of each shot memorized may be recalled by button, mouse or using a touch screen visual presentation.

Setting up a shot

A shot can be framed up by means of a joystick, and by adjusting the camera height by way of the elevation unit. Once framed up, the shot can be stored and the speed of any zoom in/out can be adjusted and preset so that when the shot is recalled, the rehearsed position of panning head and lens angle/focus is quickly obtained. There is always the need to preview a stored camera position because whereas the camera parameters may be precise, presenters are human and their body position or chair position may have shifted. Trimming the shot to adjust headroom and composition may be necessary on preview or on shot.

Storing a shot

A number of shots can be programmed and quickly accessed either through a keypad recalling alphanumeric code for each shot, or by a touch screen displaying a mosaic of freeze frames of shots available. Whatever the system in use, there is always the essential requirement of maintaining an up-to-date index describing each shot stored so that it can be accurately recalled.

Recalling a shot

The accuracy of the robotic system's repeatability (i.e. returning to the same shot), is measured either in arcsec or degrees (60 arcsecs = 0.01 degrees). Most systems are accurate enough to accommodate shots of presenters who are unlikely to be absolutely immobile as they are usually paid to be animated and vivacious. A more important consideration is the speed of repositioning between shots. The robotic speed is unlikely to match a manual operator because of the servo motor's design requirement to avoid overshoot and oscillation at maximum speed, and the need to provide imperceptible movement 'on-shot' at the slowest speed.

Robotic control

Basic requirements for any robotic system of camera control are:

- silent operation
- remote control of pan, tilt, zoom, and focus
- rapid repositioning, fast acceleration, swift motor responses
- tight damping without oscillation or overshoot
- imperceptible control of movement on-shot
- movement on-shot using pivot points
- storage of a number of preset positions of pan/tilt settings, zoom and focus setting with a designated code or description
- preview facilities of each camera's output – these can be displayed on the same screen
- cue/tally light indicating which camera is currently selected at the vision mixing panel

X-Y servo pedestals

With x-y function fitted, the pedestal can be remotely repositioned or remotely moved on-shot. Over time, if a pedestal is moved around a studio, there may be a tendency for the base to move out of its original alignment and to twist, causing errors when recalling a stored pedestal position. One method of correcting this is to lay black and white squares on the studio floor, and then store their position in the remote control memory. When this position is recalled, the pedestal moves to the squares and uses their alignment to reorientate the base of the pedestal.

Touch screen display

Touching any picture on the screen will select the shot.

Introduction to TV sound

Television programme sound can have a significant emotional effect on the audience and yet remain quite unnoticeable. Sound does not simply complement the image, it can actively shape how we perceive and interpret the image. Most TV crafts such as lighting, camerawork, editing use a form of invisible technique which achieves its effects without the audience being aware that any artifice has been employed. If the audience does becomes aware of the methods employed, they often become less involved in the production and may even suspect that the programme maker is manipulative. The production contribution of sound is usually the most unobtrusive and difficult for the audience to evaluate – until it is badly done. Visual awareness appears to take precedence over audible awareness and yet intelligibility, space and atmosphere are often created by sound. The selection and treatment of audio shapes our perception and can be used to focus our attention just as effectively as the selection of images.

What is sound?

When there is a variation of air pressure at frequencies between approximately 16 to 16,000 Hz, the human ear (depending on age and health), can detect sound. The change in air pressure can be caused by a variety of sources such as the human voice, musical instruments, etc. Some of the terms used to describe the characteristics of the sounds are:

- **Sound waves** are produced by increased air pressure and rarefaction along the line of travel.
- **Frequency** of sound is the number of regular excursions made by an air particle in one second (see figure opposite).
- **Wavelength** of a pure tone (i.e. a sine wave, see figure opposite) is the distance between successive peaks.
- **Harmonics** are part of the sound from a musical instrument which are a combination of frequencies that are multiples of the lowest frequency present (the fundamental).
- **Dynamic range** is the range of sound intensities from quietest to loudest occurring from sound sources. This may exceed the dynamic range a recording or transmission system are able to process without distortion.
- **The ear's response**: to hear an equal change in intensity, the sound level must double at each increase rather than changing in equal steps.
- **Decibels** are a ratio of change and are scaled to imitate the ear's response to changing sound intensity.
- **Loudness** is a subjective effect. An irritating sound may appear to be a great deal louder than a sound we are sympathetic to (e.g. the sound of a neighbour's cat at night compared to our own practice session on a violin!).
- **Phase** of a signal becomes important when signals are combined. Signals in phase reinforce each other. Signals out of phase subtract from or cancel out each other (see figure opposite).
- **Pitch** is the highness or lowness of the frequency of a note.

78

Wavelength and frequency

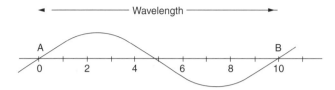

The time taken for a complete cycle of pure tone (A) to begin to repeat itself (B) is the frequency of the signal and is measured in cycles per second (Hz), e.g. 50 Hz = 50 cycles per second. Frequency is inversely proportional to wavelength. For example, a high frequency sound source of 10,000 Hz produces sound with a short wavelength of 3.4 cm. A low frequency sound source of 100 Hz produces sound with a longer wavelength of 3.4 m. Frequency multiplied by wavelength equals the speed of sound (335 m/sec) in cold air. It is faster in warm air.

Phase

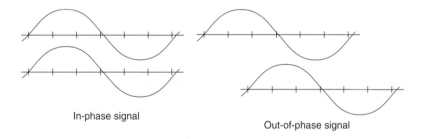

In-phase signal

Out-of-phase signal

Acoustics

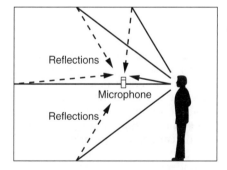

Reverberation relates to the time delay before sounds reflected from the wall and other surfaces reach the microphone.

Standing waves effect is due to the room having resonances where the parallel walls enhance certain frequencies.

Microphones

Choosing which microphone to use in a specific production environment will require consideration to be given to some or all of the following factors affecting a microphone's performance:

- nature of the sound source (e.g. speech, pop group drums, bird song, etc.)
- matching the technical characteristics of the microphone to the sound source (e.g. frequency response, transient response, ability to handle high/low levels of sound (sensitivity), and directional properties)
- mechanical characteristics such as size, appearance, robustness, wind shields, affected by humidity, stability, reliability, etc.
- compatibility – cable plugs, connectors and adaptors, matching electrical impedance, cable run required, interface with other audio equipment
- powering arrangements (see condenser microphone below)
- programme budget, microphone cost/hire and availability.

Frequency response of a microphone

Microphones convert acoustical energy (sound waves) into electrical power either by exposing one side of a diaphragm (pressure-operated) to air pressure variations or by exposing both sides of the diaphragm (pressure-gradient). Directional response of the microphone will depend upon which method is chosen or a combination of both and the physical design of the microphone. Response of the microphone is also related to frequency of the audio signal. Directional response can be plotted on a polar diagram which places the microphone in the centre of a circular graph indicating the sensitivity at each angle with respect to the front axis of the microphone (see polar diagram opposite).

There are three basic types of microphone: moving coil, ribbon, and condenser.

- **The moving coil**: The polar diagram of this microphone can be omnidirectional or cardioid, i.e. having a dead side to the rear of the microphone. This type of microphone can be used as a reporter's 'hand held' but care must be taken in its handling.
- **The ribbon**: This microphone's polar response is 'figure of eight' – open front and rear, but closed to the sides. This microphone has been used mainly in radio studios with the interviewer and interviewee sitting across a table facing one another.
- **The condenser**: The condenser microphone achieves the best quality of the three and requires a power supply to make it operate. Initially the power was supplied by a separate mains driven unit but this was superseded by an 'in line' battery supply. Today most condenser microphones will be powered directly from the audio mixer unit, the supply being known as the 48 volt phantom power. There are other forms of condenser microphone power supply known as 12 volt A/B and 'T' power. Always check that the mic power supply matches the microphone to be used *before* connection.

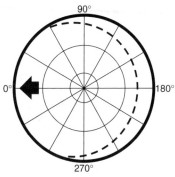

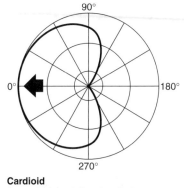

Omnidirectional
Sensitivity is more-or-less equal all round.

Cardioid
Some degree of directionality is introduced to produce a heart-shaped response curve.

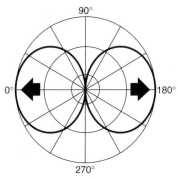

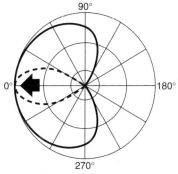

Figure-of-eight
Bi-directional sensitivity allows equal response in opposite directions.

Highly directional
Special constructions, such as the gun microphone, allow small sources to be pinpointed.

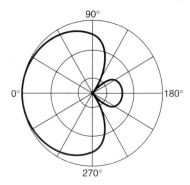

Hypercardioid
Has dead points about 45° off the rear.

— — — — high frequencies
———————— low frequencies

81

Audio monitoring

Sound intensity range: The intensity of sound is a function of the pressure variation set up in the atmosphere. Intensity is proportional to pressure squared. A microphone is used to convert sound energy into electrical energy and the voltage produced is proportional to the sound pressure. The range of intensities from quietest to loudest is the dynamic range of that sound situation. For example, the ratio of the loudest sound produced by an orchestra to the quietest sound can be as much as 60–70 db in an orchestral performance. This dynamic range is greater than can be transmitted and therefore sound control and possibly sound compression is required when recording large variations in sound levels.

Decibels: Our ears do not respond to changes in sound intensity in even, linear increments. To hear an equal change in intensity, the sound level must double at each increase rather than changing in equal steps. To match the ear's response to changes in sound intensity, it is convenient to measure the changes in the amplitude of the audio signal by using a logarithmic ratio – decibels (dB). Decibels are a ratio of change and are scaled to imitate the ear's response to changing sound intensity. If a sound intensity doubles in volume then there would be a 3 dB increase in audio level. If it was quadrupled, there would be a 6 dB increase.

Zero level voltage: Just as light is converted into a TV signal with a standard peak amplitude of 0.7 V so sound energy when it is converted into electrical energy requires a standard signal, a baseline voltage to which all changes can be referred. This is known as zero level and the standard voltage selected is 0.775 V – the voltage across 600 Ω (a common input and output impedance of audio equipment) when 1 mW is developed. 1000 Hz is the frequency of the standard zero level signal. Increasing or decreasing sound intensity will alter the level of this voltage.

Sound monitoring

The first and last evaluation of sound quality is by ear, but meters are a valuable aid in monitoring signal strength to prevent overloading the audio system's maximum permissible transmitted or recording level. Beyond this point the signal will be progressively distorted without increasing the perceived loudness. The relative levels between each sound source must be balanced by careful monitoring. The mix heard on loudspeakers, or headphones should be used to establish the correct balance of the various sound sources, using meters as a guide to ensure that the technical requirements are correctly fulfilled. Two main types of meter are used to measure and monitor changes in audio level. A peak programme meter (PPM) measures peaks of sound intensity. A programme volume meter (VU) measures average level of sound and gives a better indication of loudness but at the expense of missing brief high-intensity peaks that could cause distortion.

VUs (volume units)

- VU meters give an average reading of signal volume and are calibrated from –20 to +3 dB (some may have extended scales) and are good for reading continuous signals such as tone, and the zero position may be used for line-up.
- Care is needed to interpret programme material and it is difficult to read low level signals. Some high peak, low energy material may cause distortion before any real level is shown on the meter.
- VU meters do not respond well to short transients signals and may indicate as much as 10 dB below the actual level. Many transient sounds will barely move the meter. Be careful when judging the recording level with VU meters as their slow response time may prevent them from showing short duration peaks present in voice recordings (especially female voices). It is good practice to peak 3 to 6 dB below zero VU if limiting of the signal is to be avoided.
- Decay and rise time are identical and may be too fast to read the signal.
- Being relatively cheap to manufacture, many sound sources can be individually metered avoiding switching signals to a single meter.
- As a guide to help prevent over-modulation, speech may be held back to –6 dB or lower (50% mod.), some transient musical instruments to –10 dB, loud crowds or compressed material can reach 0 dB.
- Ensure signals do not peak beyond 0 dB (100%) to avoid distortion.

PPM (peak programme meter)

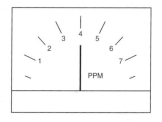

- The PPM is designed to have a very fast rise time, allowing short duration peaks likely to cause overloads to be clearly seen but give little indication of the perceived loudness of the material.
- PPMs are designed with different scales (e.g. BBC, EBU, IRT/DIN, etc.), but all have the same mechanical characteristics. The BBC version, for example, is calibrated from 1 to 7 with 4 dB steps between graduations on a linear scale.
- PPM 4 is used as a reference line-up, representing a signal of 1 mW (0.775 V into 600 ohms). PPM 6 represents the maximum allowable signal.
- PPMs are very expensive as the mechanical construction has to be very accurate and requires associated electronics to enable the parameters to be adjusted.
- The audio may be allowed to peak up to 6 but needs to be controlled according to the programme material and its loudness, monitored on loudspeakers.
- Speech should be normally peaking 5 with only occasional peaks to 6, some acoustic instruments might be allowed to peak 5 as well but more complex music mixes will need to be lower, compressed music (e.g. rock bands) will need to be held to a maximum of 4, small crowds may peak 5 but very energetic ones only 4.
- Background effects behind a voice should be no greater than PPM 2 to 3.
- Compression can be seen on the meter as the range of levels becomes reduced and loudspeaker monitoring will require close attention.

Audio control

A television production usually involves combining a number of visual and audio sources. The vision mixing panel (see Introduction to vision mixing, page 170) switches the visual sources whilst the sound mixing console is designed to handle all programme audio sources. To process a variety of different audio inputs during a live transmission or recording into a single controlled output signal, the sound mixer will require some or all of the following facilities:

- **Audio assignment** assigns an audio input to its associated channel by means of a jack field, matrix or routeing switcher.
- **Input select and gain:** Input signals to the desk may originate at line level (e.g. tape machines or incoming lines) or low level output signals from microphones with the availability to adjust the gain depending on the type of microphone in use.
- **Routeing:** Each channel output can be assigned to a group fader or direct to the main output fader.
- **Channel fader** allows individual level control and audio processing of each sound source. A mono channel will be fitted with a pan control to allow the signal to be positioned at the required image position (see Stereo, page 94). A stereo channel has two identical paths to allow processing of left and right signals and a balance control to adjust the relative levels of the left and right signals.
- **Group fader** allows all assigned sources (usually grouped for a common production purpose) to be combined in whatever proportion required.
- **Master fader** controls the combined output of the sound desk and will normally be set at a calibrated 'zero' position or at 10 dB below maximum.
- **Auxiliary outputs** are additional outputs to the main desk output and allow for foldback feeds, etc.
- **Equalization** is the process of adjusting the frequency response of the signal usually banded into control of high, medium and low frequencies. Switched filters are used to remove low frequency rumble, etc.
- **Monitoring** of the output of the audio signal is achieved by means of high quality loudspeakers installed in a good, acoustically adequate, listening area (i.e. the room should have no significant effect on the sound). As well as the final production mix, provision is often required to allow monitoring of network audio and/or other linking audio sources to the production. The correct output of signal level is checked by an audio level meter (see figures on page 83). Meters may also be fitted to group faders, channel faders or switchable to a selected combination.
- **Pre-fade listen (PFL)** is the facility on an individual channel to pre-hear the designated audio source without affecting the mixer's main output.
- **Limiters** prevent the signal from exceeding a predetermined level.

Compression: The dynamic range of some sound sources (e.g. an orchestral concert) can exceed that which can be transmitted. If manually riding the level is not always feasible, sound compression can be used. The aim is to preserve as much of the original dynamic range by judicious use of 'threshold' (the level at which compression starts); 'slope or ratio', which controls the amount of adjustment; and 'attack and release', which determines the speed at which the compression equipment will react to changes.

Reverberation uses digital delay to the audio signal to simulate the effect of audio echo. Audio delay is also required when a visual source has been delayed by a frame store or satellite link. The sound is delayed to match the timing of the image.

Audio record and playback facilities available to a sound desk include, gram decks, ¼ inch tape, mini disc, audio cartridge machines and telephone hybrid. This allows an interface with the sound desk, compensating for line resistance and received levels, of a two wire telephone system.

Other facilities available from a sound console include phantom power supply for condenser microphones, communications and talkback to audio source originators for production purposes.

A digital console converts analogue inputs into a digital signal to be combined with the input from digital devices. Signal routeing between audio source and channel can be displayed on liquid crystal displays (LCD) or computer screens. Menus display information about all operational aspects of the desk and allow adjustment of any audio parameter. Sometimes this can be less flexible than manual adjustment if the required control can only be accessed by way of a number of menu page selections.

Loudspeaker monitoring

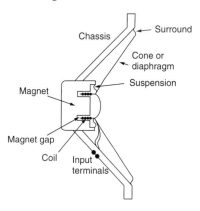

Assessing audio quality requires:

■ quality loudspeakers that produce a flat frequency response and can reproduce fast transients or changes in level.

■ a quiet listening environment with suitable acoustics that have no significant effect on the sound.

■ a clear understanding of how to interpret the chosen metering method (see page 83).

Audio rig

A television studio requires isolation from external sound, a reverberation time suitable for the production content, and sets which are designed to be compatible with good audio pick-up (e.g. the avoidance of curved hard surface backings). Ventilation noise, talkback leakage, equipment and staff movement during production can all add to unwanted background noise.

Audio rigging
Wall boxes around the studio are the means of connecting audio feeds and associated power to and from the sound control room. A number of dedicated microphone inputs, feeds for foldback speakers, production and sound control talkback are available on these panels. Care should be taken to avoid cross talk between low level signal output from microphones and the higher level foldback or talkback feeds. Use the nominated input/output on the box with the correctly screened cable and tie off the cables at the wall box to avoid disconnection if the cable is accidentally pulled.

Cabling
Start at the microphone position and run the cable back to its wall box or 'break-out' or 'stage box', a unit which can handle many microphones and take their feed on one cable back to the studio wall. Keep sound cables tidy and attempt to find cable runs across sets that are visually unobtrusive, are not endangered by other studio 'traffic', and do not run parallel or adjacent to lighting cables connected to dimmer circuits. If a microphone stand or boom is required to be repositioned during the production, make certain that surplus cable is neatly coiled and immediately available to be used as required. Any cable crossing fire lanes or entrances/exits should be ramped or flown (i.e. tied securely above head height).

Foldback
Programme sound not originating in the studio is often required. Prerecorded inserts or reports, feeds from outside sources, etc., need to be heard by presenters and guests if they form part of a discussion. Music tracks or sound effects may form part of speech or action cue. The location of the speaker and the level of foldback are critical to avoid pick-up by live microphones. Musicians require foldback of amplified instruments and voice often at a level that may cause coloration and/or prevent other production staff hearing talkback. This type of foldback is often controlled on the floor from a separate mixer.

Audience foldback
Many productions are staged in front of an audience who require to hear the content of the programme. In some discussion or game shows, members of the audience may also participate in the programme and appropriate techniques need to be employed to avoid howl-round.

Fisher microphone boom

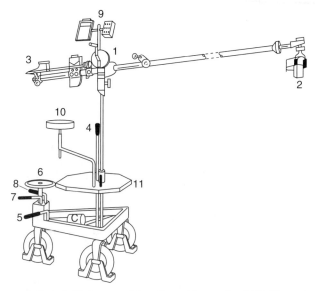

The boom arm's length (3–6 metres) is adjusted by a wheel (1). The microphone (2) can be tilted and rotated by a control lever (3), (squeeze for microphone tilt, turn for microphone turn).

The overall height of the boom arm and platform can be hydraulically adjusted (4) between 1 and 1.5 m. A pump handle (5) can be used to recharge the hydraulic cylinder. The boom pram is steerable with wheel (6) and can be held stationary by a brake (7). The back wheel drive can be disengaged (8) from the two front wheels to allow the boom to be manoeuvred. (9) Talk-back microphone, script board, programme junction box, mini-monitor. (10) Seat. (11) Platform allows operator 360° movement.

Clean feeds

If a discussion or interview is conducted with individuals who are located away from the main studio, all participants need to hear each other without hearing their own voice delayed. This requires an elimination in the recipients' fold-back of their own contribution. Clean feed is the output of the audio desk minus one or more of the sources going into it. In the USA, clean feed is more accurately called 'mix minus' and can be derived from a purpose designed clean feed output from the desk group outputs, or it may be provided for each channel on the sound control desk. This becomes more complex where there are many remote studios (e.g. an election coverage), requiring a number of clean feeds, allowing each location/studio to hear all the other sound sources.

XLR connectors

XLR (eXternal, Live and Return) type connectors are used for all balanced microphone connections and balanced high level signals. The connector has three pins – earth, live and return – and follows the convention that cable connectors with holes are inputs to the mixing/monitoring point. Connectors with pins point in the direction of the signal source.

Recording sound

There are two broad categories of audio recording:

- **analogue** – where the magnetization of a tape varies with the amplitude of the audio signal
- **digital** – where the audio signal is converted into a digital code (see pages 38–39) and then recorded.

Analogue recording

When an electrical current flows through a wire conductor it produces a magnetic field around the conductor proportional to the original current. This magnetic field can be intensified by wrapping the wire around magnetizable material to form an electromagnet. If the electric current flowing through the electromagnet has been created by an audio signal and a specially coated tape capable of being magnetized is driven past this varying magnetic field at constant speed, the fluctuating magnetic field will be imprinted onto the tape in proportion to the original signal's amplitude and frequency. This method of recording sound has a number of shortcomings and solutions:

- Tape has poor magnetic retention and does not record in a linear fashion. A fixed level bias frequency (100–200 kHz) is added to the audio to 'bias' the tape to a more linear part of its operating range.
- Tape hiss due to the finite size of the individual tape particles can be corrected by noise reduction circuits (see opposite).
- Pre-emphasis and replay equalization ensure a flat frequency response output to compensate for losses in the magnetic recording/replay process.
- Head alignment is important to ensure the head gap is at right angles to the tape, otherwise an azimuth error may cause a loss in the recording or replay of high frequencies.
- Magnetic saturation is reached when all tape particles are fully magnetized and any further increase in signal level will fail to produce a change in recorded level. Maximum recording levels must be controlled to avoid trying to produce a magnetic field that the system cannot achieve.
- The speed and tension of the tape must be constant otherwise wow and flutter will be detected in the replayed signal. In broadcasting, tape machines are often required on cue, to have instant start-up to correct operational speed.
- Tape heads and guides need to be clean to avoid a build up of tape coating deposited on the heads affecting the machine's performance.
- Tape drop out is caused if there are irregularities in the tape coating. Off-tape monitoring or a replay check on a recording and the use of high quality tape are the only methods of avoidance.
- Print through is caused by a modulated tape inducing its magnetism into an adjacent level of tape resulting in a pre- or post-echo. Storing master tapes 'tail out' (i.e. not rewinding after recording or replay) is a standard industry practice to reduce this degradation.

Recorded noise

Noise such as hiss, hum and other interference may exist alongside the required analogue audio signal. If the recorded tape is dubbed onto another tape the problem is increased on each recording. Methods of reducing this unwanted portion of the recording include:

■ **Correct levels** of recording and replay are always applied.

■ **Pre-emphasis** amplifies the high frequency portion of the wanted signals before recording to allow a reduction of high frequencies on replay, reducing high frequency noise whilst leaving the original audio unaffected.

■ **Dolby A** divides the signal into four frequency bands having its maximum effect when the level is 40 dB below reference. The system provides between 10 and 15 dB of noise reduction.

■ **Dolby B** is primarily a system of equalization with some compression applied to the signal. This can increase the signal-to-noise ratio of domestic cassette to about 60 dB.

■ **Dolby C** uses a larger compression and expansion ratio as well as frequency adjustments and can produce an improvement of around 10 dB over Dolby B.

■ **Dolby SR** (Spectral Recording) system uses ten separate bands of frequency processing operating signal compression that varies with its level. The result can be a reduction in noise of approximately 25 dB.

■ **DBX** uses compression across the whole frequency range. There is frequency pre-emphasis and corresponding de-emphasis on replay, the whole system providing up to 30 dB of improvement in the system signal-to-noise. There are two versions of the system, type 1 installed in professional equipment and type 2 used in the domestic market.

■ **Noise gates** define a set level below which the signal gain is reduced or even cut altogether. This process can be very unpleasant if not used with care. One example might be the feed to an audience PA system. Here, setting the gate threshold to around 20 dB (ref. 0.775 V) would ensure the speakers had no output unless the signal exceeded this level, thus reducing unwanted hum from the speakers.

Digital audio recording

Video recording resolved the problem of recording a much higher frequency spectrum than analogue audio on tape by means of a rotating record/replay head as well as moving the tape. Digital stereo audio needs to record at 1.4 Mhz (see Digital audio, p. 92) and the DAT (digital audio tape) system was developed to meet this criteria. For editing purposes, an identical analogue audio track is added (sometimes called cue track) as rocking a slow moving digital signal past a head produces no sound, unlike an analogue signal.

The frequency response and signal-to-noise ratio of digital recorders are superior to analogue machines and repeated copying results in far less degradation. Drop out can be corrected and print through has less significance or is eliminated. Wow and flutter can be corrected by having a memory reservoir system (see Frame store, p. 194) from which data is extracted at a constant rate eliminating any variation in the speed at which it was memorized. In general, when a signal is converted to digital, there is more opportunity to accurately rebuild and rectify any imperfections and to allow signal manipulation.

Audio and programme production

The selection and treatment of sound in a production shapes the perception of the audience and involves a range of audio techniques. These include:

- **Adjustment of loudness** in order to emphasize production content; to indicate priority (e.g. dialogue louder than background traffic); to exploit the dynamic range of sound (e.g. quiet contrasted with loud passages in orchestral music).
- **Pitch** is a subjective quality of the frequency of sound vibrations and each frequency band, similar to colour, has associated feelings.
- **Timbre** is the tonal quality of a sound as judged by the ear. It describes the texture or feel of a sound, and can be manufactured for specific production purposes (e.g. the use of distort for a telephone voice).
- **Reverberation** is the reflections from surfaces and can be artificially created to suggest environment.
- **Fades and mixes** mark the transition between sound sources, production sections or complete programmes. The rate at which a sound dies away can be highly evocative.
- **Sound effects** heighten realism, add space and atmosphere, reinforce the action, and can guide the audience to a new situation or scene. Combining sound effects can create an aural impression that is greater than its parts.
- **Smooth transitions** between contrasting images can be created by effects or music.
- **Anticipation** or preparing the audience for change can be achieved by sound leading picture (e.g. the sound of the incoming scene beginning at the end of the outgoing scene).
- **Sound perspective** focuses the attention of the audience on the visual space depicted (e.g. close-up sound for foreground action, distant sound for long shot). Sometimes dialogue clarity is more important than the realism of sound perspective. For example, the sound level of orchestral instruments in close-up are not normally boosted to match picture content. The overall orchestral balance is an integral part of the performance and therefore takes precedence.
- **Off-stage sound** suggests space and a continuing world beyond the frame of the image. It can also be used to introduce or alert the audience to new events. Sound from an unseen source creates space and mystery.
- **Narration** voice-over acts in a similar way to the thoughts of a reader. Careful balance between voice, effects, and music combine to give a powerful unity and authority to the production.
- **Music** is a sound source that has immense influence on the audience's response. It can create pace, rhythm, emotion, humour, tension, and requires a very subtle balance to weave the music in and out of effects and speech in order to create unity in the final production.
- **Silence** is an attribute of sound that has no visual equivalent. It emphasizes or enhances a production point but only in a sound film can silence be used for dramatic effect.

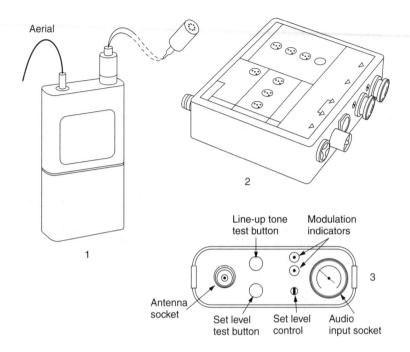

Aerial

Line-up tone
test button

Modulation
indicators

1

Antenna
socket

Set level
test button

Set level
control

Audio
input socket

2

3

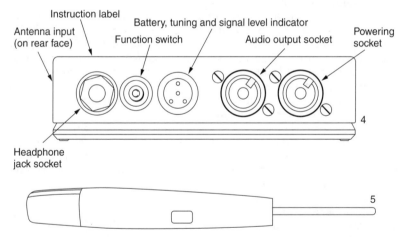

Instruction label

Antenna input
(on rear face)

Battery, tuning and signal level indicator

Function switch

Audio output socket

Powering
socket

Headphone
jack socket

4

5

Radio microphone equipment
1. Transmitter.
2. Receiver.
3. Transmitter top panel.
4. Receiver front panel.
5. Hand held radio microphone.

Digital audio

It is important to have a basic understanding of how audio is converted into digital information so that errors are not made, particularly when recording on digital camera/recorders.

Sampling

The audio signal is sampled at a constant rate like a series of pulses. For each of these pulses, the level of the sound is checked and this value is given a number. This number is transferred into binary code and this code is recorded as the digital information. The actual recording is therefore a string of codes, each representing the level of the audio at a particular moment in time. In order to achieve a good frequency response, the sampling is carried out at a very high frequency; 48,000 samples per second (48 kHz) is used for most professional systems. The level of the sound to be converted into binary numbers must also have sufficient steps to ensure accuracy, this is the quantization. With the 16 bit system employed by most camera/recorders, 65,536 finite levels can be represented. Put simply, this means that in order to encode and decode the signals, all the systems must operate at the same sampling rate and the signal level must never exceed the maximum quantization step or no value will be recorded.

Digital audio meters

The audio meter on a digital camera is very different to that on an analogue device as it shows values up to the maximum signal that can be encoded. This is calibrated from infinity (no signal) to zero (maximum level). It will also be noted that a line-up level (–20 dB) may be marked with a solid diamond shape or square on the scale (see figure opposite). This –20 dB point is used as the reference when aligning an external device such as a separate mixer. When taking a level prior to recording, it is safe to allow peaks to be well below 0 (maximum level). –12 dB to –8 dB is fine for normal peaks, ensuring the signal is properly encoded and the safety margin allows for any unexpected peak. Limiters are built into the system to prevent loss of signal should levels become too high, but as signal noise is not a problem (unlike analogue systems) holding the levels down is acceptable.

Digital camera/recorders

Most professional systems have four digital audio tracks. These all have the same specifications and can all be recorded with the picture or used for insert editing. The camera/recorder will have the ability to select any of these as mic or line inputs and will provide phantom voltages for the mics if required. On many digital camera/recorders, audio input/channel selections are not made with switches on the camera but are enabled via a menu displayed on an LCD screen positioned on the side of the camera. Many allow for other adjustments like audio limiters or the introduction of low frequency filters to help reduce unwanted noise at the time of the recording.

On camera digital audio meters

Viewfinder displays are different to analogue camera/recorder viewfinders. In the DVCPRO system, for example, there are indicators for –40 dB, –30 dB, –25 dB, –20 dB, –15 dB, –8 dB and 0 dB.

The Sony DVW-700 series uses the following display:

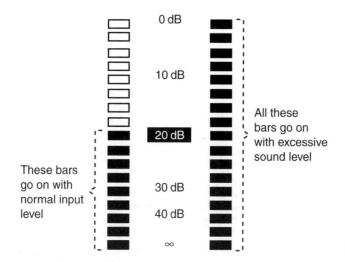

Note that unlike analogue systems, where signals above the maximum permitted level become progressively more distorted, digital signals do not exist above the maximum quantized level. The digital meters are calibrated from infinity (∞) to 0 (maximum level). Many have a calibration mark at –18 dB which is intended to be aligned with tone at zero VU. In fact some signals may produce digital clipping when aligned in this way and in the UK many users align 0 VU to –20 dB which places the zero level of 0.775 volts at –24 dB.

Cue track

As well as the four digital audio tracks, the digital formats also allow for a longitudinal audio cue track. This can be used for time code or have a guide version of the sync., or feature audio to assist in editing. This track will be easier to listen to when the tape is being played at a non-standard speed whereas digital tracks will be decoded in bursts, omitting material when played faster than standard and repeating material when slower.

The cue track can be recorded at any time, either with the picture or inserted separately. The information to be recorded on the cue track is normally set via the set-up menu in the viewfinder or on the camera/recorder output.

On the higher specification camera/recorders, a return output of audio from the camera/recorder to separate audio mixer no longer needs to come from the tiny headphone socket. Instead it is fitted with a male XLR socket on the rear of the camera. The track or mix of tracks and the level of the signal to be fed from this socket may also be adjusted via the menu-driven software on the camera/recorder.

Stereo

Normal hearing provides depth and space, perspective and separation, effects and atmosphere by 360 degree spatial hearing. Television mono sound originates from a single speaker but television stereo sound attempts to provide an approximation of this sound experience.

For effective stereo reception, it is recommended that the listener and the two stereo speakers are positioned at the three points of an equilateral triangle. Many stereo television sets fix their speakers either side of the screen (a distance of approximately three feet) with the viewer positioned six feet or more away. This limits the full potential of television stereo sound even though an effective stereo signal is transmitted. The stereo 'sound stage' that is transmitted is much wider than the screen size but it enhances the illusion of a 'third dimension' missing from a two-dimensional image.

Many television sets in use are not equipped with stereo sound and therefore stereo transmissions must be compatible with mono reception.

Locating stereo sound

Effective stereo sound requires the 'on screen' sound to be augmented with 'off screen' sound. Stereo adds to the screen image sound, background sound located left or right of the screen whilst still being compatible with mono listening. If approximately 15° is the central wedge of sound image on screen, everything else that does not have an obvious geographical relationship to the picture is 'elsewhere'.

Microphone placement

A stereo effect will occur if the time of arrival of an audio signal at two coincident microphones is different and this difference is faithfully reproduced on two loudspeakers. This inter-channel difference can also be artificially replicated from a mono source by the use of a pan-pot which determines which proportion of the mono signal is directed to each stereo channel.

The angle of acceptance of the two microphones, which are usually positioned 90 degrees to each other, will depend on their polar diagrams and their position relative to the sound source. Similar to the angle of view of a lens (see The zoom lens, page 50), the closer the pair of microphones are to the sound source, the greater the sound image will fill the region between the monitoring loudspeakers. The sound can originate from a point source such as a voice (excluding reverberations, etc.) or occupy a wide physical area such as a symphony orchestra. As television stereo sound pick-up is normally required to match the field of view of the displayed image, the width of the sound image and the polar diagram of the microphones are important. For example, a figure-of-eight ribbon microphone close to a camera will pick-up sound in front as well as behind the camera.

The M and S system – using cardioid and a figure-of-eight microphone

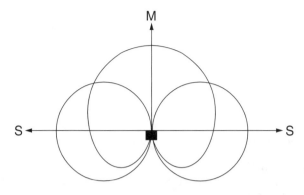

The middle and side (M and S) pair of microphones above consists of a cardioid facing forward, providing the M (middle/main) signal or centre image and a figure-of-eight microphone providing the S (side) signal.

Advantages of the M and S technique in news and documentary production are:

■ The proportion of side component can be decided and adjusted away from pressure of location work.
■ A good mono signal is available if stereo problems occur in post production.
■ The middle forward-facing microphone gives a clear indication of the direction the microphone is facing.

The main disadvantage for location work is that the S microphone (a figure-of-eight response) is prone to wind noise and rumble.

Stereo on location

Points to consider when recording stereo sound on location exteriors when there is likely to be less control of placement and choice of microphone are:

■ Are the left–right position images correct relative to the picture?
■ Are there any time delays between picture and sound?
■ Are there any time delays between the left and right legs of a stereo signal producing a hollow sound, lacking clear imagery?
■ Do the sounds appear at the correct distance from the camera (perspective)?
■ Is the relationship between the primary sound sources and the background effects satisfactory, and is the effect of the acoustic suitable?
■ Does the sound match the picture?

Preparation for location

Introduction

There are many advantages in recording items or complete programmes on location. Often the subject of the insert is the location or activity and must be recorded as found. The disadvantage is that away from base, a unit must be self-sufficient in all that is required to complete the assignment. Before travelling to a site it is worthwhile, if you are inexperienced, to make time to check over all equipment that will be needed to complete the job. Experience will teach you that frequently the shoot is not as the brief or script predicts and a few equipment 'extras' will enable you to salvage what could have been a wasted journey.

Pool equipment

Some camera users work or study with organizations where there is a pool of shared or hired-in equipment. They may be less experienced and may operate with several different cameras of unknown serviceability. To work with an unfamiliar camera each day is much more exacting than to work with a predictable and familiar camera. A start-of-day check on pool cameras and mounts is vital to eliminate problems with the equipment *before* arriving at the location.

Inventory check

Check that every item of equipment is there. Location work can be rushed and it is not unknown on a quick 'wrap' for a small item to be overlooked and left behind. Check the main equipment and then the smaller items such as power and connecting cables for mains adaptor, wet weather cover, dichroic filter on battery lamp, etc. And remember to check over the equipment you bought to a location when you leave the location.

Battery and electronic checks

Clip on battery and turn the power switch to on. Check the state of charge of the battery indicated in the display window. Find out when they were on charge and in what condition they were before the charge. A battery that has been charged and not used for several days may not remain fully charged. Individual cells discharge at different rates and the battery may have become unequalized. It may not respond to a fast charge before you leave. Run the camera up and carry out a quick check of all the main controls. Make certain that each switch is set to the mode you wish to operate in.

Mechanical checks

Check all mechanical parts for security and stability. A common problem is the interface between tripod adaptor and the pan/tilt head. Check that the tripod adaptor on the pan/tilt head is suitable for the camera and that the locking mechanism will hold the camera secure.

Adjusting the back focus

Flange-back (commonly called back focus) is the distance from the flange surface of the lens mount to the image plane of the pick-up sensor. Each camera type has a specific flange-back distance (e.g. 48 mm in air) and any lens fitted to that camera must be designed with the equivalent flange-back. There is usually a flange back adjustment mechanism of the lens with which the flange-back can be adjusted by about ±0.5 mm. It is important when changing lenses on a camera to check the flange-back position is correctly adjusted and to white balance the new lens.

Lens chart or any fine
detail/high contrast
subject

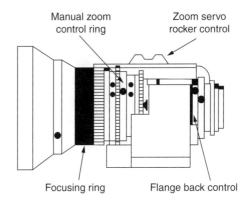
Manual zoom
control ring

Zoom servo
rocker control

Focusing ring

Flange back control

1 Open lens to its widest aperture and adjust exposure by adding ND filters or adjusting shutter speed.
2 Select the widest lens angle.
3 Adjust for optimum focus with the flange back control on the lens.
4 Zoom the lens in to its narrowest angle on an object at a distance from the camera and adjust the zoom focus for optimum sharpness.
5 Zoom out and repeat steps 2–4 of the above procedure until maximum sharpness is achieved at both ends of the zoom range.
6 Lock off the flange-back control taking care that its sharpest focus position has not been altered.

Operational checks at base

Remove lens and inspect rear element and filter wheel for finger marks or scratches. Refit lens if clean. Check that auto-iris and auto-zoom are set to AUTO position if you wish to operate in this mode.

A front-of-lens screw-in filter such as an ultraviolet (UV) is the best protection for the front element of a zoom. The cost of replacement, if damaged, is insignificant compared to the cost of repairing or replacing the zoom front element. Lens tissue and breathing on the front-of-lens filter is the most common and the simplest method of removing rain marks or dust. Dirt and dust can be removed with an air blower or wiped off gently with a lens brush. Never vigorously rub the lens surface or damage to the lens coating may result. Where there is oil, fingerprints or water stains, apply a small amount of commercial lens cleaner to a lens tissue and clean in a circular movement from centre to edge of lens.

Moisture and humidity
Protect lens from driving rain. Dry off lens casing with a cloth and front element with lens tissue. Place lens in a plastic bag overnight, with a desiccant such as silica gel. Check that the HUMID indicator is off in display window before inserting tape cassette.

Menu
Most digital camera functions and parameters such as gain, shutter, etc., can be programmed from a computer menu displayed in the viewfinder or external monitor. Each set of memorized variables is called a scene file and is stored either on a removable memory card or in a memory system integral to the camera. There are usually four or five different categories of file available.

1 A default scene file containing values which have been preset by the manufacturer. This should be selected when using a camera following on from other users.
2 There may be a scene file which has been customized by an organization for a group of users such as students (e.g. a standard zebra setting).
3 A blank scene file can save any adjustment to the camera variables displayed on the menu. It is advisable to name the file to indicate its application (e.g. J. Smith File or Preset Studio, etc.).
4 An engineering file may be locked to prevent accidental adjustment to crucial camera settings (e.g. Linear Matrix Table).
5 There is usually a self-diagnostic programme which checks the camera/recorder electronics and reports on the status of each section.

Check the menu settings and select *default* or *factory setting* if another user of the camera has reprogrammed the set-up card.

Viewfinder: brightness and contrast

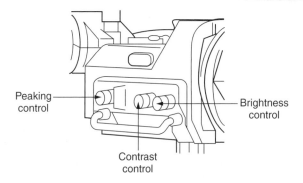

Peaking control

Brightness control

Contrast control

The monocular viewfinder is the first and often the only method of checking picture quality for the camcorder cameraman. The small black and white image has to be used to check framing, focusing, exposure, contrast and lighting. It is essential, as the viewfinder is the main guide to what is being recorded, to ensure that it is correctly set up. This means aligning the brightness and contrast of the viewfinder display. Neither control directly affects the camera output signal. Indirectly, however, if the brightness control is incorrectly set, manual adjustment of exposure based on the viewfinder picture can lead to under or over-exposed pictures. The action of the brightness and contrast controls therefore needs to be clearly understood.

■ **Brightness:** This control alters the viewfinder tube bias control and unless it is correctly set-up the viewfinder image cannot be used to judge exposure. The brightness control must be set so that any true black produced by the camera is just not seen in the viewfinder.

If, after a lens cap is placed over the lens and the aperture is fully closed, the brightness is turned up, the viewfinder display will appear increasingly grey and then white. This obviously does not represent the black image produced by the camera. If the brightness is now turned down, the image will gradually darken until the line structure of the picture is no longer visible. The correct setting of the brightness control is at the point when the line structure just disappears and there is no visible distinction between the outside edge of the display and the surrounding tube face. If the brightness control is decreased beyond this point, the viewfinder will be unable to display the darker tones just above black and distort the tonal range of the image. There is therefore only one correct setting of the brightness control which once set, should not be altered.

■ **Contrast:** The contrast control is in effect a gain control. As the contrast is increased the black level of the display remains unchanged (set by the brightness control) whilst the rest of the tones become brighter. This is where confusion over the function of the two viewfinder controls may arise. Increasing the contrast of the image increases the brightness of the image to a point where the electron beam increases in diameter and the resolution of the display is reduced. Unlike the brightness control, there is no one correct setting for the contrast control other than an 'over-contrasted' image may lack definition and appear subjectively over-exposed. Contrast is therefore adjusted for an optimum displayed image which will depend on picture content and the amount of ambient light falling on the viewfinder display.

■ **Peaking:** This control adds edge enhancement to the viewfinder picture as an aid in focusing and has no effect on the camera output signal.

Road craft

Tape problems

The tape is manufactured to a high tolerance and requires care in handling. Check for tape slack and tighten reels before loading. Do not force the cassette into the VTR. When battery voltage is almost below the level required to operate, the cassette can be removed. With some formats, when the voltage falls below this point, the cassette cannot be ejected or the cassette holder closed.

Batteries

For many years nickel cadmium (Ni-Cd) batteries have been the standard power for portable video cameras. With the growth of portable computers and mobile phones, new battery technologies using nickel metal hydride (NiMH) and rechargeable lithium have been developed but at present NiCad batteries form the main proportion of professional video batteries in use. The camera/recorder is normally powered by a 13.2 V or 14.4 V nickel-cadmium rechargeable battery which is clipped to the back of the recorder. There are a range of different capacity batteries available to give extended running times or several batteries can be grouped together and worn on a belt.

Capacity

The capacity of a battery is often rated in ampere-hours, which is the maximum current flow (amps) in one hour before the battery is completely discharged. A more useful measure is how long a specific battery will run a specific make of camera. The nominal run time is calculated by multiplying the battery voltage by its ampere hour rating to determine a watt hour figure which is then divided by the power rating of the camera/recorder, e.g. a 12 volt/5 AH battery = 12 (volts) × 5 (AH) = 60 watt hours which will give a 2.5 hours run time for a camera drawing 24 watts (60 ÷ 24). For the same camera, a 14.4 volt/5 AH battery = 14.4 × 5 (AH) = 72 watt hours will give a 3 hour run time (72 ÷ 24).

Battery voltage range

Another crucial camera specification is the operating voltage range. Most cameras will specify a minimum voltage below which the camera will not operate and an upper voltage beyond which, operating the equipment will cause damage or trigger the power breaker. The value of this power figure is stated, for example, as 12 V (−1 +5) which means that the camera will function over the voltage supply range of 11 V through to 17 V.

Tape problems that can occur include:

■ Head clogging caused by a build up of invisible metal particles. You must use a cleaning cassette to maintain tape path performance but do not exceed the recommended timetable of cleaning as excessive cleaning can shorten the life of the head.

■ Tape dropout can be caused by imperfections in the coating and by worn heads with insufficient contact between tape and head. After considerable use, the head may need replacing. Also, any part of the recorder that the tape comes into contact with (guides and rollers, etc.) should be periodically checked and cleaned.

■ Excessive humidity or low humidity can cause problems. Although the tape is manufactured with a built in lubricant to reduce tape wear, high humidity causes stiction and increases the risk of head clogging. At lower humidities electro-static charging will be more pronounced resulting in greater attraction of dust and an increase in dropout. Allow tapes to acclimatize if they have been subject to extremes of temperature or humidity.

■ Moisture condensation on the drum assembly may occur if the camera is moved from a cold to a warm location or if the unit is used in a very humid place (e.g. an enclosed swimming pool). This may cause the tape to stick to the head and damage head and tape. Avoid this occurring by removing cassette when changing from cold to hot locations and, with the power on, check that the HUMID indicator in the display window does not light. Do not insert cassette until the HUMID indicator light goes off.

■ Cinching of the tape is caused by badly adjusted playback recorders which abruptly stop and cause several layers of tape to slip and bunch between themselves. Remember that the tape from the camera is the master tape and irreplaceable. It should not be used to repeatedly view the day's shooting. Transfer to VHS for production viewing and guard the use of the master tape until it arrives in post production.

Safety hazards when charging a battery

■ **Cold temperature charging:** The fast charging of a cold battery is one of the most dangerous hazards associated with NiCad batteries and can result in a violent explosion. When a NiCad is fast charged at temperatures below +5°C (+41°F), the internal charging reaction cannot proceed normally and a significant portion of the charge current can be diverted into producing highly explosive hydrogen gas. A spark can ignite this gas causing an explosion that can turn the battery into a grenade. *Cold batteries must be allowed to reach room temperature before being placed on a charger.*

■ **Fire hazards:** NiCad batteries and chargers have been identified as the source of several fires and toxic smoke incidents over the years. One major TV network instructed their cameramen that batteries must not be charged in their hotel bedrooms. Most of these incidents are connected to fast chargers that failed to recognize when a battery reached full charge. The continuing current produces heat and eventually smoke or fire. This can be avoided by the use of a thermal fuse in the power circuit which will disconnect the battery from the charger if dangerous temperatures are detected. A similar fire hazard can also occur if there is a mismatch between the charger and battery on a slow charge. Always provide for air circulation around batteries and do not charge batteries in a bag or flight case.

■ **Physical shock:** If a battery is internally damaged by physical impact or being accidentally dropped, internal wires can be short circuited and become red hot elements causing the battery to burst into flames. Take every precaution to avoid subjecting batteries to violent physical impact.

■ Most of the above hazards can be avoided or eliminated by using an interactive charger that continuously interrogates the battery while charging.

Safety

Health and safety legislation obliges you to take reasonable care of your own health and safety and that of others who may be affected by what you do or fail to do. You also have a responsibility to co-operate, as necessary, to ensure satisfactory safety standards. If you comply with the requirements for safety and something goes wrong, then your employer will be held to account. If you fail to comply, you may lose any claim for compensation for injury and could even be prosecuted as an individual. What you must do is:

- Follow the safety requirements and any instructions you are given, especially in relation to emergencies (e.g. know the location of fire exits).
- Ask for further information if you need it and report accidents (or a near miss!), and any dangerous situations or defects in safety arrangements.
- Do not interfere with or misuse safety systems or equipment, or engage in horseplay that could be dangerous.
- Work within the limits of your competence, which means a knowledge of best practice and an awareness of the limitations of one's own experience and knowledge.

Assessing risk

The key to good, safe working practices is to assess any significant risk and to take action to eliminate or minimize such risks. The procedure is:

- identify precisely what is required in the production
- identify any potential hazards in that activity
- identify the means by which those risks can be controlled.

The key terms in risk assessment are:

- **Hazard** – the inherent ability to cause harm.
- **Risk** – the likelihood that harm will occur in particular circumstances.
- **Reasonably practicable** – the potential improvement in safety is balanced against the cost and inconvenience of the measures that would be required. If the costs and inconvenience do not heavily outweigh the benefits, then the thing is reasonably practicable and should be done.
- **Residual risk** – the risk remaining after precautions have been taken.

An example

It is proposed to shoot from a camera hoist near overhead power lines. The power lines are a **hazard**. Touching them could result in death. What is the likelihood (**risk**) that harm will occur in particular circumstances? There may be the risk of a high wind blowing the hoist onto the power lines. Is the weather changeable? Could a high wind arise? What is **reasonable and practical** to improve safety? The obvious action is to reposition the hoist to provide a usable shot but eliminate all risk of it touching the power lines. As weather is often unpredictable, the hoist should be repositioned as the costs and inconvenience do not heavily outweigh the benefits. There remains the **residual risk** of operating a camera on a hoist which can only be partially reduced by wearing a safety harness.

A check list of potential location safety hazards

- **Boats**: It is essential to wear life lines and life-jacket when operating on a boat or near water such as on a harbour wall.
- **Confined spaces:** Check the quality of air and ventilation when working in confined spaces such as trench, pipes, sewer, ducts, mines, caves, etc.
- **Children** are a hazard to themselves. When working in schools or on a children's programme, check that someone is available and responsible to prevent them touching or tripping over cables, floor lamps, camera mountings, etc.
- **Explosive effects and fire effects** must be regulated by a properly trained effects operator and especial care should be taken with those effects that cannot be rehearsed.
- **Excessive fatigue** is a safety problem when operating equipment that could cause damage to yourself or others and when driving a vehicle on a long journey home after a production has finished.
- **Fork lift trucks** must have a properly constructed cage if they are to carry a cameraman and camera.
- **Lamps:** All lamps should have a safety glass/safety mesh as protection against exploding bulbs. Compact source discharge lamps must always be used with a UV radiation protective lens. Lamps rigged overhead must be fitted with a safety bond. Check that lamp stands are secured and cabled to avoid being tripped over and that they are securely weighted at the base to prevent them being blown over.
- **Location safety:** In old buildings, check for weak floors, unsafe overhead windows, derelict water systems and that the electrical supply is suitable for the use it is put to. Check the means of escape in case of fire and the local methods of dealing with a fire. Check for the impact of adverse weather and in remote locations, the time and access to emergency services.
- **Noise:** High levels of location noise (machinery, etc.), effects (gunshots, explosions) as well as close working to foldback speakers can damage hearing. Stress will be experienced attempting to listen to talkback with a very high ambient noise. Wear noise-cancelling headsets. If wearing single sided cans, use an ear plug in the unprotected ear.
- **Stunt vehicles:** Motor vehicles travelling at speed involved in a stunt are likely to go out of control. Leave the camera locked-off on the shot and stand well away from the action area in a safe position agreed with the stunt-coordinator.
- **Filming from a moving vehicle:** Camera must be either securely mounted or independently secured on safety lanyards. Operators should be fitted with seat belts or safety harness attached to safety lines securely anchored.
- **Roadside working:** Wear high visibility gear and get the police to direct traffic if required. Police may give permission for a member of the crew to direct traffic but motorists are not obliged to obey such instructions.

Video recording formats

ENG format cameras
A variety of digital recording formats have been developed particularly the upgrading of hitherto domestic digital video recording formats to facilitate cheaper and less complex cameras/recorders to match the different production requirements of video acquisition.

Betacam format specification
The picture is recorded on a ½ in Beta tape cassette using two adjacent video heads. The luminance signal (Y) is recorded on one track and on the other track the chroma consists of a compressed time division multiplex of the colour difference signals (red – Y and blue – Y). Two audio longitudinal tracks are recorded at the top of the tape with longitudinal control and time code tracks at the bottom of the tape. Betacam SP recording on metal particle tape provides two additional audio FM channels recorded with the chrominance signal. They allow improved sound quality but cannot be edited independently of the video and must be layed-off to be edited.

Digital Betacam
Digital working provides greater control over the look of the picture with the ability to alter gamma, knee point, skin tone, detail enhancement, matrix, etc. Also the ability for precise colour matching in a multi-camera shoot using a wide range of gamma curves programmed into the camera. Linear matrix coefficients can be varied and two sets of the coefficients stored in memory. Additional control over image appearance is now possible with such variables as horizontal detail enhancement to match scene content, detail clip level to avoid excessive highlight detail and stepped lines along slanted picture edges. A skin tone detail function allows selective reduction to be applied to face tones. This can reduce or eliminate facial imperfections while maintaining detail enhancement to the rest of the image.

Betacam SX
The Betacam SX format has the following additional features. Auto-tracing white (on B position) which will white balance when moving between different colour temperature light (e.g. moving between interior and exterior). Its automatic selected value cannot be stored. Pressing 'return' on the lens during a recording places a 'good shot' marker on the tape which can be picked up by the edit machine. The camera operator can identify and code up to 198 selected shots while shooting. These codes are stored on the tape and can be read-out during the edit. In addition to the selectable three gain positions positioned on the side of the SX range of cameras, there is an instant turbo gain button providing an immediate 36 dB gain (equal to 6 stops). Time code regeneration facility (in record run) can pick up on the existing recorded time code of any tape placed in the camera. Dockable Betacam SX recorders can be used with analogue cameras.

The DV format was originally intended for the domestic camcorder market as the DV format cameras did not meet the basic ENG requirements of operational features and ruggedness. The picture quality, however, was good enough for broadcasters to use the format in productions that required small, inexpensive lightweight kit.

DVCPRO and DVCAM are upgrades of the DV format primarily designed for news acquisition. The two formats have an improved recording specification and a number of broadcast operational facilities not found on consumer DV cameras. The camera/recorders are smaller, lighter and cheaper, and with less power consumption than previous ENG formats, coupled with smaller cassettes, allow longer recording times. The lightweight cameras allow easier handling in ENG work and have the ability to provide colour playback. With low power consumption, a two-machine editor can provide rapid, portable editing on location and stories can be put to air more quickly.

■ **Digital-S:** Digital-S uses the same size half-inch tape and cassette as S-VHS and records on metal particle tape. Certain Digital-S studio VTRs can replay standard analogue S-VHS tapes allowing continuing access to previous S-VHS tape libraries. Digital-S uses 4:2:2 processing with a video data rate of 50 Mega bits per second with a 3.3:1 compression. The half-inch width tape allows 2 linear audio cue-tracks for audio access in edit shuttle and 4 digital audio (16 bit, 48 kHz) tracks and for 2 lines for uncompressed video for closed captioning. Up to 104 minutes of material can be recorded.

■ **Disk camera:** The Camcutter format records direct to disk in the camera/recorder. This allows certain edit functions to be performed in the camera. Whereas digital formats required downloading from tape to disk, the Camcutter's FieldPak (a disk drive in the camera) can be removed and inserted into the desktop FieldPak adaptor and non-linear edited. Each FieldPak can be reused many thousands of times. The disk recording unit is available in two configurations: as an add-on to a suitable existing Ikegami camera or as an integrated single-piece camera/recorder unit.

Disk recording allows the additional production facilities on camera of:

■ **RetroLoop:** This facility constantly records in a pre-defined loop of time selectable from 15 to 60 seconds. When the record button is pressed, video/audio stored in the RetroLoop is kept as part of the new clip. This stored 15–60 seconds of material is added to the new shot.

■ **Intelligent recording:** This facility allows immediate recording without cueing-up blank tracks even during playback. The new data is written onto free tracks avoiding over-recording previous material. Automatic clip numbering on every separate shot/recording.

■ **Time lapse recording:** This function enables intermittent recording at predetermined intervals for a predetermined period of time. Disk cameras can be preprogrammed to record one frame at predetermined intervals.

■ **Lip-synching:** Audio can be recorded while video is played back. While video is played, a pre-scripted narration can be recorded.

■ **Location control:** Access to any desired point on the disk can be selected by use of camera report or time code without the need to shuttle. Simple editing can be done with the camera/recorder.

■ **Erasing unwanted video:** In camera, previous recordings may be reviewed and unnecessary clips deleted. This function enables only necessary scenes to be left on the disk. About 15–20 minutes (2.2 Gb) of recording time is normally attainable with a single FieldPak. Thirty minutes of record time is available on the higher density FieldPak.

White balance

Processing of the output from the red, green and blue sensors is normalized to signal levels produced by a scene lit with tungsten lighting (3200 K). When the camera is exposed to daylight, it requires significant changes to the red channel and blue channel gains to achieve a 'white balance'. Many cameras are fitted with two filter wheels which are controlled either mechanically, by turning the filter wheel on the left-hand side at the front of the camera, or by selecting the required filter position from a menu displayed in the viewfinder. The filter wheels contain colour correction and neutral density filters and possibly an effects filter. The position of the various filters varies with camera model.

Filter selection
Set the filter selectors to match the colour correction filter appropriate to the light source and light intensity. A common combination of colour correction and neutral density filters are:

position [1] 3200 K   sunrise/sunset/
tungsten/studio
position [2] 5600 K + ¼ ND (neutral density) exterior, clear sky
position [3] 5600 K   exterior, cloud/rain
position [4] 5600 K + 1/16 ND (neutral density) exterior, exceptionally bright.

Neutral density filters are used when there is a need to reduce the depth of field or in circumstances of a brightly lit location. The 3200 K is a clear glass filter whereas a 5600 K filter (with no ND) is a minus blue filter to cut out the additional blue found in daylight. All colour correction filters decrease the transmission of light and therefore the minus blue filter cuts down the light (by approximately one stop) where most light is available – in daylight. A white balance is required after changing filter position.

To white balance
To white balance, select the appropriate filter according to the lighting condition and fill the frame with a white object lit by the predominant subject illumination. Check that the gain is at 0 or as low as possible and that any contrast control facility is switched out.

There are usually two memory buttons associated with each filter. Select A or B on the white balance selector and set the IRIS to automatic iris control. Push the AUTO W/B BAL switch to WHT. The adjustment will be completed in about one second and the adjusted value will be stored in the A or B memory selected. If the white balance was unsuccessful the viewfinder may display a message such as 'WHITE:NG' – white balance no good – and an explanatory message. If you set the WHITE BAL selector to the PRST (preset) the white balance will be set to the factory-preset value of 3200 K if the filter position is set to the 3200 K filter position.

Peak white clippers: There are three peak white clippers, one in each colour channel, and their function is to limit any part of the scene that would produce a signal greater than a pre-set value. Their effect is to render all gradations in brightness above the 'clip' level as white – to burn out any overexposed parts of the picture. This can be difficult for the cameraman to see if his viewfinder is not correctly adjusted.

Knee

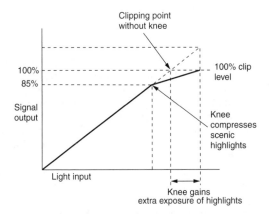

The 'knee', which is introduced into the camera head amplifiers, progressively compresses highlights which otherwise would be lost in the peak white clipper. It extends the camera's response to a high contrast range but with some loss of linearity.

Variable slope highlight control

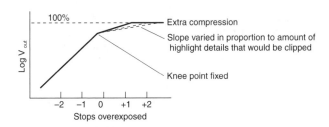

Variable knee point highlight control

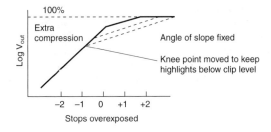

107

Exposure

Contrast range

Every shot recorded by the camera/recorder has a variation of brightness contained within it. This variation of brightness is the contrast range of the scene. The relationship between the brightest part of the subject and the darkest part is the contrast ratio. Normally, exposure is adjusted to allow the contrast range of the scene to be accurately reproduced on the recording. The aim is to avoid losing any variation between shades and at the same time maintaining the overall scene brightness relationships.

Achieving the correct exposure for any specific shot therefore requires reproducing the detail in the highlights as well as in the shadows of the scene. Additionally, if a face is the subject of the picture then the skin tones need to be set between 70% and 75% of peak white (may be a wider variation depending on country and skin tones). Whereas the contrast ratios of everyday location and interiors can range from 20:1 to 1000:1, a video camera can only record a scene range of approximately 32:1. Peak white (100%) to black level (3.125%) is equivalent to 5 stops. The contrast range can be extended by compressing the highlights using a non-linear transfer characteristic when translating light into the television signal (see page 107). The amount of compression on the highlights can be further increased by switching in contrast control circuits. The result of recording a contrast range greater than the camera can handle is highlights of the scene will appear a uniform white – details in them will be burnt out and the darker tones of the scene will be a uniform black. The limiting factor for highlight detail in high contrast scenes is the peak white clipper circuits and the 'knee' of signal amplification in the camera.

Auto-exposure

Exposure can be determined by using the auto-iris exposure circuit built into the camera or by manually using a light meter and the viewfinder picture, or using the zebra indicator in the viewfinder. Auto-exposure works by averaging the picture brightness and therefore needs to be used intelligently. In some cameras, different portions of the frame can be monitored and the response rate to the change of exposure can be selected. In general, expose for the main subject of the shot and check that the auto-iris is not compensating for large areas of peak brightness (e.g. overcast sky) in the scene.

Zebra exposure indicator

The zebra pattern is a visual indicator in the viewfinder when areas of the picture have reached a certain signal level. If the zebra exposure indicator is switched on, those elements of the image that are above this pre-set level are replaced by diagonal stripes in the picture. The cameraman can respond by closing the iris until part or all of the zebra diagonals have been removed.

Exposure and the reduction in contrast range

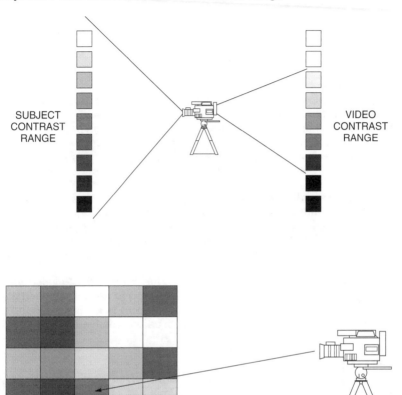

SUBJECT
CONTRAST
RANGE

VIDEO
CONTRAST
RANGE

The auto exposure system measures the range of subject brightness and sets an f-number which will reproduce a mid-tone grey at 50% of peak white. 50% of peak white is equivalent to the light from a subject with 18% reflectance.

Time code

Time code enables every recorded frame of video to be numbered. This allows precise identification when editing. There are two methods of recording the identification number.

Longitudinal time code

Longitudinal time code (LTC) is recorded with a fixed head on a track reserved for time code. It can be decoded at normal playback speed and at fast forward or rewind but it cannot be read unless the tape is moving as there is no replayed signal to be decoded. It is recorded once every frame as a series of pulses (binary digits) whose repetition rate changes according to whether it is recording 0s or 1s.

Vertical interval time code

Vertical interval timecode (VITC) numbers are time-compressed to fit the duration of one TV line and recorded as a pseudo video signal on one of the unused lines between frames. It is recorded as a variation in signal amplitude once per frame as binary digits. 0 equals black and 1 equals peak white.

The 300/400 series Beta format cameras have the ability to insert VITC twice on two non-consecutive lines. They are factory-set to insert the VITC signal between lines 19 and 21 for PAL but there is provision for another choice of line position for VITC insertion independent of the first choice.

Code word

Every frame contains an 80 bit code word which contains 'time bits' (8 decimal numbers) recording hours, minutes, seconds, frames and other digital synchronizing information. All this is updated every frame but there is room for additional 'user bit' information.

User bit

User bit allows up to 9 numbers and an A to F code to be programmed into the code word which is recorded every frame. Unlike the 'time bits', the user bits remain unchanged until re-programmed. They can be used to identify production, cameraman, etc.

There are two ways of starting time code – record run and free run.

Record run

Record run only records a frame identification when the camera is recording. The time code is set to zero at the start of the day's operation and a continuous record is produced on each tape covering all takes. It is customary practice to record the tape number in place of the hour section on the time code. For example, the first cassette of the day would start 01.00.00.00 and the second cassette would start 02.00.00.00. Record run is the preferred method of recording time code on most productions (Free run, see opposite).

110

Time code

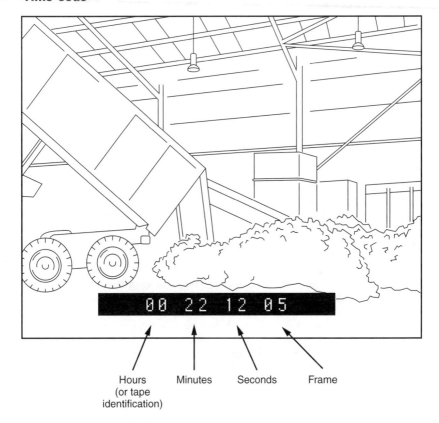

Hours (or tape identification)　Minutes　Seconds　Frame

Free run

In free run, the time code is set to the actual time of day and when synchronized is set to run continuously. Whether the camera is recording or not, the internal clock will continue to operate. When the camera is recording, the actual time of day will be recorded on each frame.

This mode of operation is useful in editing when covering day-long events such as conferences or sport. Any significant action can be logged by time as it occurs and can subsequently be quickly found by reference to the time-of-day code on the recording.

In free run (time of day) a change in shot will produce a gap in time code proportional to the amount of time that elapsed between actual recordings: missing time code numbers can cause problems with an edit controller when it rolls back from intended edit point and is unable to find time code number it expects there (i.e. the time code of the frame to cut on, minus the pre-roll time).

Time code setting

If you are using time code and user bits, set user bits first. If you set time code first, the time code value will not be correct because the time code generator stops while the user bits are being programmed.

111

Structure

Single camera working

There are broadly three requirements for all location camerawork. The camera operator must produce a technically acceptable picture (e.g. correctly exposed, white balanced, etc.), he/she must ensure the shots provided can be edited together (e.g. size of shot, camera angle, camera movement, etc., see page 114, Shooting for editing), and lastly, and most importantly, the shot coverage of the event or activity has a rough structure which can communicate the intended message. A series of isolated, unconnected shots will not provide a structured visual message.

Separate shots

Whether shooting news or a magazine item, the transmitted item will be shaped by the editor to connect a sequence of shots either visually, by voice-over, atmosphere, music or by a combination of all of them. Essentially the cameraman or director must organize the shooting of separate shots with some structure in mind. Any activity must be filmed to provide a sufficient variety of shots that are able to be cut together following standard editing conventions (e.g. avoidance of jump cuts, not crossing the line, etc.) and that there is enough variety of shot to allow some flexibility in editing. Just as no shot can be considered in isolation (what precedes and what follows always has an effect), every sequence must be considered in context with the overall aims of the production.

Structuring a sequence of shots for news and magazine items

- When shooting an event or activity, have a rough mental outline of how the shots could be cut together and provide a mixture of changes in camera angle, size of shot and camera movement.
- Avoid too restricted a structure in type of shot give some flexibility to the editor to reduce or expand the running time.
- Keep camera movement short with a greater proportion of small significant moves that reveal new (essential) information.
- Avoid long inconsequential pans and zooms.
- When shooting unrehearsed events, steady the shot as soon as possible and avoid a sequence of rapid, very brief shots.
- Get the 'safe' shot before attempting the ambitious development.
- Provide some type of establishing shot and some general views (GVs) that may be useful in a context other than the immediate sequence.
- In general, wide shots require a longer viewing time than big close-ups.

Checklist of questions before recording

■ What is the purpose of the shot?
■ Is the shot fact or feeling? Will the image attempt to be factual and objective and allow the viewer to draw their own conclusions or is it the intention
  to persuade or create an atmosphere by careful selection?
■ In what context will the shot be seen: what precedes, what follows?
■ What will be the most important visual element in the shot?
■ Why has this specific lens angle and camera position been chosen:
  ■ to emphasize the principal subject?
  ■ to provide variation in shot size?
  ■ to give added prominence to the selected subject?
  ■ to provide more information about the subject?
  ■ to provide for change of angle/size of shot to allow unobtrusive intercutting?
  ■ to allow variety of shot and shot emphasis?
  ■ to create good shot composition?
  ■ to favour the appearance of the performer?
  ■ to alter the internal space in the shot by changing camera distance and
    lens angle?
  ■ to alter size relationships in shot?
  ■ to improve the eyeline?
  ■ to comply with the lighting rig or natural light?

113

Shooting for editing

News editing requirements

There are many ways to assist the editor to get the best out of your camerawork. Shooting with editing in mind is essential. A series of disconnected shots have to be meaningfully edited together and this relies on the cameraman thinking and providing edit points. Nothing is more time consuming than the attempt to edit a pile of cassettes of ill-considered footage into some intelligent and intelligible form. To avoid this, the editor requires from the cameraman maximum flexibility with material supplied and the nucleus of a structure.

■ **Brevity and significance**: The value of a shot is its relevance to the story in hand. One single 10-second shot may sum up the item but be superfluous in any other context. Check that the vital shots are provided and at the right length before offering visual decoration to the item. Editing for news means reducing to essentials.

■ **Variety of shot**: In order to compress an item to essential information, the editor requires a variety of options. This means a variety of relevant shots in order to restructure a continuous event (e.g. a football match, a conference speech) and to reduce its original time scale to the running order requirement.

■ **Continuity**: Be aware of possible continuity mismatch between shots in background as well as foreground information. As well as changes over time (weather, light, face tones) watch for changing background action that will prevent intercutting.

■ **Speed of access:** A large portion of an editing session can be taken up simply finding the relevant shot. Shuttling back and forth between different tapes is time consuming and the edit is greatly speeded up if thought is given to the order in which shots are recorded whenever this is possible.

■ **Shot size**: Avoid similar size shots, whether in framing, scale, horizon line, etc., unless you provide a bridging shot. In general, television is a close-up medium. Big wide-angle shots do not have the same impact they might have on a larger screen.

■ **Leaving frame**: Do not always follow the action (especially on 'VIP' items where the temptation is to keep the 'notable' in shot at all times). It can sometimes help in editing if the subject leaves frame.

■ **5-second module**: News items tend to be constructed on an approximate 5 second module. To allow maximum flexibility for the editor, try to shoot in multiples of 5 seconds. Keep zooms and pans short. e.g. 10 second hold at start of zoom (or pan); 5/10 second zoom (or pan); 5/10 second hold at end of movement. This allows the editor a choice of three shots.

■ **Shooting ratio:** Be aware of the editing time available. Over-shooting a topic without any structure in mind will result in most of the material being unable to be previewed let alone used: a waste of location and editing time.

Crossing the line

Every shot of a sequence should stay the same side of an imaginary line drawn between the speakers. It is easy to forget eyeline direction when recording questions or 'noddies' after an interview has been recorded, particularly with a three-hander or when equipment is being demonstrated or explained. Make certain that the camera stays on one side only of the imaginary line drawn between the interviewer and interviewee.

Time code

Except for some sport (e.g. football) and occasionally all day conferences, where reference in editing to time of day is important, ensure that the recorder is switched to **RECORD RUN** time code. This records a numerically continuous code from the beginning to the end of the tape. **REAL TIME** will give discontinuous time code, dependent on the time of day the shots were recorded. This can cause problems in the 'pre-roll' when editing.

Length of pan

Avoid long panning or development shots. Although it may be difficult, depending on the circumstances, try to begin and end camera movement cleanly. It is difficult to cut into a shot which creeps into or out of a movement. Be positive when you change framing. Use a tripod whenever possible as unsteady shots are difficult to cut and a distraction to the viewer.

Editing checklist

- Record 30 seconds of bars (and tone if available) at the front of each new cassette.
- In general use record run time code.
- Avoid recording when the camera is in a stand-by mode with the tape unlaced.
- Record for 6 seconds (depending on camera model) before essential action.
- For news, remember the 5-second module and keep camera movement short.
- Hold a steady frame at front and end of movement and use a tripod if possible.
- Be positive when you change framing.
- Give the editor as many options as possible to allow items to be shortened or restructured.
- Avoid jump cut situations.
- Identify by sound, cutaways of people and objects if it is not obvious who they are.
- Check white balance when you become aware of a changing colour temperature.
- Provide the editor with plenty of cutaways to allow an event (such as sport) to be cut to a fraction of its running time.
- Use time-of-day time code for sport if significant action can be logged.
- Provide a continuous master shot/soundtrack of musical numbers.

115

Interviews

Providing cutting points

Most interviews will be edited down to a fraction of their original running time. Be aware of the need for alternative shots to allow for this to happen.

Brief the presenter/journalist to start talking when you cue (i.e. approximately 5 or 6 seconds after start of recording) and to precede interview with interviewee's name and status to 'ident' interview. Also not to speak over the end of an answer or allow the interviewee to speak over the start of a question. If necessary, change framing during questions but not answers unless you make the camera movement smooth and usable.

Backgrounds

If an interview is being conducted against a changing background (e.g. a tennis match or a busy shopping arcade) reverse questions must be shot because a two-shot, shot after the interview will not match. If an interview or 'presenter to camera' is staged in front of a discussed building or object (e.g. crash scene) which is an essential part of the item, make certain that cutaways of the building or object are sufficiently different in angle and size to avoid jump cuts.

Cutaways

Make sure your two-shots, cutaways, reverse questions, noddies, etc., follow the interview immediately. Not only does this save the editor time in shuttling but light conditions may change and render the shots unusable. Match the interviewee and interviewer shot size. If the interview is long, provide cutaways on a separate tape. Listen to the content of the interview which may suggest suitable cutaways.

Vox pops

Alternate the direction the interviewees are looking in the frame so that the editor can create the feeling of a dialogue between consecutive speakers and to avoid jump cuts between subjects who are looking in the same direction.

Think about sound as well as pictures

If the interview is exterior, check for wind noise and shield the microphone as much as possible by using a windshield or using the presenter/interviewee's body as a windbreak. Check background noise, particularly any continuous sound such as running water which may cause sound jumps in editing. Record a 'wild track' or 'buzz track' of atmosphere or continuous sound after the interview to assist the editor.

Standard interview

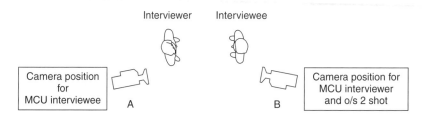

Interviewer   Interviewee

Camera position
for
MCU interviewee   A

Camera position for
MCU interviewer
and o/s 2 shot   B

C

Camera position
for
wide 2 shot

■ Set interviewee's position, first ensuring good background and lighting.
■ Then set interviewer beside camera lens (A) to achieve a good eyeline on the interviewee.
■ Record the interviewee's shot first changing size of shot on the out of frame questions.
■ Reposition for the interviewer's questions and 'noddies' (B). An over-the-shoulder 2 shot from this position can be useful to the editor when shortening the answers.
■ Match the MCU shot size on both participants.
■ A wide 2 shot of the two participants talking to each other (without sound) can be recorded after the main interview if the shot is sufficiently wide to avoid detecting the lack of lip synch if the shot is used for editing purposes in mid-interview (C).

Provide the editor with information

Identify on sound at the start or at the end of a shot, any specific cutaways especially people whose identity may not be known to the editor (e.g. court case – identify by description – 'the man in the blue anorak is the defendant, Joe Bloggs'). Make certain your sound ident is clear of significant action or effects.

Identify on the sound track and by written ident on the tape box the priority of sound tracks if necessary (e.g. **TRACK ONE** interview and sync sound, **TRACK TWO** wild track atmos).

Consider the possible problems of using auto iris and auto gain during the interview.

Avoid using **AUTO GAIN** in situations where a high level background noise may suddenly occur (e.g. a lorry passing) and severely attenuate the interviewee's voice level.

The nature of light

Lighting and communication

The most important element in the design of television images is light. Apart from its fundamental role of illuminating the subject, light determines tonal differences, outline, shape, colour, texture and depth. It can create compositional relationships, provide balance, harmony and contrast. It provides mood, atmosphere and visual continuity. Light is the key pictorial force in television production.

One of the simplest definitions of the aim of any TV production was stated succinctly as 'whatever is happening on screen, the viewer wants to see it and usually wants to hear it'. Good television lighting does a great deal more than simply enabling the viewer to see programme content, but usually the first basic technical requirements are to supply sufficient light to enable cameras to be correctly exposed, at the appropriate colour temperature, and to help modify or create a suitable contrast range for the subject in order to meet the requirements of TV broadcasting (see page 108).

These technical requirements can be satisfied fairly easily if sufficient luminaires and power are available but washing the subject with light may produce flat, dead pictures that fail to engage the audience's attention. The controlled use of light to satisfy and enhance production requirements is also the aim and objective of studio and location lighting.

The nature of light

In order to control light it is necessary to understand how light behaves and have some means of measuring its physical characteristics.

What the human eye can detect (the visible spectrum from red to violet), is only part of a range of electromagnetic radio waves that enable radio and television to be transmitted, radar and microwaves to operate, and also includes ultraviolet radiation, X-rays and gamma rays. They can be categorized by their individual wavelength – the distance from wave peak to wave peak – which in visible light is measured in nanometres.

The eye begins to register wavelengths at about approximately 700 nm (red) through to a peak response to wavelengths of 555 nm (green) up to shorter wavelengths of approximately 400 nm (blue). This non-uniform average response to visible light when plotted is known as the photopic curve and any useful meter to measure light should mimic this curve.

Measurement of light

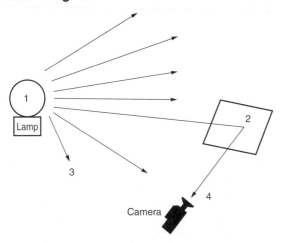

1 LIGHT SOURCE has a luminous intensity (*I*) measured in *candelas*

2 ILLUMINATION (*E*): luminous flux incident onto a surface, measured in lumens/m² = *lux*

3 LUMINOUS FLUX (*F*): radiant energy (*F*) weighted by the photopic curve, measured in *lumens*

4 LUMINANCE (*L*): measure of the reflected light from a surface, measured in *apostils*

Luminous flux emitted into the solid cone from a source of 1 candela = 1 lumen

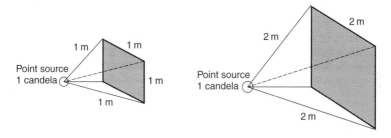

- ■ **Inverse square law:** Doubling the distance from light to subject quarters the level of illumination (lux) falling on the subject.
- ■ **Cosine law:** If the angle of a light beam to a surface it is illuminating is less than 90°, the illuminance of that surface is reduced by a factor determined from the cosine law.
- ■ **Incident light meter:** These meters are designed to measure the light falling on the subject. To calculate the ratio between key and fill, place the meter close to the face of subject and point in turn at the key light and the fill. The ratio of the two readings will provide the contrast ratio of light on the face.

Visual perception

There have been many theories about perception and many visual experiments. Most conclude that perception is instantaneous and not subject to extended judgement. It is an active exploration rather than a passive recording of the visual elements in the field of view and is selective and personal. The mind makes sense of visual elements by grouping elements into patterns. Any stimulus pattern tends to be seen in such a way that the resulting structure is as simple as the given conditions permit.

Although perception seeks visual unity, a detailed visual communication requires contrast to articulate its meaning. Morse code can be understood if the distinction between a dot and a dash is accentuated. Communication is achieved by contrast. The communication carrier – sound or light – provides a message by modulation. There is a need for polarities, whether loud or soft, dark or light, dot or dash. Meaning is made clear by comparison. A television image requires the same accentuation of contrast in order to achieve coherent meaning. Light, by supplying contrast of tones, can remove visual ambiguity in a muddle of competing subjects but the wrong tonal contrast can produce a confused and misleading 'message'.

The choice between harmony and contrast

Visual arts have traditionally employed two competing systems – **harmony**, which tends to balance out conflict of mass, and **contrast**, which stresses differences and therefore makes meaning clear. Harmony is the weakening or toning down of irregularity. It is epitomized by the perfect distribution of ratio and balance accomplished in classical art. There are no visual ambiguities or uncertainties of what is displayed either in the objectives of the visual designer or in the perception of the viewer. But perceptual attention demands stimulation whereas harmony tends towards the elimination of visual conflict. There is a visual design need to introduce tension through contrast to achieve clarity of communication. In its most extreme form, middle tones are eliminated to provide a simplification of the image to the bare essentials. If the purpose of a television image is to convey ideas, information or feeling, then contrast is required to articulate the image and to focus on the meaning of the message.

Hard and soft

Within this broad generalization, two qualities of light are used in television production – hard and soft. Usually hard light produces the greatest contrast, modelling and texture. It creates depth, shape and relationships. All light, hard or soft can reveal modelling, texture, contrast – it is a matter of shadow structure which determines the 'sharpness' of the effects. Diffused light is often applied to reduce the contrast introduced by a hard light source and to create an integrated harmony of tones.

Use of colour

The individual response to colour may be a product of fashion and culture – a learnt relationship – or may be an intrinsic part of the act of perception. People's colour preferences have been tested and in general western people choose in order of preference blue, red, green, purple, orange, yellow. This choice is modified when the colour is associated with an object that has a specific use. Below is a very generalized checklist of points to bear in mind when using colour:

■ Many colours have a hot or a cold feel to them. Red is considered hot and blue is felt as cold. It will take other strong design elements within a shot to force a foreground blue object to exist in space in front of a red object. The eye naturally sees red as closer than blue unless the brightness, shape, chroma value and background of the blue are so arranged that in context it becomes more dominant than the desaturated, low brightness of the red.

■ Colour effects are relative and no one set of guidelines will hold true for all colour relationships. For example, the intensity of a hot colour can be emphasized by surrounding it by cool colours. The intensity of the contrast will affect balance and to what part of the frame the eye is attracted.

■ The perception of the apparent hue of any coloured object is likely to vary depending on the colour of its background and the colour temperature of the light illuminating it. Staging someone in a yellow jacket against green foliage will produce a different contrast relationship to staging the same person against a blue sky.

■ Complementary contrast balance can be achieved by opposing a colour with its complementary. The complementary of red is green, the complementary of blue is orange, the complementary of yellow is violet. These complementary pairings consist of a hot and a cold colour. Complementaries placed alongside each other will appear to have more vividness and vitality than colours that are adjacent in the colour wheel. Visual equilibrium however is not simply achieved by equal areas of complementary pairs. Blue needs a greater area to balance its complementary orange. Red needs approximately the same area of green whereas yellow needs a relatively small area of violet to achieve visual equilibrium.

■ Colour can communicate experience or feeling by association. Red is often described as passionate, stimulating and exciting. Blue is seen as sad and depressing. Yellow is serene and gay whilst green is thought of as restful and stable. Strong prolonged stimulation of one colour has the effect of decreasing the sensitivity to that colour but sensitivity to its complementary is enhanced.

■ The balancing of area and the shape of a coloured object has a strong impact on the unity of an image. A small area of intense colour can unbalance a composition and continually attract the eye. If its location coincides with the main subject of the shot then the right emphasis is achieved. If it exists near the edge of frame or away from the dominant subject then it acts as a second subject of interest and is a distraction.

■ Paintings often achieve a strong visual impact by restricting the range of colours used. A limited palette of colours on a set can create unity and impact. A number of sequences in a variety show can each be given their own individual identity by using colours which compliment or contrast with the artiste's costume colour.

■ Colour temperature: A piece of iron when heated glows first red and then, as its temperature increases, changes colour through yellow to 'white hot'. The colour of a light source can therefore be conveniently defined by its colour temperature. Strictly speaking this only applies to incandescent sources (i.e. sources glowing because they are hot). The most common incandescent source is the tungsten filament lamp. Colour temperature is measured in Kelvin equivalent to °C +273. The colour temperature of domestic tungsten light is 2760 K, while that of a tungsten halogen source is 3200 K.

121

Lighting a face

A 'talking head' is probably the most common shot on television. Whether news, drama, sport or entertainment, people like watching people. The reflectivity of the human face varies enormously by reason of different skin pigments and make-up. In general, Caucasian face tones will tend to look right when a 'television white' of 60% reflectivity is exposed to give peak white. Average Caucasian skin tones reflect about 36% of the light. As a generalization, face tones are approximately one stop down on peak white. But as well as achieving correct exposure, lighting a face also involves making decisions about how a specific face is to be portrayed. Most professional presenters know their 'good' side and their 'bad' side. This may be to do with blemishes or their nose line but usually it is because faces are often asymmetrical about the centre-line. Depending on its position, the keylight modelling will either make the shadowed side of the face appear to be narrower (to be avoided if it is already the narrow side of the face) or broader.

The lighting treatment must take into account blemishes ('key' into the blemish), emphasizing or adjusting the overall shape of the face, the shape or the jaw line, the line of the eyes, the line of the mouth, etc. If a subject with a bent nose is keyed the same way as the bend of the nose, this will exaggerate the nose bend. If keyed in the opposite direction it will tend to straighten out the bend. The American cine-matographer Gordon Willis used top lighting on Marlon Brando in *The Godfather* to help reduce Brando's jowls but this also had the effect of putting his eyes in shadow and making him more mysterious and threat-ening. Presenters with deep set eyes can lose contact with their audience unless a way is found to get light on to their eyes. A catch light reflected in the eyes often lifts the personality of the face and allows the viewer 'eye contact' with the most important part of the face.

Multi-camera shooting requires lighting which provides for different angles and many faces on the same set. Location lighting may only have to accommodate one face and one camera position, but the shot may include a natural lighting source such as a window or the direct light from the sun. Ideally, the aim is to light artistes separately to their back-grounds as this enables control of the lighting of both areas to be achieved.

Hard and soft light

A light source can be identified as being 'hard' or 'soft' depending on the type of shadow it produces. A hard source (e.g. direct sunlight) produces a hard edge shadow, reveals texture and is usually a point source or of a small area. A 'hard' lamp can be focused and have its beam shaped by barndoors and is more controllable than a 'soft' source. Soft light produces overlapping shadows with soft edges. It tends to obliterate texture and because it needs a large originating area to be soft, it is difficult to control.

122

Three point lighting

Key light

A single strong directional light gives the best modelling and structure to a shot. The key light provides the necessary exposure and brings out the three dimensional aspects of the subject. As we have discussed, when keying faces, the decisions to be made are: where should the nose shadow fall (or should there be a nose shadow?), are deep-set eyes lit, does the angle and position of the key suit the structure of the subject's face, are there reflections in spectacles, and are any facial imperfections exaggerated or concealed? Does it throw unwanted shadows on the background of the shot?

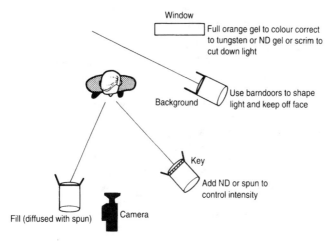

Fill

Wherever the key is placed, the strong shadows it creates need to be modified to reduce the contrast range and normally to lighten the mood of the shot. This is achieved by a fill light usually on the opposite side of the lens to the key, which is a soft source of light produced by a reflector or a diffused flooded lamp or an overcast sky but not direct sunlight. The key-to-fill ratio on the face is the contrast range and can be balanced by using a meter or estimated by eye to match the required mood of the shot. An average is between 2:1 and 3:1.

Backlight

It is usually necessary to find some visual way of separating the subject from its background so that attention can be focused on the subject. Check for suitable unobtrusive background detail when positioning camera and subject and use a hard light source directed from behind the subject to highlight the head. This will give sparkle to the hair and rim light the shoulders. Try to avoid too high an intensity – the backlight should hardly be perceptible.

Background light

To avoid people being shot in limbo, some light needs to be directed to the space behind them. The aim should be to light sufficient background to provide some indication of location whilst avoiding overpowering the foreground. A lit background gives space and mood to the shot, but on location, ensure that it conforms to the main source of light.

123

Lighting levels

How light is shaped, balanced and distributed within a shot plays a vital part in television production but there are a number practical considerations when deciding the overall level of light that is to be used. These include:

- satisfying exposure requirements which depend on camera sensitivity
- creating an appropriate depth of field
- providing a good environment for artists performance
- heat generation, ventilation, number of luminaires available, total capacity and cost of the power supply.

Camera sensitivity

Camera sensitivity is usually quoted by camera manufacturers with reference to four interlinking elements – a subject with peak white reflectivity, scene illumination, f-number, and signal-to-noise ratio for a stated signal. It is usually stated as being the resulting f-number when exposed to a peak white subject with 89.9% reflectance lit by 2000 lux and also quoting the signal/noise ratio. For most current cameras this is f8 with some achieving f11 and better. The sensitivity of the camera could be increased by simply greater and greater amplification of weak signals but this degrades the picture by adding 'noise' generated by the camera circuits. In a great deal of 'actuality' location work (e.g. news gathering, sports coverage, etc.), the gain of the head amplifiers can be increased if insufficient light is available to adequately expose the picture.

Depth of field

Lighting level will determine f-number for correct exposure, which in turn will decide depth of field (see Zoom lens, page 50). The range of subjects in focus within the frame will have a significant effect on the visual appearance of the production. The chosen depth of field can therefore be a production design element as well as having a crucial impact on the ability to find and hold focus in ad lib camerawork. Other factors which affect exposure include shutter speed, lens range extenders, zoom ramping, filters, prompt devices and the lighting environment to accommodate performance and mood.

Mood and atmosphere

With highly sensitive cameras, it is possible to achieve correct exposure with very low light levels – levels which may appear to be darker than the corridor approach to the studio. This may be appropriate for some types of drama but it can have a depressing effect on other types of TV productions.

Economics

Luminaires require a power supply and, in an enclosed space like a studio, ventilation to extract heat that tungsten lamps can generate. The number and cost of luminaires available to a production, the total capacity of the power supply and the deployment of the rig, is another practical controlling factor in lighting design.

Types of location lighting

■ **Reflector:** A reflector board or sheet requires no power and takes up very little space. It is invaluable for fill-in lighting by bouncing light from daylight or lamp into shadow.

■ **Battery lamps:** These are fixed to the top of the camera and powered from the camcorder battery or, preferably, a separate battery belt. When working in daylight they require a dichroic filter to correct the colour temperature of the lamp to daylight. Dichroic filters are made of glass and are therefore more fragile than gel filters, but their advantage is that they transmit approximately 15% more light than gels.

■ **Flight kit (portable lighting kit):** This is a two or three lamp kit that derived its name from its compact size – small enough to fit into a metallized container for quick stowage and easy transportation.

■ **Redhead:** This is a 800 W lamp drawing 3.3 A, weighing 3 kg including barn-door and safety glass, with an output of approximately 6000 candelas (cd) flooded and 24,000 cd spotted when over 4 m.

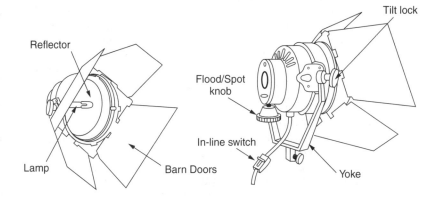

■ **Blonde:** This is a 2000 W lamp drawing 8.3 A and weighting 6 kg with barndoor and safety glass. It produces approximately 25,000 cd flooded and 150,000 cd spotted when over 6 m. Because of their weight and flexibility and their low power consumption they can be rigged and derigged quickly and plugged into most domestic power supplies.

■ **Discharge lamps**: Discharge light sources such as HMI lamps produce light by ionizing a gas contained in the bulb. They have greater efficiency than tungsten, are lighter and cooler in operation and produce light which approximates to daylight. They require an EHT supply to ionize the gas and a current limiting device. This may be a simple inductive choke or in the form of a flicker free electronic ballast. A 1.2 kW HMI, which is one of the most useful on a small unit with conventional ballast, will draw 12 A when switched on but settle to 6.4 A when warmed up. It can therefore be used on a domestic 13 A ring main circuit providing no other lamps are connected when it is switched on.

■ **Ballast:** The use of high-frequency dimmable ballasts operating above 40 kHz provide a flicker free output and allow dimming with a simple 0–10 V control (or 100 kΩ potentiometer) to achieve reduction in lighting levels with little change in colour (unlike dimmed tungsten sources).

125

Luminaires

There are many different types of luminaire that have been developed to satisfy different aspects of lighting (see figure page).

- **Fresnel spotlights (a):** This is a general purpose luminaire used in a wide range of applications that require a good modelling light (e.g. keylight, backlight, set light or hard fill-light). It is available in a number of operating wattage ranging from 100 W up to 24 kW and is fitted with a Fresnel lens and a reflector/lamp assembly that can be moved to alter the beam angle from wide angle (full flood) to narrow angle (full spot). The light output from the luminaire can be directed by a pan/tilt and a spot/flood mechanism, and if required, this can be adjusted by a pole when the lamp is rigged at a height. Fresnel spotlights are usually fitted with barndoors to control the beam shape.
- **Soft source (b):** Soft sources are large area sources which produce light on the subject from many directions resulting in multiple overlapping shadows. They need to be of a large area (such as light bouncing off a large white surface), to be truly soft and are useful for controlling the density of shadows, creating gradations of tone, improving the appearance of a face (e.g. hiding blemishes), creating a shadowless backlight, and for lighting shiny or glossy surfaces (e.g. car commercials). Soft luminaires are often grouped together to create a large effective area.
- **Transparency projectors (c):** Transparency projectors are luminaires with condenser optics and a projection lens to project still or moving effects, e.g. clouds, flames, etc.
- **Silhouette projector (d):** A luminaire which has a lens system to produce a sharply focused disc of light or to project a customized metal cut-out called a gobo (e.g. logo, abstract pattern, etc.). The projector includes metal shutters within it to shape the beam and may have a single lens or twin lens optics, and they are also available with a rotatable gobo holder.
- **PAR cans beam light (e):** Parabolic aluminized reflector lights produce a very intense and narrow beam of light which, when used with smoke, results in the production of dramatic shafts of light. The lamp and reflector are part of a sealed unit with a front element that may be plain, diffused or in the form of a lens. A gel slot is fitted to the front of the can and the design of the lamp filament allows the lamp to be rapidly switched on and off. They are available in various beam spreads from wide flood to very narrow spot.
- **Ground row (f):** Ground row units are used to light cycloramas and are positioned on the floor or hung from hoists. The angle of the row and its distance from the cyc are critical in achieving an even lit cyc from top to bottom. They are available as single units fitted with frosted 625 W or 500 W linear tungsten halogen lamp that are slotted together, or as groups of four, six, etc. Each open faced luminaire can be fitted with an individual coloured gel and are separately wired to allow for the grouping and mixing of colours.

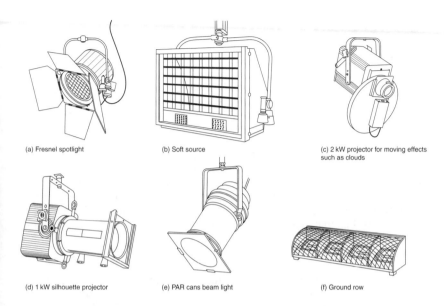

(a) Fresnel spotlight

(b) Soft source

(c) 2 kW projector for moving effects such as clouds

(d) 1 kW silhouette projector

(e) PAR cans beam light

(f) Ground row

There are many other types of luminaires including:

- **Fluorescent luminaires (cold lights):** Fluorescent luminaires usually use several lamps to produce a practical light source, hence they are soft sources. Control of the light beam shape is either by a fine structured 'egg-crate' or 'honeycomb' fitment. Improved phosphors have made the fluorescent lamp acceptable for television and film and are available to provide tungsten matching and daylight matching colour temperatures.

- **Dual source luminaires:** These are basically a hard source and a soft source bolted together with pole-operation of pan, tilt, spot/flood, hard/soft and power switching.

- **Follow spot:** The follow-spot is used to light artistes at long throws in complete isolation, and to follow any artiste movement. It is a narrow angle version of a twin-lens hard-edged projector, designed to use a tungsten halogen or discharge light source, depending on the lamp throw required.

- **Moving lights (intelligent lights):** A moving light achieves its effects by moving the complete luminaire or by moving a mirror to move the beam. A variety of effects are available, e.g. pan and tilt, colour change of light beam (infinite or limited colour wheel), beam angle change, beam focus change, gobo wheel, rotating gobo effects, diffusion, colour correction, mechanical dimmer. Some are designed to remotely 'follow' the performer by way of a small transmitter carried by the artiste which sends signals to receivers around the edge of the performing area. The information received is used to process the controlling signals sent to the moving lights.

127

Controlling light

To rehearse, record or transmit multi-camera studio productions it is necessary to have continuous control of the luminaires. The lighting console allows the lighting director to set and adjust dimmer levels, scrollers, moving lights and practicals. The luminaires can be grouped and their levels adjusted for lighting changes and then computer memorized. For purposes of rigging and/or adjustments during rehearsal, the console should have the ability to be remotely controlled from the studio floor. Usually the console will be equipped with a mimic board which allows a quick visual check of which lamps are currently in use. The third essential element in the control of light is a high quality switchable monitor or monitors displaying the programme production and close liaison with the vision controller. There is also a requirement for load meters to be installed alongside the lighting console so that the load current for each phase can be monitored.

Dimmers

The lighting console provides the necessary control signals to remotely operate dimmers. Modern consoles usually achieve this by generating a digital number for sequential transmission over one pair of wires using a digital multiplexing system (DMX 512). Whenever possible there should be a dimmer for each lighting circuit (outlet) matched to its associated lighting channel number (dimmer number).

In the past, the thyristor or silicon controller rectifier (SCR) was the preferred electronic method for controlling the current to a luminaire, and hence its light output. These were superseded by transistor dimmers which were quieter in operation and avoided large current surges on 'switch-on' and could be rack mounted or located, if required, on lighting hoists.

Modern digital dimmers use the DMX data signal directly for processing the control of the dimmer, using a 'number' not an analogue voltage and allow a cheaper, more reliable, accurate dimmer, with a faster response to level changes, protection against overloads and short circuits and with a choice from a number of dimmer laws. The dimmer law is the relationship between the fader setting and light output.

Digital Multiplex 512 (DMX 512)

DMX 512 provides a digital multiplex system capable of handling the control information for 512 channels, as a single data channel. The fader setting between 0 and +10 V (analogue signal) is sampled in channel sequence at a regular interval and converted into an 8-bit binary number, this provides 255 discrete fader levels plus OFF. This data is sent as a sequence down a single cable to all devices using DMX 512.

- **Neutral density filters:** A recurring problem with location interiors is to control and balance the intensity of daylight from windows with the much lower light levels from lamps. Neutral density (ND) filters will reduce the level of daylight without changing its colour temperature. They are made of flexible gelatin or thin acrylic sheets and are available in a range of grades. They can also be combined with colour correction filters. The filters are fixed to windows in a method that will avoid being seen on camera. Although ND gel can buckle and produce flares it is easily transportable in rolls. The acrylic sheet needs to be cut, is difficult to move and is expensive.
- **Plastic 'scrim':** a perforated material silver on one side and black on the other, can also be used on windows (black side in) to act as a neutral density filter (0.6 ND). It is more robust than ND gels and not so prone to flare. Check that its perforated pattern cannot be seen on camera.
- **Polarizing filters** on the camera lens reduce reflections and glare, darken blue skies and increase colour saturation. They are useful in eliminating reflections in glass such as shop windows, cars and shooting into water. The filter must be rotated until the maximum reduction of unwanted reflection is achieved.
- **Spun or diffusion,** a fibreglass-type material, is used in front of lamps to diffuse or soften the light. It also reduces the lamp intensity. It can be used to cover partially a portion of the lamp's throw to soften edges and to produce a reduction in brightness in part of the shot. It is available in a range of grades and can be doubled up in use to increase diffusion.
- **Colour filters:** Polyester filters have a clear plastic base coated with a coloured pigment. Polycarbonate filters have the base material mixed with the pigment. They are referred to as high temperature (HT) filters and are not affected by heat as much as the polyester filters.
- **Colour correction filters** are used to correct the light sources to a common colour temperature, e.g. tungsten sources to daylight (5500 K), daylight to tungsten (3200 K) or to correct both sources to an intermediate value (see location lighting figures, page 135).
- **Barndoors** are metal flaps fitted to the front of the lamp lens and can be adjusted in a number of ways to keep light off areas in shot and to shape, soften and produce gradations on surfaces.

Studio lighting

Programme planning

Daily multi-camera TV production from a studio complex requires the same precision in planning as any 'conveyor belt' industrial process. There is neither the time nor staff to simply arrive in a studio without pre-planning where sets, furniture and artistes will be positioned. This information is crucial to the lighting director's need to produce a lighting plot for the pre-rigging of luminaires before rehearsal begins. Production content, style and artistes' movement is required so that a lighting strategy can be evolved. The lighting director needs to visualize the production and plan the lighting treatment accordingly.

Lighting plot

The lighting plot is usually a 1:50 scale drawing of the studio detailing the type, position and aiming direction of all luminaires, colour filters, any flags, cutters, half wires, etc., floor luminaires, practical lamps, e.g. wall lights, table stands, any special lighting requirements. There is no internationally agreed set of symbols for use on a television lighting plot and many television companies use their own 'in-house' signs and codes (figure opposite). It is important that any changes to the lighting rig during set and light, or rehearsal, are indicated on the lighting plot to keep it up to date.

Using a copy of the lighting plot, the electricians rig all the appropriate lighting equipment, filters, etc. The lighting director, using a remote rigger panel, together with the electricians, will then set each luminaire to the correct height and adjust it to light the required area.

Rehearsal and levels

A rough lighting balance may be obtained during the setting process, but usually it is when shots are available during the rehearsal that a satisfactory balance can be achieved. The lighting team of lighting director, console operator and vision control operator work together to produce a satisfactory lighting balance and exposure. Often the vision control operator will avoid exposure adjustment to cameras until the lighting balance has been set. Because of the interaction between lighting levels, lighting balance, camera exposure and black level on picture quality, the process of balancing the lighting levels requires the use of Grade 1 monitors which have been correctly aligned and are available as a common reference.

Recording/transmission

All the lighting conditions set during rehearsal, lighting cues and lighting changes have to be executed as rehearsed during the recording/transmission period as well as responding to the unplanned and the unexpected.

Setting a lamp – checklist

It is useful to adopt a definite procedure when setting luminaires, say start upstage and work downstage or the reverse. For each Fresnel spotlight:

■ Check that the height is correct.

■ Rotate barndoors to the configuration you think you require. This avoids the disturbance of a 'set' luminaire if you leave this to last. Many barndoors develop a reluctance to rotate smoothly, requiring some additional force which often displaces the luminaire setting!

■ Open barndoors so that you can see the hot spot.

■ Adjust pan/tilt as necessary to 'set' luminaire. Useful to check that illuminance is satisfactory for keylights.

■ Adjust barndoors as necessary.

■ Avoid trying to set a luminaire with others on.

■ When all the luminaires are set, have a look at each lighting condition.

■ Check illuminance and make up basic memories.

■ Finally set the line-up lamp.

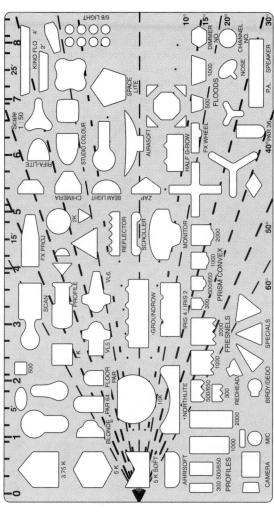

Stencil symbols for a lighting plot

Vision control

One of the principal aims of a television production is to create a stream of pictures that convinces the viewer that they are watching continuous action in 'real' time. Direction, camerawork, sound, lighting, vision mixing all practise an 'invisible' technique designed to hide the mechanics of bringing the image to the screen in order to emphasize the content of the programme. The vision controller plays a crucial part in this strategy by ensuring image continuity in exposure, colour and picture quality. In order to achieve this, he/she must continuously monitor the output of all cameras making any appropriate adjustments to iris, black level and colour as needed. This can only be achieved if each shot is assessed on a Grade 1 monitor coupled to a waveform monitor/vectorscope.

Matching pictures is usually achieved by using a joystick control for each camera which, when depressed, switches that camera's output to the assessment monitor. Rotating the top of the joystick allows the black level to be set, and moving the joystick forwards or backwards opens/closes the iris. The ratio of joystick movement to iris movement can be altered by a FINE and a COARSE setting. For studio work, the iris control is normally operated in the FINE mode, which allows one f-stop either side of the central position; the central position having been set to the nominal lens aperture. The COARSE iris control is normally used on outside broadcasts where large changes in lighting levels can be expected!

In a studio production, exposure will be dependent on lighting levels and variation in levels. It is common practice for the lighting director to attempt to balance out lighting levels during rehearsal before the vision control operator begins exposure correction. To maintain the 'invisible' technique there should be no evidence of vision control adjustment in the recorded/transmitted picture. Usually each shot will be previewed before it is used but sometimes (e.g. spontaneous actuality events under sunlight), adjustment on shot is unavoidable. Picture matching is focused on exposure, matching face tones and background, and black level. A small adjustment of black level has a greater effect on the TV image than a similar alteration to iris. To summarize, the operational role of the vision control operator may include:

■ align the cameras prior to rehearsal and transmission/recording
■ align vision/lighting control room monitors
■ check incoming/outgoing vision sources to the vision mixer
■ adjust black level, iris setting of each shot and colour match if required
■ set the appropriate contouring detail for each shot and adjust gamma and knee as appropriate
■ switch appropriate mixed viewfinder feeds to camera viewfinders as required and identify any vision faults and arrange for the necessary adjustment.

Assessment of picture quality

There are a number of video signal measurements that can be objectively checked with a vectorscope and waveform monitor, but essentially picture matching has to be done visually using a monitor. Picture monitor alignment is of critical importance if correct picture assessment is to be achieved.

Many monitors are designed with an automatic alignment system using a sensor placed against the face of the monitor. Another method of assessing monitor line-up is by feeding the monitor display with a special test signal from an external picture line-up generating equipment known as PLUGE.

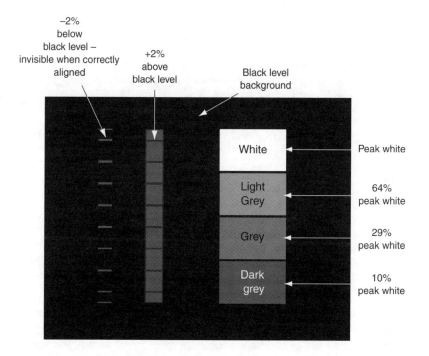

PLUGE test signal

The PLUGE test signal allows accurate setting of brightness and contrast. Brightness is adjusted so that the lighter bar is just visible, but the darker bar is not visible. Using a spotmeter, the contrast is adjusted to give 25 foot lamberts off the peak white signal. The other 'steps' may be used to check the gamma of the monitor. Ideally, brightness and contrast should be remotely controlled from the Vision Controller's desk.

A method of checking chroma is by feeding colour bars to the monitor and switching the monitor to blue only. Under this condition, the three right-hand colour bars should look the same brightness. Precise assessment can be improved by turning down the brightness control (to be reset later) and/or viewing the screen through a suitable ND filter. All adjustments of monitors should be done under normal control room operating lighting levels.

Location lighting

Minimum exposure

One of the prime reasons for using lamps on location interiors is to boost existing lighting levels to the minimum level required for exposure. With camera sensitivity increasing with each new camera/recorder that is developed and with the ability to switch in additional gain it would seem that usable pictures could be recorded anywhere and at any time. This may be acceptable for emergency hard news coverage but there are many situations which require an additional light source not only to produce a noise-free picture but also to bring modelling and therefore legibility to the image.

Modelling the picture

Controlling the direction and intensity of light on a face and background brings space and form to a picture. It allows for better compositions and it focuses attention on the main subject in the frame. It can also, if it is skilfully handled, help to express the character or enhance the appearance of the person who is being recorded. These are important considerations when a three-dimensional world is depicted on a two-dimensional screen.

Modifying contrast range

Using artificial light or reflectors with daylight can help improve the rendering of detail in highlights and shadows. The most common example is a face lit by the sun. With a clear sky and a bright sun, the contrast between the sunlit part of the face and the shadows will produce a contrast of about 8:1. Using a reflector board to bounce the sunlight on to the unlit side of the face can lift the shadow so that detail can be seen and a more acceptable portrait produced.

Source of light

When adding to existing light, try to make certain that the new illumination and shadows created are consistent and logical with any original light sources that appear in the frame. A window in an interior shot will be seen by the audience as the main source of light. Additional lighting should be positioned out of frame to reinforce the direction of the perceived main source of light. The keyed side of the face should be on the same side as any lit practical in frame (e.g. table lamp beside the subject). If there is no apparent source of light within the frame, then lamps can be placed to suit the subject depending on the practicalities of placing the lighting stands and the requirements of the shot. Think ahead before lighting the first shot to be recorded because lighting continuity in subsequent shots will require the same direction and apparent source of light to be consistent. The questions to ask are: will it be possible to light reverses from the same direction, is there room to place and direct lamps, will that direction be suitable for the subject, and how long will it take to relight?

Colour correction

Whether shooting interior or exterior, a fundamental problem with location work is dealing with a mixture of light of different colour temperatures. If the light remains uncorrected, faces and subjects may have colour casts which look unnatural and distracting.

The two most common light sources on location are daylight, which has a range of colour temperatures but averages around 5600 K, and tungsten light which is often produced by lamps carried to the location which are approximately 3200 K.

Colour correction filters

There are two basic types of correction filter used when attempting to combine mixed lighting of tungsten and daylight.

■ An orange filter which converts daylight to tungsten and is most often seen attached to windows for interior shots.
■ A blue filter which converts tungsten to daylight and is often used on tungsten lamps.

Any correction filter will reduce the amount of light it transmits and therefore a balance must be struck between colour correction and sufficient light for adequate exposure. A filter for full colour conversion from daylight to tungsten will have a transmission of only 55% which means nearly half of the available light is lost. A filter for full colour correction from tungsten to daylight has an even smaller transmission factor of 34% – it cuts out nearly two thirds of the possible light from a lamp. This is a more serious loss because whereas daylight is usually more than adequate for a reasonable exposure, reducing the light output of a lamp (say a redhead) by blue filtering to match daylight may leave an interior lit by blue filtered lamps short of adequate light.

All light sources at same colour temperature

The choice when shooting an environment which has a mixture of daylight and tungsten is to decide whether to correct all sources to daylight or all sources to tungsten. If the choice is tungsten, any window which is in shot or producing light which is reaching the shot requires filtering. It needs a full orange filter squeegeed onto the glass or fastened by double sided tape onto the frame.

Orange filters can be obtained which have additional light reduction by combining with neutral density filters. This is helpful when attempting to balance out a very bright window with the interior lit by lamps.

135

Lighting an interview

Many multi-camera studio productions will involve lighting two or three people in an interview situation. A single camera location interview allows lamps to be reset between each set-up but a continuous live multi-camera interview requires all faces in shot to be lit simultaneously. There are a number of standard interview shots to be lit (see Interviews page, 178) ranging from close-ups of each participant to over-the-shoulder two-shots and a wide or establishing shot. The normal eye-line of the participants will be towards each other and each face needs to be keyed with respect to the camera that will be shooting their closest shot. Usually this puts the keylight 'upstage' of the participant to create modelling shadow on the downstage side of their face. When setting keylights and backlights on an interview semi-circle, careful barndooring is necessary to prevent unwanted light falling on the wrong subject.

Multi-purpose luminaire

A Fresnel spotlight can be used on wide beam so two artistes can be covered easily with one luminaire. Although it is advisable to have separate backlights for each participant for individual control to avoid, for example, a conflict of lighting levels when a bald headed interviewee is placed alongside a dark haired participant, it is sometimes possible (provided there is sufficient artiste separation) for a key light to double as a backlight. Usually, the backlight needs only be half the power of the keylight, and therefore because the luminaire will be closer as a backlight and consequently be of too high intensity, a bottom half-wire (doubled or overlapped as necessary) should be fitted to obtain the correct backlight illumination. This half-wire should be clear of the inner three rings of the Fresnel lens to ensure that the lamp which is acting also as keylight, is accurately 'centred' on the artiste to be keyed with no loss of Illuminance.

Mood and programme style

Lighting sets the mood of a shot and therefore consideration should be given to the lighting style and if it matches the aims of the programme. News, magazine and current affairs programmes often attempt to present an objective viewpoint. A set which is fussily lit, with odd washes of colour or looks like Elsinore Castle on a foggy day is unlikely to give credibility to the truthfulness of the presentation or visually engage the viewer. Match your lighting style to the content of the programme. Leave obtrusive lighting styles to pop concerts and entertainment shows. Attempt to make your lighting technique invisible and keep it simple.

Electrical and location safety checklist

■ **Location electrical supplies:** It is important to check the power supply fuse rating and the condition of the wiring before using a domestic supply. Blown fuses can waste time but burnt out wiring could start a fire. Also check cable runs, especially around doors and tops of stairs. Check where you place lamps. They get hot and so will anything touching them.

■ **More haste:** Location recording is often a scramble to rig, record, wrap and move on to the next set-up. There is always the urgency to get the job done but, pressurized as this may be, it is never expedient to cut corners on safety. A couple of minutes saved by not making safe a cable crossing the top of a flight of stairs may result in injury and many hours of lost time. You have a responsibility to ensure that the condition and the method of rigging lamps and cables at a location is safe to yourself and to members of the public.

■ **Electrical condition:** Check the earthing and safety of lamps. Make certain the safety glass or wire is fitted and not damaged in any way. Check the condition of cables for frayed or worn insulation and that they are earthed correctly.

■ **HMIs**: Discharge light sources such as HMI lamps produce light by ionizing a gas contained in the bulb. Because of a high bulb pressure they are liable to explode and they also produce a harmful level of ultra-violet radiation. Therefore all discharge sources must be fitted with a glass filter as a safety glass. Usually an inter-lock will prevent the supply of EHT if the safety glass is broken or missing. Check that any HMI you are using has a safety glass fitted.

■ **Placement of lamps:** Adequate time should be allowed for the selection of suitable sites for the safe placement of lamps and for their setting up.

■ Lamps should be placed so that they do not obstruct entrances, exits or passageways. They should be placed in such a way that there is no risk of them being knocked over.

■ Stands should be sited on firm, level ground and set at a height to ensure maximum stability. Use portable sand bags to weigh stands down.

■ Particular care should be taken when placing lamps so that any heat generated can do no damage nor cause a risk of fire.

■ Cables should not run across thoroughfares unless they do not cause a tripping hazard or they are at a suitable height. Any cables which are flown (unsupported) must be securely tied off at a suitable height.

■ If a lamp is knocked over it should be switched off, allowed to cool and not used again until it has been examined.

Introduction to video editing

There is an old Hollywood saying which claims that 'a good cutter cuts his own throat', cutter meaning a film editor. What does this mean? Well, simply that the skills and craft employed by the film editor to stitch together a sequence of separate shots persuades the audience that they are watching a continuous event. They are unaware of the hundreds of subtle decisions that have been made during the course of the film. The action flows from shot to shot and appears natural and obvious. The editing skills and techniques that have achieved this are rendered invisible to the audience, and therefore the unenlightened may claim, 'But what has the editor done? What is the editor's contribution to the production?' The editor has become anonymous and apparently his/her skills are redundant. As we have seen, nearly all TV craft skills employ invisible techniques.

A technical operator who is required to edit will usually be assigned to news or news feature items. This section examines the technique required for this type of programme format. Obviously the craft of editing covers a wide range of genres up to, and including the sophisticated creative decisions that are required to cut feature films. However, there is not such a wide gap between different editing techniques as first it would appear.

What is editing?

Essentially editing is selecting and coordinating one shot with the next to construct a sequence of shots which form a coherent and logical narrative. There are a number of standard editing conventions and techniques that can be employed to achieve a flow of images that guide the viewer through a visual journey. A programme's aim may be to provide a set of factual arguments that allows the viewer to decide on the competing points of view; it may be a dramatic entertainment utilizing editing technique to prompt the viewer to experience a series of highs and lows on the journey from conflict to resolution; or a news item's intention may be to accurately report an event for the audience's information or curiosity.

The manipulation of video, sound and picture, can only be achieved electronically, and an editor who aims to fully exploit the potential of television must master the basic technology of the medium. To the knowledge of technique and technology must be added the essential requirement of a supply of appropriate video and audio material. As we have seen in the section on camerawork, the cameraman, director or journalist needs to shoot with editing in mind. Unless the necessary shots are available for the item, an editor cannot cut a cohesive and structured story. A random collection of shots is not a story, and although an editor may be able to salvage a usable item from a series of 'snapshots', essentially editing is exactly like the well known computer equation which states that 'garbage in' equals 'garbage out'.

138

Video editing terms (1)

- **Burnt-in time code:** In order for edit decisions to be made in a limited off-line preview facility, time code is superimposed on each picture of a copy of the original for easy identification of material.

- **Logging:** Making a list of shots of the recorded material speeds up the selection and location (e.g. which cassette) of shots. When this is compiled on a computer it can be used as a reference to control which sections of the recorded images are to be digitalized.

- **Edit decision list (EDL):** The off-line edit decisions can be recorded on a floppy disk giving the tape source of the shot, its in and out time code or duration. In order to work across a range of equipment there are some widely adopted standards such as CMX, Sony, SMPTE, and Avid.

- **Conform:** The set of instructions contained in the EDL can be used to directly control conforming in an on-line edit suite dubbing from source tape to master tape adding any effects or special transitions between shots as required.

- **Auto assemble:** Editing process using an edit controller programmed with the required edit point identified by time code, which automatically runs the source tape back for the requisite run-up time and then runs both source and master VTRs to make a perfect edit transition.

- **Uncommitted editing:** This technique can only be achieved in a true random access edit suite where the source material has been digitalized and stored on high density memory chips (integrated circuits). Hard disk video storage systems require more than one TV interval (1.6 ms or less) to reposition their read/write heads (typically 10 ms) to access any part of the disk, so replay is limited to accessing the next track, rather than any track and therefore any picture. Uncommitted editing allows any shot to be played out in any order in real time under the control of the EDL. Because the playout is not re-recorded in a fixed form, it is uncommitted and trimming any cut or re-cutting the material for a different purpose is relatively simple.

- **Timebase corrector (TBC):** Most VTRs have a TBC to correct the timing inaccuracies of the pictures coming from tape.

- **Tracking:** Tracking is adjusting the video heads of the VTR over the picture information recorded on tape to give the strongest signal. The position of the heads should also be in a constant relationship with the control track.

- **Pre-roll:** The pre-roll is the time needed by a VTR to reach the operating speed to produce a stable picture. With some VTRs this can be as little as a single frame. When two or more transports are running up together, it is highly unlikely that they will all play, lock and colour frame within a few frames as they each chase and jockey to lock up correctly. For this reason, virtually all transport based editing systems provide for an adjustable pre-roll duration. This cues the machine to a predefined distance from the required in-point in order that, with a suitable cue, all synchronized devices can reliably lock in time for the required event. VTRs also have to achieve a predetermined time code off-set to each other – so lengthening the overall lock-up time.

- **Preview:** Previewing an edit involves rehearsing the point of a transition between two shots without switching the master VTR to record to check that it is editorially and technically acceptable.

- **Split edit:** An edit where the audio and video tracks are edited at different points.

139

The technology of news editing

Video and audio can be recorded on a number of mediums such as tape, optical, hard disk, or high density memory chips (integrated circuits). Tape has been the preferred method of acquisition because of its storage capacity and cost. An edit suite will be defined by the format of its principal VTR machines, but will often be equipped with other VTR machine formats to allow transfer of acquisition material to the main editing format, or to provide lower quality copies for off-line editing or previewing.

The other defining technology of the edit suite is if the edited tape has been recorded in analogue or digital format, (see Television engineering, pages 34–47), and the format of the finished master tape.

Video editing

Recorded video material from the camera almost always requires rearrangement and selection before it can be transmitted. Selective copying from this material onto a new recording is the basis of the video editing craft. Selecting the required shots, finding ways to unobtrusively cut them together to make up a coherent, logical, narrative progression takes time. Using a linear editing technique (i.e. tape-to-tape transfer), and repeatedly re-recording the material exposes the signal to possible distortions and generation losses. Some digital VTR formats very much reduce these distortions. An alternative to this system is to store all the recorded shots on disc or integrated circuits to make up an edit list detailing shot order and source origin (e.g. cassette number, etc.) which can then be used to instruct VTR machines to automatically dub across the required material, or to instruct storage devices to play out shots in the prescribed edit list order.

On tape, an edit is performed by dubbing across the new shot from the originating tape onto the out point of the last shot on the master tape. Simple non-linear disk systems may need to shuffle their recorded data in order to achieve the required frame-to-frame sequence whereas there is no re-recording required in random access editing, simply an instruction to read frames in a new order from the storage device.

Off-line editing

Off-line editing allows editing decisions to be made using low-cost equipment to produce an edit decision list (EDL, see Glossary), or a rough cut which can then be conformed or referred to in a high quality on-line suite. A high-quality/high-cost edit suite is not required for such decision making, although very few off-line edit facilities allow settings for DVEs, colour correctors or keyers. Low-cost off-line editing allows a range of story structure and edit alternatives to be tried out before tying up a high-cost on-line edit suite to produce the final master tape.

140

Video editing terms (2)

- **Digital video effect (DVE):** This is the manipulation of a digitalized video signal such as squeezing, picture bending, rotations and flipping, etc. These effects can be used as an alternative to a cut or a dissolve transition between two images (see Section 9: Vision mixing).

- **Video graphics:** Electronically created visual material is usually provided for an editing session from a graphics facility, although character generators for simple name-supers are sometimes installed in edit suites.

- **Frame store:** Solid state storage of individual frames of video. Frames can be grabbed from any video source, filed and later recovered for production purposes.

- **Jam/slave time code:** Sometimes time code needs to be copied or regenerated on a re-recording. Slave and jam sync generators provide for the replication of time code signals.

- **Crash record/crash edit:** This is the crudest form of editing by simply recording over an existing recording without reference to time code, visual or audio continuity.

- **Colour framing:** It is necessary when editing in composite video, to maintain the correct field colour phase sequencing. In PAL, it is possible to edit different shots on every second frame (4 fields) without the relocking being visible. Analogue and digital component formats have no subcarrier and so the problem does not exist.

- **Match frame (edit):** An invisible join within a shot. This is only possible if there is no movement or difference between the frames – the frames have to match in every particular.

- **A and B rolls:** Two cassettes of original footage either with different source material are used to eliminate constant cassette change (e.g. interviews on one tape A, cutaways on tape B) or the original and a copy of the original to allow dissolves, wipes or DVEs between material originally recorded on the same cassette.

- **Cutting copy:** An edited, low quality version used as a guide and reference in cutting the final, full quality editing master.

- **Trim (edit):** A film editing term for cutting a few frames of an in or out point. It is possible to trim the current edit point in linear editing, but becomes difficult to attempt this on a previous edit. This is not a problem with random access editing.

Editing compressed video
Care must be taken when editing compressed video to make certain that the edit point of an incoming shot is a complete frame, and does not rely (during compression decoding), on information from a preceding frame.

Archive material
When editing news and factual programmes, there is often a requirement to use library material that may have been recorded in an older, and possibly obsolete video format (e.g. 2 inch Quadruplex, U-matic, etc.). Most news material before the 1980s was shot on film, and facilities may be required to transfer film or video material to the current editing format when needed.

Insert and assembly editing

An edit suite is where the final edit is performed in full programme quality. Each shot transition and audio will be selected and dubbed onto the master tape. The alternative to the high cost of making all edit decisions using broadcast equipment, is to log and preview all the material, and choose edit points on lower quality replay/edit facilities. These edit decision lists can then be used to carry out an auto-transfer dub in the on-line edit suite. Preparation in an off-line suite will help save time and money in the on-line facility.

Linear editing

Cameras recording on tape are recording in a linear manner. When the tape is edited, it has to be spooled backwards and forwards to access the required shot. This is time consuming with up to 40% of the editing session spent spooling, jogging and previewing edits. Although modern VTRs have a very quick lock-up, usually less than a second, which allows relatively short pre-rolls, normally all edits are previewed. This involves performing everything connected with the edit except allowing the record machine to record. The finished edited master has limited flexibility for later readjustment, and requires a return to an edit session with the originating tapes if a different order of shots is required. Nevertheless, this method of editing video has been in use since the 1950s, and has only been challenged as the standard technique in the late 1980s when technology became available to transfer, store and edit video material in a non-linear way. Tape-to-tape editing then became known as linear editing. There are two types of linear editing:

- **Insert editing** records new video and audio over existing recorded material (often black and colour burst) on a 'striped' tape. **Striped tape** is prepared (often referred to as blacking up a tape) before the editing session by recording a continuous control track and time code along its complete length. This is similar to the need to format a disk before its use in a computer. This pre-recording also ensures that the tape tension is reasonably stable across the length of the tape. During the editing session, only new video and audio is inserted onto the striped tape leaving the existing control track and time code already recorded on the tape, undisturbed. This minimizes the chance of any discontinuity in the edited result. It ensures that it is possible to come 'out' of an edit cleanly, and return to the recorded material without any visual disturbance. This is the most common method of video tape editing and is the preferred alternative to assemble editing.
- **Assemble editing** is a method of editing onto blank (unstriped) tape in a linear fashion. The control track, time code, video and audio are all recorded simultaneously and joined to the end of the previously recorded material. This can lead to discontinuities in the recorded time code and especially with the control track if the master tape is recorded on more than one VTR.

Video edit suite

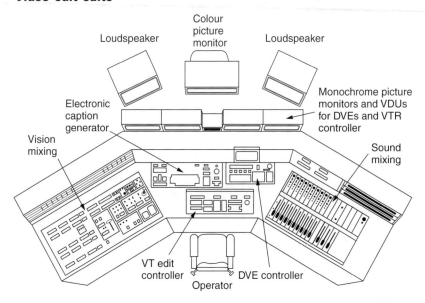

Line-up

A start-of-day check in an edit suite would include:

- Switch on all equipment.
- Select machine source on edit controller.
- Check routeing of video and audio.
- Line-up video monitors with PLUGE or bars.
- Check bars and tone from replay to record machine.
- Check playback of video/audio from playback and record machine.
- If available, check the operation of the video and audio mixing panels.
- Black-up tape: record on a complete tape, a colour TV signal (without picture information), plus sync pulses, colour burst, and black level for use for insert editing.

The master tape is the result of the editing session. It can also exist as an edit playout list for shots stored on disc.

143

Time code

Video editing can only be achieved with precision if there is a method of uniquely identifying each frame. Usually at the point of origination in the camera (see Working on location, pages 96–117), a time code number identifying hour, minute, second, and frame is recorded on the tape against every frame of video. This number can be used when the material is edited, or a new series of numbers can be generated and added before editing. A common standard is the SMPTE/EBU which is an 80 bit code defined to contain sufficient information for most video editing tasks.

- **Code word:** every frame contains an 80 bit code word which contains 'time bits' (8 decimal numbers), recording hours, minutes, seconds, frames and other digital synchronizing information. All this is updated every frame but there is room for additional 'user bit' information.
- **User bit**: user-bit allows up to nine numbers and an A to F code to be programmed into the code word which is recorded every frame. Unlike the 'time bits', the user bits remain unchanged until re-programmed. They can be used to identify production, cameraman, etc.

There are two types of time code – record run and free run.

- **Record run:** record run only records a frame identification when the camera is recording. The time code is set to zero at the start of the day's operation, and a continuous record is produced on each tape covering all takes. It is customary practice to record the tape number in place of the hour section on the time code. For example, the first cassette of the day would start 01.00.00.00, and the second cassette would start 02.00.00.00. Record run is the preferred method of recording time code on most productions.
- **Free run:** in free run, the time code is set to the actual time of day, and when synchronized, is set to run continuously. Whether the camera is recording or not, the internal clock will continue to operate. When the camera is recording, the actual time of day will be recorded on each frame. This mode of operation is useful in editing when covering day-long events such as conferences or sport. Any significant action can be logged by time as it occurs and can subsequently be quickly found by reference to the time-of-day code on the recording. In free run, a change in shot will produce a gap in time code proportional to the amount of time that elapsed between actual recordings. These missing time code numbers can cause problems with the edit controller when it rolls back from an intended edit point, and is unable to find the time code number it expects there (i.e. the time code of the frame to cut on, minus the pre-roll time).

144

Time code tracks on Beta tape

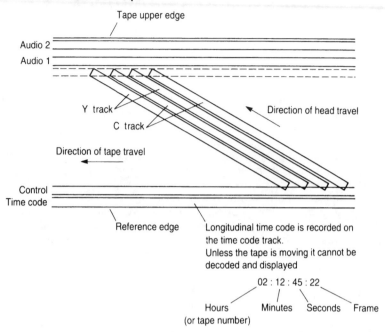

Tape upper edge

Audio 2
Audio 1

Y track
C track

Direction of head travel

Direction of tape travel

Control
Time code

Reference edge

Longitudinal time code is recorded on the time code track.
Unless the tape is moving it cannot be decoded and displayed

02 : 12 : 45 : 22

Hours   Minutes   Seconds   Frame
(or tape number)

Perennial editing techniques

Film began with recording images of actuality events such as a train arriving at a station, or workers leaving a factory. These were viewed by the audience as a single shot lasting as long as the amount of film that was wound through the camera. Within a few years, the audiences developed a taste for a story, a continuity element connecting the separate shots, and so narrative film techniques began to be developed. The visual storytelling methods chosen ensured the audience understood the action. Shooting and editing had to develop ways of presenting the causal, spatial and temporal relationship between shots. This was a completely new craft, and other story-telling disciplines such as theatre or literature were of little help in providing solutions to the basic visual problems faced by these early pioneers.

Film makers soon learnt how to make a cut on action in order to provide a smoother transition between two shots, and invented a number of other continuity editing techniques. The classical grammar of film editing was invented and understood not only by the film makers, but also by the film audience. It is the basis of most types of programme making to this day.

Continuity editing
Continuity editing ensures that:

- shots are structured to allow the audience to understand the space, time and logic of the action
- each shot follows the line of action to maintain consistent screen direction so that the geography of the action is completely intelligible
- unobtrusive camera movement and shot change directs the audience to the content of the production rather than the mechanics of production
- continuity editing creates the illusion that distinct, separate shots (possibly recorded out of sequence and at different times), form part of a continuous event being witnessed by the audience.

The birth of 'invisible technique'
As the early film pioneers discovered, it is not possible, without distracting the audience, to simply cut one shot to another unless certain basic continuity rules are followed. The aim is to ensure the spectator understands the story or argument by being shown a variety of shots, without being aware that in fact the shots are changing. Visual story-telling has two objectives – to communicate the required message, and to sustain the interest of the audience. Changing shot would appear to interrupt the viewer's flow of attention, and yet it is an essential part of editing technique in structuring a sequence of shots, and to control the audience's understanding of the intended message. There are a number of ways to make the transition from one shot to the next (see Visual transitions, page 174 for a full description).

Preparation for editing

- Check script or brief for tape numbers.
- Select and check tape cassette for correct material.
- If time allows preview all material with reference to any shot list or running order that has been prepared.
- Check the anticipated running time of the piece.
- Transfer bars and tone and then the ident clock onto the front of the final edit cassette (master tape).

The technical requirements for an edit

- Enter the replay time code in and out points into the edit controller.
- Enter the record tape time code in-point.
- Preview the edit.
- Check sync stability for the pre-roll time when using time-of-day time code.
- Make the edit.
- Check the edit is technically correct in sound and vision and the edit occurs at the required place.
- When two shots are cut together, check that there is continuity across the cut and the transition (to an innocent eye) is invisible.

The importance of audio

Audio plays a crucial part in editing and requires as much attention as video. See Section 5: Audio technical operations.

Perception and shot transition

Film and television screens display a series of single images for a very short period of time. Due to the nature of human perception (persistence of vision), if these images are displayed at more than 24 times a second, the viewer no longer sees a series of individual snapshots, but the illusion of continuous motion of any subject that changes position in succeeding frames.

It takes time for a change of shot to be registered, and with large discrepancies between shot transitions, it becomes more apparent to the viewer when the composition of both shots is dissimilar. If the programme maker aims to make the transition between shots to be as imperceptible as possible in order to avoid visually distracting the viewer, the amount of eye movement between cuts needs to be at a minimum. If the incoming shot is sufficiently similar in design (e.g. matching the principal subject position and size in both shots), the movement of the eye will be minimized and the change of shot will hardly be noticeable. There is, however, a critical point in matching identical shots to achieve an unobtrusive cut (e.g. cutting together the same size shot of the same individual), where the jump between almost identical shots becomes noticeable.

Narrative motivation for changing the shot (e.g. 'What happens next? What is this person doing?' etc.) will also smooth the transition. A large mismatch between two shots, for example, action on the left of frame is cut to when the previous shot has significant action on extreme right of frame, may take the viewer four or five frames to catch up with the change, and trigger a 'What happened then?' response. If a number of these 'jump' cuts (i.e. shot transitions that are noticeable to the audience), are strung together, the viewer becomes very aware of the mechanics of the production process, and the smooth flow of images is disrupted. This 'visual' disruption, of course, may sometimes be a production objective.

Matching visual design between shots

When two shots are cut together, the visual design, that is the composition of each shot, can be matched to achieve smooth continuity. Alternatively, if the production requirement is for the cut to impact on the viewer, the juxtaposition of the two shots can be so arranged to provide an abrupt contrast in their graphic design. The cut between two shots can be made invisible if the incoming shot has one or more similar compositional elements as the preceding shot. The relationships between the two shots may relate to similar shape, similar position of dominant subject in the frame, colours, lighting, setting, overall composition, etc. Any similar aspects of visual design that is present in both shots will help the smooth transition from one shot to the next.

Matching spatial relationships between shots

Editing creates spatial relationships between subjects which need never exist in reality. A common example is a passenger getting into a train at a station. The following shot shows a train pulling out of the station. The audience infers that the passenger is in the train when they are more probably on an entirely different train or even no train at all. Any two subjects or events can be linked by a cut if there is an apparent graphic continuity between shots framing them, and if there is an absence of an establishing shot showing their physical relationship. Portions of space can be cut together to create a convincing screen space provided no shot is wide enough to show that the edited relationship is not possible.

Matching tone, colour or background

Cutting between shots of speakers with different background tones, colour or texture will sometimes result in an obtrusive cut. A cut between a speaker with a bright background and a speaker with a dark background will result in a 'jump' in the flow of images each time it occurs. Colour temperature matching and background brightness relies on the cameraman making the right exposure and artiste positioning decisions. Particular problems can occur, for example, with the colour of grass which changes between shots. Face tones of a presenter or interviewee need to be consistent across a range of shots when cut together in a sequence. Also, cutting between shots with in-focus and defocused backgrounds to speakers can produce a mismatch on a cut. Continuity of colour, tone, texture, skin tones, and depth of field, will improve the seamless flow of images.

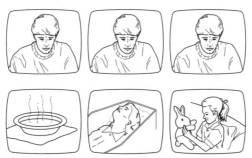

Kuleshov and I made an interesting experiment. We took from some film or other several close-ups of the well known Russian actor Mosjukhin. We chose close-ups which were static and which did not express any feeling at all – quiet close-ups. We joined these close-ups, which were all similar, with other bits of film in three different combinations.

In the first combination the close-up of Mosjukhin was looking at the soup. In the second combination the face of Mosjukhin was joined in shots showing a coffin in which lay a dead woman. In the third the close-up was followed by a shot of a little girl playing with a funny toy bear. When we showed the three combinations to an audience which had not been let into the secret the result was terrific. The public raved about the acting of the artist. They pointed out the heavy pensiveness of his mood over the forgotten soup, were touched and moved by the deep sorrow which looked on the dead woman, and admired the light, happy smile with which he surveyed the girl at play. But we knew that in all three cases the face was exactly the same.

Film Technique and Film Acting
V.I. Pudovkin

Matching shots

Matching rhythm relationships between shots

The editor needs to consider two types of rhythm when cutting together shots; the rhythm created by the rate of shot change, and the internal rhythm of the depicted action.

Each shot will have a measurable time on screen. The rate at which shots are cut creates a rhythm which affects the viewer's response to the sequence. For example, in a feature film action sequence, a common way of increasing the excitement and pace of the action is to increase the cutting rate by decreasing the duration of each shot on screen as the action approaches a climax. The rhythms introduced by editing are in addition to the other rhythms created by artiste movement, camera movement, and the rhythm of sound. The editor can therefore adjust shot duration and shot rate independent of the need to match continuity of action between shots; this controls an acceleration or deceleration in the pace of the item.

By controlling the editing rhythm, the editor controls the amount of time the viewer has to grasp and understand the selected shots. Many productions exploit this fact in order to create an atmosphere of mystery and confusion by ambiguous framing and rapid cutting which deliberately undermines the viewer's attempt to make sense of the images they are shown.

Another editing consideration is maintaining the rhythm of action carried over into succeeding shots. Most people have a strong sense of rhythm as expressed in walking, marching, dancing, etc. If this rhythm is destroyed, as for example, cutting together a number of shots of a marching band so that their step becomes irregular, viewers will sense the discrepancies, and the sequence will appear disjointed and awkward. When cutting from a shot of a person walking, for example, care must be taken that the person's foot hits the ground with the same rhythm as in the preceding shot, and that it is the appropriate foot (e.g. after a left foot comes a right foot). The rhythm of a person's walk may still be detected even if the incoming shot does not include the feet. The beat of the movement must not be disrupted. Sustaining rhythms of action may well override the need for a narrative 'ideal' cut at an earlier or later point.

Matching temporal relationships between shot

The position of a shot in relation to other shots (preceding or following) will control the viewer's understanding of its time relationship to surrounding shots. Usually a factual event is cut in a linear time line unless indicators are built in to signal flash-backs or very rarely, flash-forwards. The viewer assumes the order of depicted events is linked to the passing of time. The duration of an event can be considerably shortened to a fraction of its actual running time by editing if the viewer's concept of time passing is not violated. The standard formula for compressing space and time is to allow the main subject to leave frame, or to provide appropriate cutaways to shorten the actual time taken to complete the activity. While they are out of shot, the viewer will accept that greater distance has been travelled than is realistically possible.

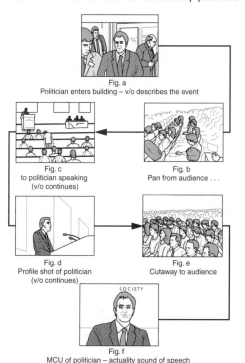

Fig. a
Politician enters building – v/o describes the event

Fig. c
to politician speaking
(v/o continues)

Fig. b
Pan from audience . . .

Fig. d
Profile shot of politician
(v/o continues)

Fig. e
Cutaway to audience

Fig. f
MCU of politician – actuality sound of speech

For example, a politician enters a conference hall and delivers a speech to an audience. This whole event, possibly lasting 30 minutes or more, can be reduced to 15 seconds of screen time by cutting between the appropriate shots. In the first shot (Fig. a), the politician is seen entering the building with a voice-over giving details of the purpose of the visit. A cutaway to an audience shot with a pan to the politician on the platform (Figs b and c), allows all the intervening time to be collapsed without a jump cut, and also allows the voice-over to paraphrase what the politician is saying. A third, closer, profile shot of the politician (Fig. d), followed by a shot of the listening audience (Fig. e), continues with the voice-over paraphrase, ending with a MCU of the politician (Fig. f), with his actuality sound, delivering the key 'sound bite' sentence of his speech. A combination of voice-over and five shots that can be cut together maintaining continuity of time and place allows a 30 minute event to be delivered in 15/20 seconds.

Provided the main subject does not leap in vision from location one immediately to location two, and then to three and four, there will be no jump in continuity between shots. The empty frames and cutaways allow the editing-out of space and time to remain invisible. News editing frequently requires a reduction in screen time of the actual duration of a real event. For example, a 90 minute football match recording will be edited down to 30 seconds to run as a 'highlights' report in a news bulletin. Screen time is seldom made greater than the event time, but there are instances, for example, in reconstructions of a crime in a documentary, where time is expanded by editing. This stylistic mannerism is often accompanied by slow motion sequences.

151

Basic editing principles

Rearranging time and space

When two shots are cut together, the audience attempts to make a connection between them. For example, a man on a station platform boards a train. A wide shot shows a train pulling out of a station. The audience makes the connection that the man is in the train. A cut to a close shot of the seated man follows, and it is assumed that he is travelling on the train. We see a wide shot of a train crossing the Forth Bridge, and the audience assumes that the man is travelling in Scotland. Adding a few more shots would allow a shot of the man leaving the train at his destination with the audience experiencing no violent discontinuity in the depiction of time or space. And yet a journey that may take two hours is collapsed to thirty seconds of screen time, and a variety of shots of trains and a man at different locations have been strung together in a manner that convinces the audience they have followed the same train and man throughout a journey.

Basic editing principles

This way of arranging shots is fundamental to editing. Space and time are rearranged in the most efficient way to present the information that the viewer requires to follow the argument presented. The transition between shots must not violate the audience's sense of continuity between the actions presented. This can be achieved by:

- **Continuity of action:** action is carried over from one shot to another without an apparent break in speed or direction of movement (see figure opposite).
- **Screen direction:** if the book is travelling left to right in the medium shot, the closer shot of the book will need to roughly follow the same direction (see figure opposite). A shot of the book moving right to left will produce a visual 'jump' which may be apparent to the viewer.
- **Eyeline match:** the eyeline of someone looking down at the book should be in the direction the audience believes the book to be. If they look out of frame with their eyeline levelled at their own height, the implication is that they are looking at something at that height. Whereas if they were looking down, the assumption would be that they are looking at the book.

There is a need to cement the spatial relationship between shots. A subject speaking and looking out of the left of frame will be assumed by the viewer to be speaking to someone off camera to the left. A cut to another person looking out of frame to the right will confirm this audience expectation. Eyeline matches are decided by position, (see crossing the line on page 69), and there is very little that can be done at the editing stage to correct shooting mismatches except flipping the frame to reverse the eyeline which alters the continuity of the symmetry of the face and other left/right continuity elements in the composition such as hair partings, etc.

(a)

In a medium shot, for example (Fig. a), someone places a book on a table out of shot. A cut to a closer shot of the book (Fig. b), shows the book just before it is laid on the table. Provided the book's position relative to the table and the speed of the book's movement in both shots is similar, and there is continuity in the table surface, lighting, hand position, etc., then the cut will not be obtrusive. A close shot that crosses the line (Fig. c) will not cut.

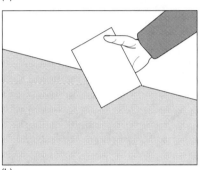

(b)

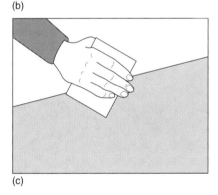

(c)

Shot size

Another essential editing factor is the size of shots that form an intercut sequence of faces. A cut from a medium close up to another medium close up of another person will be unobtrusive provided the eyeline match is as above. A number of cuts between a long shot of one person and a medium close up of another will jump and be obtrusive.

153

Types of edit

There are a number of standard editing techniques that are used across a wide range of programme making. These include:

- **Intercutting editing** can be applied to locations or people. The technique of intercutting between different actions that are happening simultaneously at different locations was discovered as early as 1906 to inject pace and tension into a story. Intercutting on faces in the same location presents the viewer with changing viewpoints on action and reaction.
- **Analytical editing** breaks a space down into separate framings. The classic sequence begins with a long shot to show relationships and the 'geography' of the setting followed by closer shots to show detail, and to focus on important action.
- **Contiguity editing** follows action through different frames of changing locations. The classic pattern of shots in a western chase sequence is where one group of horsemen ride through the frame past a distinctive tree to be followed later, in the same framing, by the pursuers riding through shot past the same distinctive tree. The tree acts as a 'signpost' for the audience to establish location, and as a marker of the duration of elapsed time between the pursued and the pursuer.
- **The point-of-view shot.** A variant of this, which establishes the relationship between different spaces, is the point-of-view shot. Someone on-screen looks out of one side of the frame. The following shot reveals what the person is looking at. This can also be applied to anyone moving and looking out of frame, followed by their moving point-of-view shot.

Summary of perennial technique

These editing techniques form the basics of an invisible craft which has been developed over nearly a hundred years of film and video productions. There are innovation and variation on these basic tenets, but the majority of television programme productions use these standard editing conventions to keep the viewers' attention on the content of the programme rather than its method of production. These standard conventions are a response to the need to provide a variety of ways of presenting visual information coupled with the need for them to be unobtrusive in their transition from shot to shot. Expertly used, they are invisible and yet provide the narrative with pace, excitement, and variety.

An alternative editing technique, such as, for example, pop promotions, uses hundreds of cuts, disrupted continuity, ambiguous imagery, etc., to deliberately visually tease the audience, and to avoid clear visual communication. The aim is often to recreate the 'rave' experience of a club or concert. The production intention is to be interpretative rather than informative.

Previewing

The restraints of cutting a story to a specific running time, and having it ready for a broadcast transmission deadline, is a constant pressure on the television editor. Often there is simply not enough time to preview all the material in 'real' time. Usually material is shuttled though at a fastforward speed stopping only to check vital interview content. The editor has to develop a visual memory of the content of a shot and its position in the reel. One of the major contributions an editor can make is the ability to remember a shot that solves some particular visual dilemma. If two crucial shots will not cut together because of continuity problems, is there a suitable 'buffer' shot that could be used? The ability to identify and remember the location of a specific shot, even when spooling and shuttling, is a skill that has to be learnt in order to speed up editing.

Solving continuity problems is one reason why the location production unit need to provide additional material to help in the edit. It is a developed professional skill to find the happy medium between too much material that cannot be previewed in the editing time available, and too little material that gives the edit no flexibility of structure, running time, or story development changes between shooting, and editing the material.

Repeating a shot of a distinctive group of trees can be used to indicate location and time passing.

Fact or fiction?

The editing techniques used for cutting fiction and factual material are almost the same. When switching on a television programme mid-way, it is sometimes impossible to assess from the editing alone if the programme is fact or fiction. Documentary makers use story telling techniques learned by audiences from a life time of watching drama. Usually, the indicator of what genre the production falls into is gained from the participants. Even the most realistic acting appears stilted or stylized when placed alongside people talking in their own environment. Another visual convention is to allow 'factual' presenters to address the lens and the viewer directly, whereas actors and the 'public' are usually instructed not to look at camera.

- **Communication and holding attention**: The primary aim of editing is to provide the right structure and selection of shots to communicate to the audience the programme maker's motives for making the programme, and secondly, to hold their attention so that they listen and remain watching.
- **Communication with the audience**: Good editing technique structures the material and identifies the main 'teaching' points the audience should understand. A crucial role of the editor is to be audience 'number one'. The editor will start fresh to the material and he/she must understand the story in order for the audience to understand the story. The editor needs to be objective and bring a dispassionate eye to the material. The director/reporter may have been very close to the story for hours/days/weeks – the audience comes to it new and may not pick up the relevance of the setting or set-up if this is spelt out rapidly in the first opening sentence. It is surprising how often, with professional communicators, that what is obvious to them about the background detail of a story, is unknown or its importance unappreciated by their potential audience. Beware of the 'I think that is so obvious we needn't mention it' statement. As an editor, if you do not understand the relevance of the material, say so. You will not be alone.
- **Holding their attention**: The edited package needs to hold the audience's attention by its method of presentation (e.g. method of story telling – what happens next, camera technique, editing technique, etc.). Pace and brevity (e.g. no redundant footage), are often the key factors in raising the viewers' involvement in the item. Be aware that visuals can fight voice-over narration. Arresting images capture the attention first. The viewer would probably prefer to 'see it' rather than 'hear it'. A successful visual demonstration is always more convincing than a verbal argument – as every successful salesman knows.
- **Selection**: Editing, in a literal sense, is the activity of selecting from all the available material and choosing what is relevant. Film and video editing requires the additional consideration that selected shots spliced together must meet the requirements of the standard conventions of continuity editing.

Cutaway and cut-in

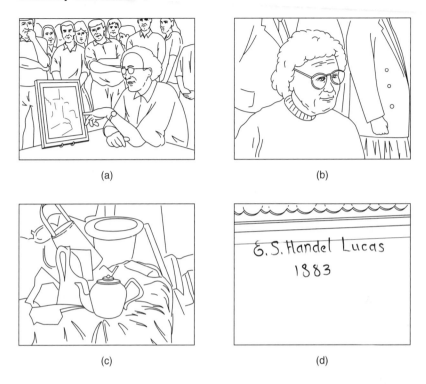

(a)

(b)

(c)

(d)

A cutaway literally means to cut away from the main subject (a) either as a reaction to the event, e.g. cutting to a listener reacting to what a speaker is saying (b), or to support the point being made.

A cut-in usually means to go tighter on an aspect of the main subject. For example, an art expert talking in mid-shot (a) about the detail in a painting would require a cut-in close shot of the painting (c) to support the comment, and an even closer shot (d), to see a signature for the item to make sense to the viewer.

Stings and bridges

Sometimes there is a requirement for a visual and sound bridge between two distinct sequences that nevertheless need to be connected. For example, a round-up of all sporting activity that has taken place over a weekend may have several different sports activities that are to be shown together in one package. Between each separate sporting activity, a bridging graphic or visual with a sound 'sting' (a short self-contained piece of music lasting no more than 5 seconds), will be spliced in. The bridging visual can be repeated on each change of topic in the report, and can be, for example, the tumbling last frame of the end of one activity introducing the next activity or possibly a customized digital video effect.

Telling a story

The strongest way of engaging the audience's attention is to tell them a story. In fact, because film and television images are displayed in a linear way – shot follows shot – it is almost impossible for the audience not to construct links between succeeding images whatever the real or perceived relationships between them. Image follows image in an endless flow over time and inevitably the viewer will construct a story out of each succeeding piece of information.

The task of the director/journalist and editor is to determine what the audience needs to know, and at what point in the 'story' they are told. This is the structure of the item or feature and usually takes the form of question and answer or cause and effect. Seeking answers to questions posed, for example, 'what are the authorities going to do about traffic jams?' or 'what causes traffic jams?', involves the viewer and draws them into the 'story' that is unfolding. Many items can still be cut following the classical structure of exposition, tension, climax, and release.

The story telling of factual items is probably better served by the presentation of detail rather than broad generalizations. Which details are chosen to explain a topic is crucial both in explanation and engagement. Many issues dealt with by factual programmes are often of an abstract nature which at first thought, have little or no obvious visual representation. Images to illustrate topics such as inflation can be difficult to find when searching for precise representations of the diminishing value of money. The camera must provide an image of something, and whatever it may be, that something will be invested by the viewer with significance.

That significance may not match the main thrust of the item and may lead the viewer away from the topic. Significant detail requires careful observation at location, and a clear idea of the shape of the item when it is being shot. The editor then has to find ways of cutting together a series of shots so the transitions are seamless, and the images logically advance the story. Remember that the viewer will not necessarily have the same impression or meaning from an image that you have invested in it. A shot of a doctor on an emergency call having difficulty in parking, chosen, for example, to illustrate the problems of traffic congestion, may be seen by some viewers as simply an illustration of bad driving.

A linking theme

Because the story is told over time, there is a need for a central motif or thread which is easily followed and guides the viewer through the item. A report, for example, on traffic congestion may have a car driver on a journey through rush hour traffic. Each point about the causes of traffic congestion can be illustrated and picked up as they occur such as out-of-town shoppers, the school run, commuters, traffic black spots, road layout, etc. The frustrations of the journey throughout the topic will naturally link the 'teaching' points, and the viewer can easily identify and speculate about the story's outcome.

Emphasis, tempo and syntax

Just as a written report of an event will use a structure of sentence, paragraph and chapter, a visual report can structure the elements of the story telling in a similar way. By adjusting the shot length and fine tuning the rate and rhythm of the cuts, and the juxtaposition of the shots, the editor can create emphasis and significance.

A piece can be cut to relate a number of connected ideas. When the report moves on to a new idea there is often a requirement to indicate visually, 'new topic'. This can be achieved by a very visible cut – a mismatch perhaps, or an abrupt change of sound level, or content (e.g. quiet interior is followed by a cut to a parade marching band), to call attention to a transitional moment.

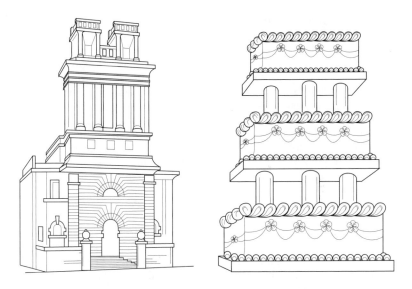

Attention can also be captured by a very strong graphic match, usually in a dissolve, where the outgoing shot has, for example, the strong shape of the archi-tecture of a church, which has substantial columns converging up to a dome which is mixed to a shot of a similar shaped wedding cake, matched in the same frame position and lens angle. The audience registers the visual connection because the connection has been overstated. The visual design match is so strong it becomes visible, and signals a change of time, place, or a new scene or topic.

Structuring a sequence

The chosen structure of a section or sequence will usually have a beginning, a development, and a conclusion. Editing patterns and the narrative context do not necessarily lay the events of a story out in simple chronological order. For example, there can be a 'tease' sequence which seeks to engage the audience's attention with a question or a mystery. It may be some time into the material before the solution is revealed, and the audience's curiosity is satisfied. Whatever the shape of the structure it usually contains one or more of the following methods of sequence construction:

- A **narrative** sequence is a record of an event such as a child's first day at school, an Olympic athlete training in the early morning, etc. Narrative sequences tell a strong story and are used to engage the audience's interest.
- A **descriptive** sequence simply sets the atmosphere or provides background information. For example, an item featuring the retirement of a watchmaker, may have an introductory sequence of shots featuring the watches and clocks in his workshop before the participant is introduced or interviewed. Essentially, a descriptive sequence is a scene setter, an overture to the main point of the story, although sometimes it may be used as an interlude to break up the texture of the story, or act as a transitional visual bridge to a new topic.
- An **explanatory** sequence is, as the name implies, a sequence which explains either the context of the story, facts about the participants or event, or explains an idea. Abstract concepts like a rise in unemployment usually need a verbal explanatory section backed by 'visual wallpaper' – images which are not specific or important in themselves, but are needed to accompany the important narration. Explanatory sequences are likely to lose the viewer's interest, and need to be supported by narrative and description. Explanatory exposition is often essential when winding-up an item in order to draw conclusions or make explicit the relevance of the events depicted.

The shape of a sequence

The tempo and shape of a sequence, and of a number of sequences that may make up a longer item, will depend on how these methods of structuring are cut and arranged. Whether shooting news or documentaries, the transmitted item will be shaped by the editor to connect a sequence of shots either visually, by voice-over, atmosphere, music, or by a combination of any of them. Essentially the cameraman or director must organize the shooting of separate shots with some structure in mind. Any activity must be filmed to provide a sufficient variety of shots that are able to be cut together following standard editing conventions (e.g. avoidance of jump cuts, not crossing the line, etc.), and that there is enough variety of shot to allow some flexibility in editing. Just as no shot can be considered in isolation, every sequence must be considered in context with the overall aims of the production.

160

Building a structure

Creating a structure out of the available material will tell a story, present an argument, or provide a factual account of an event (or all three). It starts with a series of unconnected shots which are built into small sequences. These are then grouped into a pattern which logically advances the account either to persuade, or to provide sufficient information leaving the viewer to draw their own conclusion. Usually the competing points-of-view are underlined by the voice-over, but a sequence of strong images will make a greater impact than words.

The available material that arrives in the edit suite has to be structured to achieve the clearest exposition of the subject. Also the edited material has to be arranged to find ways of involving the viewer in order to hold their interest and attention. Structure is arranging the building blocks – the individual unconnected shots – into a stream of small visual messages that combine into a coherent whole.

For example, a government report on traffic pollution is published which claims that chest ailments have increased, many work hours are lost though traffic delay, and urges car owners to only use their vehicles for essential journeys.

A possible treatment for this kind of report would be to outline the main points as a voice-over or text graphic, interviews with health experts, motorist pressure group spokesman, a piece to camera by the reporter, and possibly comments from motorist. The cameraman would provide shots of traffic jams, close-ups of car exhausts, pedestrians, interviews, etc. The journalist would decide the order of the material whilst writing his/her voice-over script, whilst the editor would need to cut bridging sequences which could be used on the more 'abstract' statistics (e.g. increase in asthma in children, etc.). Essentially these montages help to hold the viewer's attention and provide visual interest on what would otherwise be a dry delivery of facts. A close-up of a baby's face in a pram cut alongside a lorry exhaust belching diesel fumes makes a strong quick visual point that requires no additional narrative to explain. The juxtaposition of shots, the context and how the viewer reads the connections is what structures the item, and allows the report to have impact. The production team in the field must provide appropriate material, but the editor can find new relationships and impose an order to fit the running time.

Factual editing

News reportage attempts to emphasize fact rather than opinion, but journalistic values cannot escape subjective judgements. What is newsworthy? What are news values? These questions are answered and shaped by the prevailing custom and practices of broadcasting organizations. Magazine items can use fact, feeling, atmosphere, argument, opinion, dramatic reconstruction, and subjective impressions. These editing techniques differ very little from feature film storytelling. For a more detailed account of objective and subjective reporting, see the section on documentaries.

News – condensing time

A news bulletin will have a number of news items which are arranged in importance from the top story down through the running order to less important stories. This running order, compiled by the news editor, will usually allow more time to the main stories, and therefore the editor and journalist will often face the task of cutting an item to a predetermined time to fit the news agenda. There are a number of ways of chopping time out of an item. If a voice-over script has been prepared to the running time allocated, the editor can use this as a 'clock' to time the insertion of various images throughout the piece. The task then is to slim down the selection from the available material to a few essential images that will tell the story. It is a news cameraman's complaint that when the editor is up against a transmission deadline, he/she will only quickly preview the first part of any cassette, often missing the better shots towards the end of the tape. If there is time, try to spin through and review all the material. The cameraman can help the editor, wherever possible, by putting interviews on one tape and cutaways and supporting material on another cassette. This allows the editor to quickly find material without shuttling backwards and forwards on the same tape.

News – brevity and significance

The pressure of cutting an item down to a short duration will impose its own discipline of selecting only what is significant and the shots that best sum up the essence of the story. The viewer will require longer on-screen time to assimilate the information in a long shot than the detail in a close shot. Moving shots require more perceptual effort to understand than static shots.

The skill in news cutting can be summed up as:

- each shot must serve a purpose in telling the story
- more detail than geography shots or scene setting
- more close, static shots than ones with camera movement
- use short pans (no more than two seconds long) to inject pace into a story
- use a structure containing pace, shot variety, and dynamic relevant images.

Unscripted shot structure

Most news and magazine items will not be scripted when they are shot. There may be a rough treatment outlined by the presenter or a written brief on what the item should cover, but an interview may open up new aspects of the story. Without pre-planning or a shot list, the shots provided will often revert to tried and trusted formulas. A safe rule-of-thumb is to move from the general to the particular – from wide shot to close up. A general view (GV) to show relationships, and to set the scene, and then to make the important points with the detail of close-ups. The cameraman has to provide a diversity of material to provide cutting points. The editor will hope that the cameraman/journalist has provided:

■ a substantial change in shot size or camera angle/camera position for shots intended to be intercut
■ a higher proportion of static shots to camera movement. It is difficult to cut between pans and zooms until they steady to a static frame and hold
■ relevant but non-specific shots so that voice-over information (to set the scene or the report) can be dubbed on after the script has been prepared

Cutting a simple news item

■ The journalist previews the material (if there is time).
■ Decide whether the item will be cut to picture or audio.
■ Cutting to audio: the journalist writes the script identifying where interviews and essential visuals will occur.
■ The journalist records the voice-over (v/o) in the dub studio or if time is against him, or the dub studio is in use, records off a lip mic in the edit suite.
■ The VT editor then lays down as much audio that is available, e.g. v/o, interviews, etc., and then cuts pictures to the sound.
■ Atmos or music may be added after this cut.
■ Cutting to picture: Load the correct cassette and jog and shuttle to find the start of the first shot.

An appropriate shot

Every shot should be recorded for a purpose. That purpose is at its weakest if it simply seemed a good idea at the time to the cameraman or director etc., to record a shot 'just in case' without considering its potential context. No shot can exist in isolation. A shot must have a connection with the aim of the item and its surrounding shots. It must be shot with editing in mind. This purpose could be related to the item's brief, script, outline, or decided at the location. It could follow on from an interview comment or reference. It could be shot to help condense time or it could be offered as a 'safety' shot to allow flexibility in cutting the material.

163

Interviews

The interview is an essential element of news and magazine reporting. It provides for a factual testimony from an active participant similar to a witness's court statement; that is, direct evidence of their own understanding, not rumour or hearsay. They can speak about what they feel, what they think, what they know, from their own experience. An interviewee can introduce into the report opinion, beliefs and emotion as opposed to the reporter who traditionally sticks to the facts. An interviewee therefore provides colour and emotion into an objective assessment of an event and captures the audience's attention.

How long should a shot be held?
The simple answer to this question is as long as the viewer needs to extract the required information, or before the action depicted requires a wider or closer framing to satisfy the viewer's curiosity, or a different shot (e.g. someone exiting the frame) to follow the action. The on-screen length is also dependent on many more subtle considerations than the specific content of the shot.

As discussed above, the rhythm of the editing produced by rate of shot change, and the shaping of the rate of shot change to produce an appropriate shape to a sequence, will have a bearing on how long a shot is held on screen. Rhythm relies on variation of shot length, but should not be arbitrarily imposed simply to add interest. As always with editing, there is a balance to be struck between clear communication, and the need to hold the viewer's interest with visual variety. The aim is to clarify and emphasize the topic, and not confuse the viewer with shots that are snatched off the screen before they are visually understood.

The critical factor controlling on-screen duration is often the shot size. A long shot may have a great deal more information than a close shot. Also, a long shot is often used to introduce a new location or to set the 'geography' of the action. These features will be new to the audience, and therefore they will take longer to understand and absorb the information. Shifting visual information produced by moving shots will also need longer screen time.

A closer shot will usually yield its content fairly quickly, particularly if the content has been seen before (e.g. a well known 'screen' face). There are other psychological aspects of perception which also have a bearing on how quickly an audience can recognize images which are flashed on to a screen. These factors are exploited in those commercials which have a very high cutting rate, but are not part of standard news/magazine editing technique.

Cutting an interview

A standard interview convention is to establish who the interviewee is by superimposing their name and possibly some other identification (e.g. farmer, market street trader, etc.) in text across an MCU of them. The interview is often cut using a combination of basic shots such as:

- an MS, MCU or CU of the interviewee
- a matched shot of the interviewer asking questions or reacting to the answers (usually shot after the interview has ended)
- a two-shot which establishes location and relationship between the participants or an over-the-shoulder two-shot looking from interviewee to interviewer
- the interviewee is often staged so that their background is relevant to their comments

The interview can follow straightforward intercutting between question and answer of the participants, but more usually, after a few words from the interviewee establishing their presence, a series of cutaways are used to illustrate the points the interviewee is making. A basic interview technique requires the appropriate basic shots:

- matched shots in size and lens angle
- over-the-shoulder (o/s) shots
- intercutting on question and answer
- cutaways to referred items in the interview
- 'noddies' and reaction shots (N.B. reaction shots should be reactions – that is, a response to the main subject)
- cutaways to avoid jump cuts when shortening answers

Content and pace

Although news/magazine editing is always paring an item down to essential shots, due consideration should always be given to the subject of the item. For example, a news item about the victim of a civil disaster or crime, has to have pauses and 'quiet' on-screen time to reflect the feelings and emotion of the event. Just as there is a need to have changes of pace and rhythm in editing a piece to give a particular overall shape, so a news bulletin or magazine running order will have an overall requirement for changes of tempo between hard and soft items to provide balance and variety.

Cutting on movement

A change of shot requires a measurable time for the audience to adjust to the incoming shot. If the shot is part of a series of shots showing an event or action, the viewer will be able to follow the flow of action across the cut if the editor has selected an appropriate point to cut on movement. This will move the viewer into the next part of the action without them consciously realizing a cut has occurred. An edit point in the middle of an action disguises the edit point.

Cutting on movement is the bedrock of editing. It is the preferred option in cutting, compared to most other editing methods, provided the sequence has been shot to include action edit points. When breaking down a sequence of shots depicting a continuous action there are usually five questions faced by the editor:

- What is visually interesting?
- What part of a shot is necessary to advance the 'story' of the topic?
- How long can the sequence last ?
- Has the activity been adequately covered on camera?
- Is there a sufficient variety of shots to serve the above requirements?

Cutting on exits and entrances

One of the basic tenets of perennial editing technique is that each shot follows the line of action to maintain consistent screen direction so that the geography of the action is completely intelligible. Cutting on exits and entrances into a frame is a standard way of reducing the amount of screen time taken to traverse distance. The usual convention is to make the cut when the subject has nearly left the frame. It is natural for the viewer, if the subject is disappearing out of the side of the frame, to wish to be shown where they are going. If the cut comes after they have left the frame then the viewer is left with an empty frame and either their interest switches to whatever is left in the frame or they feel frustrated because the subject of their interest has gone. Conversely, the incoming frame can have the subject just appearing, but the match on action has to be good otherwise there will be an obtrusive jump in their walking cadence or some other posture mismatch. Allowing the subject to clear the frame in the outgoing shot and not be present in the incoming shot is usually the lazy way of avoiding continuity mismatches. An empty frame at the end of a shot is already 'stale' to the viewer. If it is necessary, because there is no possibility in the shots provided of matching up the action across the cut, try to use the empty frame of the incoming shot (which is new to the viewer) before the action begins to avoid continuity problems. This convention can be applied to any movement across a cut. In general, choose an empty frame on an incoming shot rather than the outgoing shot unless there is the need for a 'visual' full stop to end a sequence, e.g. a fade-down or mix across to a new scene.

Cutting on sound

Cutting to sound is an extremely effective method of creating a seamless flow of images that moves the viewer though the 'story' line. The most obvious use of sound is in an interview where shots are cut to dialogue following a question and answer pattern. A more subtle use in matching sound to visual is, for example, on a voice-over narration where the shots to illustrate the content of a report are cut on the ending of a sentence or a paragraph. A similar integration of vision and sound is employed in editing music. Cutting to the beat of accompanying music adds rhythm and fluency to a string of images that may in themselves have no continuity connections. The strong rhythm of the music sweeps across the cuts and integrates the visual sequence. When shooting a musical group, the cameraman can help the editor by providing first, a continuous shot of the musical item and then additional shots of the musicians (possibly playing another, similar tempo number), which avoids seeing synchronized hand or arm movement. These can be used to break up the long take, and add variety and pace to the cut item. The same requirement is needed in dance coverage.

In Martin Scorsese's *Raging Bull* (1980), there is a cut from a shot of Robert de Niro closing a fridge door to a shot of him sitting down on a sofa. There is no continuity match between the two shots although it forms part of continuous action. If the cut had not come on the loud clunk of the fridge door closing, the cut would have produced a visual 'jump'. The cut on the loud sound of the fridge door acted like a magician's misdirection when they distract their audience by waving their left hand in the air while the right hand is producing a rabbit from their sleeve. A loud sound can act as a similar distraction and allow an acceptable cut between two shots that are not continuity matched. The sound used to disguise the cut is usually part of the action and not an unseen background event.

The montage

Montage is a sequence of brief shots created to compress action and often to indicate a change of time or location. It is a visual convention that people have learnt to understand from films where, for example, images of calendars, falling leaves etc., are used to indicate the passing of time.

Documentary

Like news, documentary often attempts to capture spontaneous action, and present a slice of life avoiding influencing the subject material with the presence of the camera. But there is also the investigative form of documentary; an exposé of social ills.

Whereas news is generally topical information of the day, shot on the day, to be transmitted on that day, documentary themes and issues are shot over a period of time. The documentary format is often used to take a more considered look at social concerns that may have occurred in the form of a quick specific event in a news bulletin.

Conventional documentary style

A standard documentary structure, popular for many years, involves an unseen presenter (often the producer/director) interviewing the principle subject/s in the film. From the interview (the questions are edited out), appropriate visuals are recorded to match the interviewee comments which then becomes the voice-over. A professional actor is often used to deliver an impersonal narration on scientific or academic subjects. The choice of the quality of the voice is often based on the aim to avoid an overt personality or 'identity' in the voice-over whilst still keeping a lively delivery.

The camera can follow the documentary subject without production intervention, but often the individual is asked to follow some typical activity in order for the camera to catch the event, and to match up with comments made in previous interviews.

'Verite' as a style

The 'verite' style attempts to be a fly-on-the-wall simply observing events without influence. It over-relies on chance and the coincidence of being at the right place at the right time to capture an event which will reveal (subjectively judged by the filmmaker at the editing stage), the nature of the subject. With this style, the main objective of being in the right place at the right time becomes the major creative task. There is often an emphasis on a highly charged atmosphere to inject drama into the story. It may use minimum scripting and research other than to get 'inside' where the action is estimated to be. The style often incorporates more traditional techniques of commentary, interviews, graphics, and recon-struction, using hand-held camerawork and available light technique.

A variant of this approach is to use very high shooting ratios, but spend time researching subjects in order to find structures in editing whereas 'verite' has lower shooting ratios, structuring work to the requirements of the television evening schedules (e.g. six thirty-minute episodes), spending less time in situ studying the subject.

Television documentary attempts to deal with the truth of a particular situation but it also has to engage and hold the attention of a mass audience. John Grierson defined documentary as 'the creative treatment of actuality'. How much 'creativity' is mixed in with the attempt at an objective account of the subject has been the subject of debate for many years.

In one sense, any sequence of shots is a subjective construction because of the new relationships set up when one shot is placed against another (e.g. the 'noddy' filmed after the interviewee has left). Essentially the process of editing is selection. But what are the criteria used to determine the structure of a documentary? Should the standard Hollywood values of pace, excitement and tension predominate, or should there be an attempt to be true to the subject even if it bores the viewer?

There have been many instances of documentary makers being unmasked for using uncredited reconstructions – simply faking incidents they were unable to film or which never took place. Many professional programme makers protest that the viewer understands their subterfuge and fabrication and they are forgiven for the sake of entertainment, involvement and pace. Other documentary makers insist that if you are going to take liberties with the truth it needs to be sign posted or signalled to the audience otherwise they are going to be deceived. The viewer is sucked into a totally believable account of an event which is simply a piece of fiction. Faking documentary sequences has a long history. Even the father of the documentary movement, John Grierson in *Drifters* (1929), used a mocked-up part of a fishing boat on shore to film with fish bought at a local shop that were never caught by the fisherman depicted. And they were the wrong variety of fish.

The newcomer to editing should be aware that the ethics of what liberties can be taken with the documentary form are as varied as the form itself.

169

Introduction to vision mixing

Studio and master control room equipment

Vision mixing equipment is used in production control rooms, continuity and master control suites. Although there is some overlap between the different operating techniques employed, this section mainly deals with vision mixing in programme production.

Button pushing

The operational aspects of a vision mixing control panel can be mastered in a matter of hours. The ability to switch visual sources either by a cut, mix or through the digital effects bank is relatively simple to master. It would be a mistake to conclude (and this applies to all television production craft operations), that knowing which button to push will convert you into a vision mixer.

There are a number of essential skills that separate a vision mixer from someone who knows how a vision mixing panel works. A competent vision mixer is someone who can work with split second timing so that a cut is taken precisely at the point the action requires, but who is constantly monitoring the previews to see if it will conflict with the mechanics of collecting the shot. They will have the ability to divide their attention between script, director's instructions, preview monitors and audio.

Good vision mixing, like much of television production technique, is often a question of instant decision making, fast reflexes and complete operational integration with the rest of the production crew. In high-speed cutting on a complex show there is almost a telepathic link between director, vision mixer and camera crew. In ad lib situations when cutting between cameras constantly changing shot, the vision mixer and the camera crew know, from a knowledge of the programme format, what shots should be offered and taken. There is no more frustrating television than missing the right shot at the right moment. One of the skills developed by a vision mixer is knowing when to wait for directions to cut, and when to take the cut before the moment is lost.

Working in 'real' time

One of the fundamental distinctions that exists between multi-camera and single-camera techniques is that 'film-style' production splits its production decisions between acquiring the basic material and then editing the material. Live, and much of recorded television, requires all the options closed at the time of transmission/recording. Editing decisions on the precise moment of a cut have to be taken in 'real' time unlike the more considered decision making in an edit suite where a cut can be rehearsed, trimmed, rethought, and then executed.

Vision mixer's role

The basic vision mixing activity is switching visual sources when directed. With a scripted show, the cuts will be rehearsed and often the director will not call them on transmission. On an ad lib show, where the precise nature of the content is not known, the director will call most of the cuts, but at moments of high activity when they are fully engaged, they may leave an experienced vision mixer to follow the action and cut as appropriate.

As split second timing is often involved, the vision mixer must have a good sense of the programme format conventions and the customary technique used in order to stay with the director's requirements. For example, they must know the rules of the sport being covered, or have a feel for rhythm and mood when covering music, or roughly know the possible attitudes or opinions of participants in a debate. So often in live television, the speed of the technique is controlled by the content of the programme, and there is no time 'on air' to be precisely directed though all the vision mixing operations required. The director, vision mixer and camera crew activities are linked by the tempo of the event and must all be attentive to the immediate action and anticipate future events.

Vision mixing and video editing

Both vision mixing and video editing share many common techniques. Whereas a vision mixer makes an edit decision in real time with little or no opportunity to adjust the point of edit, a video editor can rehearse and find a precise edit point before laying down the edit. They both, however, follow the standard, perennial conventions of shot transition. Although some of these conventions are dealt with in this chapter, a discussion in greater detail of the requirements of shot transition are to be found in the section on Editing, pages 138–169. There is some overlap of content.

171

Vision mixing technology

Vision mixing a multi-camera production requires an understanding and how to effectively use all the facilities available on the desk in conjunction with the preview, effects and transmission monitors, and the ability to work in a team.

Although not appearing at first sight an important element of vision mixing, the physical relationship between the desk, script, monitors and control room lighting can be crucial. Every visual source required for the production should have a preview monitor or, if there are more incoming visual sources than monitors, control of the switching matrix should be easily accessible to the mixer.

The height and distance of the monitors should allow a rapid preview by the mixer without moving their body. Ideally this distance should be about six times the picture height from the viewer. There should be adequate space in front of the mixer for the script which should be directionally lit to avoid spillage on to the preview monitors. The ambient lighting in the control room should be designed to avoid reflections on the monitor display screens.

Synchronization and timing

In order that all incoming visual sources can be mixed, wiped, superimposed, and processed through the vision mixing desk, it is essential that certain conditions relating to signal timing are met otherwise it is impossible for the mixer to perform correctly. These conditions require a timing accuracy of less than 50 ns for the syncs and a phase difference of less than 5° between the subcarrier reference bursts when transmitting PAL or NTSC. Every video signal passing through the desk must be aligned to achieve these conditions if it is intended to combine it with another visual source.

Digital vision mixing

Once an analogue signal has been converted to digital or the signal originates as a digital signal then a considerable number of effects can be produced via the vision mixing panel. Digital video effects such as picture in picture, freeze frames and picture manipulation have become a staple part of programme production.

The next step on from digital mixing has been the development of computer software to control visual transitions using graphical interface units controlled by a computer mouse. Although these add enormously to the flexibility in post production work, 'real time' vision mixers on live or recorded-as-live productions usually prefer the security of buttons, faders and source selectors provided by the traditional vision mixing panel.

The importance of monitoring

All preview and effects previewing should be available on high-grade colour monitors. The phosphors should match so that skin-tones of any individual face or object colour are the same on each monitor. Each monitor should be set-up for correct contrast and brightness. Every shot requires previewing for content, composition and exposure before it is cut to line (i.e. transmitted or recorded). Any large differences between monitors will prompt a visual 'jump' each time they are previewed inducing inefficient hesitation before selection.

The importance of communications

The vision mixer needs to confirm incoming video signal's availability and where they will appear on the switching matrix before transmission/recording, and often needs to query the availability of lines and their source on transmission. Good communications between the control room and the operational point controlling switching and lines checks are therefore essential.

Visual transitions

The controls on the mixing panel allow several basic visual transitions. These include:

- **A cut** is the simplest switch between shots. One image is instantaneously replaced by another image.
- **Dissolve or mix** (also known as a cross-fade) allows the incoming shot to emerge from the outgoing shot until it replaces it on screen. Sometimes both images are held on screen (a half-mix) before completing the transition. The time taken for the dissolve to make the transition from one image to the next can vary depending on content and the dramatic point the dissolve is making (e.g. a slow mix on slow music, etc.). The proportion of each image present at any point in the mix can be varied, with one image being held as a dominant image for most of the dissolve.
- **Fade** is similar to a mix except only one image is involved and either appears from a blank/black screen (fade-in) or dissolves into a blank/black screen (fade-out). A fade-in is often used to begin a sequence whilst a fade-out marks a natural end to a sequence.
- **Superimposition** is when one image (often text, such as the name of the speaker on shot) is superimposed on top of another image. Name-super text is usually faded-in or wiped-in, held so that it can be read, and then faded-out, cut-out or wiped-out.
- **Wipes and pattern wipes** provide an edge that moves across the screen between the outgoing image and the incoming image. The edge may be soft or bordered (a soft-wipe, or a border-wipe) to add to the transition visually. Common wipe patterns are a simple box or circle, stars, heart shapes and other geometric shapes.
- **Split screen** is when two different images are held on screen separated by a hard or soft edge wipe.
- **Digital video effect (DVE).** When a picture is digitalized the image is formed by millions of separate parts called pixels. These pixels can be endlessly rearranged to produce a variety of random and mathematically defined transitions such as geometric wipes, spins, tumbles, squeezes, squashing, and transitions from one image to another, simulating the page of a book, for example, being turned to introduce the next image.
- **Colour synthesizers** is a method of producing coloured captions and other effects from a monochrome source. The synthesizers rely on an adjustable preset video level to operate a switch, and usually two or three levels can be separated and used to operate colour generators and produce different colours. The switching signal is usually derived from a caption generator.
- **Chroma key** is a method of combining two images to achieve the appearance of a single image (see Chroma key, page 190).

The vision mixing console

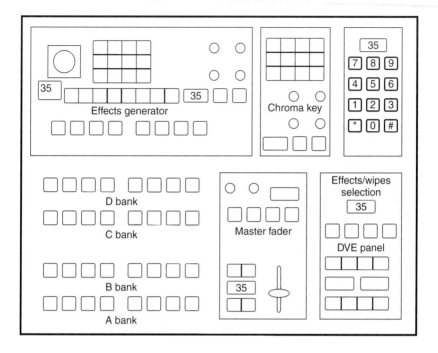

The output of the mixing panel is via a master fader although additional visual inputs can be added by a downstream keyer (see below). A basic mixer has two selection banks, normally termed A and B, and mixing or effects is performed between the two banks. Normally, each camera in use in the production has a dedicated button numbered in sequence from left to right as 1, 2, 3, 4, 5, 6, or however many cameras there are. Selection of other video sources can usually be switched to the required button with both banks duplicating the visual sources. Cutting between video sources is achieved by selecting one of the banks and then depressing the appropriate button on that bank.

Mixing between video sources is achieved by selecting the incoming video source on one bank and the outgoing source on the other bank. A pattern wipe on the transition can be achieved by routeing the mix through the effects generator.

As well as an A and B bank, a C and D bank allows previewing of pictures prior to selection on the operational banks plus the ability to mix to a combination of two visual sources. For example, an image selected on the C bank with a super-imposed caption selected from bank D can be mixed to the output of banks A and B.

A black input is available so that a correct waveform is transmitted when the pictures are faded down.

A downstream keyer is a facility in-line with the output of a vision mixing panel which allows a superimposition on the output of a mixer panel which is un-affected by any changes on the mixer panel, e.g. a caption can be superimposed over changing shots selected at the mixer.

Vision mixing techniques

A digital vision mixing panel enables the most complex and sophisticated transitions between video sources that may be required in programme production. However, the vision mixing activity that is not available on any desk, and is crucial to programme production, is which vision source should be selected, and at what precise moment should that transition occur. Technology cannot help with these production decisions, and anyone new to vision mixing will have to learn the underlying principles of why change shot and when to change shot.

As we have discussed in Section 2, Television production, continuous camera coverage of an event using a number of cameras relies on a stream of invisible shot changes. Invisible in the sense that the transition between each shot does not distract the audience. The aim is to make the shot change unobtrusive to prevent the audience's attention switching from programme content to the programme production technique. No shot can be viewed in isolation – its effect on the viewer will be related to the preceding and succeeding shot. Standard conventions are employed, when cutting between shots, to ensure a smooth flow of images to guide the viewer unobtrusively to a new viewpoint.

Basic conventions

After mastering the operational controls on the vision mixing desk, the next stage is to fully understand these editing conventions. For a shot change to be unobtrusive:

- there must be an appropriate production reason to change the shot
- the shots either side of the visual transition (cut, wipe, mix) must satisfy the editing requirements that link them.

Visual perception

Moving images in television are created by a repetition of 25 complete 'freeze' frames per second. It is human perception that combines the separate images into a simulation of movement, (see Perception and shot transition, page 148). The greater the visual discrepancy between two shots the more likely it is that the viewer will consciously notice the change of shot. A basic technique of vision mixing is to find ways of reducing the visual mismatch between two adjacent images (see text box opposite).

Matching the visual design of shots is discussed in more detail in the section on editing (pages 138–169). The majority of studio work that the technical operator may be vision mixing will concern shots of people in discussion, and the transition from live to recorded items. Most of the following topics have been dealt with in the section on multi-camera camerawork but the important points for vision mixing are emphasized below.

176

Why change the shot?

The standard production reasons for a shot change are:

- to follow the action (e.g. coverage of horse racing – as the horses go out of range of one camera, they can be picked up by another and so forth)
- presenting new information (e.g. a wide shot of an event shows the general disposition, a close-up shows detail)
- to emphasize an element of the event (e.g. a close-up shot revealing tension in the face of a sports participant
- telling a story (e.g. succeeding shots in a drama)
- to provide pace, excitement and variety in order to engage and hold the attention of the audience (e.g. changing the camera angle and size of shot on a singer)
- to visually structure an event in order to explain (e.g. a variety of shots of a cooking demonstration that show close-ups of ingredients and information shots of the cooking method).

In general, a change of shot will be unobtrusive:

- if the individual shots (when intercutting between people) are matched in size, have the same amount of headroom, have the same amount of looking space if in semi-profile, if the lens angle is similar (i.e. internal perspective is similar) and if the lens height is the same
- if the intercut pictures are colour matched (e.g. skin tones, background brightness, etc.) and if in succeeding shots the same subject has a consistent colour (e.g. grass in a stadium)
- if there is continuity in action (e.g. body posture, attitude)
- when cutting on action – the flow of movement in the frame – is carried over into the succeeding shot (e.g. a man in medium shot sitting behind a desk stands up and on his rise, a longer shot of the man and the desk is cut to)
- if there is a significant change in shot size or camera angle when intercutting on the same subject
- if there is a significant change in content (e.g. a cut from a tractor to someone opening a farm gate)
- if there is continuity in lighting, in sound, props and setting and continuity in performance or presentation

177

Interviews

Eyeline is an imaginary line between an observer and the subject of their observation. In a discussion, the participants are usually reacting to each other and will switch their eyeline to whoever is speaking. The audience, in a sense, is a silent participant and they will have a greater involvement in the discussion if they feel that the speaker is including them in the conversation. This is achieved if both eyes of the speaker can be seen by the viewer rather than profile or semi-profile shots. The cameras should be able to take up positions in and around the set to achieve good eyeline shots of all the participants. That is, both eyes of each speaker, when talking, can be seen on camera. In addition, the relationship of the participants should enable a variety of shots to be obtained in order to provide visual variety during a long interview (e.g. over-the-shoulder two-shots, alternative singles and two-shots and group shots, etc.). The staging should also provide for a good establishment shot or relational shot of the participants and for opening or closing shots.

Standard shot sizes
Because so much of television programming involves people talking, a number of standard shot sizes have evolved centred on the human body. In general, these shot sizes avoid cutting people at natural joints of the body such as neck, elbows, knees. See Section 4, Multi-camera camerawork (pages 48–77) for illustration of standard shot sizes. Precise framing conventions for these standard shot descriptions vary between studios, broadcast organizations, and country. One director's MCU may be another director's MS. The reason abbreviations are used is to speed up communication on live broadcasts. Make certain that you understand how the abbreviation is being used by the production team that you are working with.

Cross shooting
A standard cross shooting arrangement is for the participants to be seated facing each other and for cameras to take up positions close to the shoulders of the participants. The usual method of finding the optimum camera position is to position the camera to provide a well composed over-the-shoulder two-shot, then zoom in to check that a clean single can be obtained of the participant facing camera. A tight over-the-shoulder two-shot always risks masking or a poorly composed shot if the foreground figure should lean left or right.

Crossing the line
There may be a number of variations in shots available depending on the number of participants and the method of staging the discussion/interview. All of these shot variations need to be one side of an imaginary line drawn between the participants (see Section 4 Multi-camera camerawork).

Matching to other cameras

In addition to setting up the optimum position for singles, 2 shots etc, shots in a multi-camera intercutting situation need to match. The medium close-ups (MCUs), etc. should be the same size with the same amount of headroom. All cameras intercutting on singles should be the same height and if possible roughly the same lens angle (therefore the same distance from their respective subjects), especially when intercutting on over-the-shoulder 2 shots. This avoids a mismatch of the perspective of mass (i.e. the background figure is smaller or larger than the shot it is matching to). Other matching points are the same amount of looking room with semi-profile shots by placing the centre of the eyes (depending on size of shot) in the centre of frame.

Interview format

The main points about cutting an interview have already been discussed, but the following additional points should be noted.

■ The director should establish in rehearsal on which camera the presenter will make their introduction.

■ The camera coverage and the order the participants will be introduced should also be established so that vision mixer can mark up. A frequent problem in this part of the interview format is the presenter names the participants too quickly giving little or no chance for the cameras and the vision mixer to get the appropriate shot up as the person is named.

■ Try and establish who the first question will be addressed to if it is known before recording/transmission.

■ Establish with the director if he/she will call for reaction shots, although the best reactions are so quick that if the cut is not taken immediately the 'reaction' is lost.

■ A popular convention is to cut to the participant who is being asked a question before the presenter has finished the question in order to observe their reaction to the point being put to them. Check with the director if they intend to follow this convention.

■ It is not a good idea for cameras to make large repositions during an interview as the speed of question and answer may result in a camera being on the move when it is required to be on a participant. An experienced camera crew will inform the director in rehearsal if they are repeatedly having to make large off-shot movement to provide the camera coverage he or she requires. The vision mixer can only watch the preview monitors and hope that the required shot will be steady, focused, and with a matched frame when it is required.

■ If the presenter does not name the person they are coming to, watch the preview monitor of the wide shot or the presenter shot to check their eyeline to establish who he or she is addressing before making the cut. It is better to be a beat behind the answer than cut to the wrong person.

Production methods

Different programme genres have different production techniques. Sports coverage has different shot patterns and camera coverage conventions, for example, to the conventions used in the continuous coverage of music. Knowledge of these customary techniques is an essential part of the vision mixing skills that need to be acquired. There is usually no time for directors to spell out their precise requirements during a fast, live transmission. They assume that the production team is experienced and understand the conventions of the programme being transmitted.

Programme formats

For a vision mixer, a basic distinction is whether the production is scripted (e.g. cuts to dialogue or narration are pre-planned and marked up in the camera script), or if the majority of the programme speech is unscripted. With this type of ad lib production, the vision mixer will need to follow direction, and, at times, make edit decisions when the director is otherwise involved. At an early stage in rehearsal, establish with the director whether they wish to call every cut or if they are happy for the vision mixer to take the appropriate cuts in an interview when needed.

'As-directed' procedures

'As-directed' procedures require fast reflexes and an awareness of the development in programme content. Sometimes a programme will have sections which have a rehearsed shot structure interspersed with 'as-directed' sequences. The danger point is the junction between the two. It is easy to be caught in the 'as-directed' mode of operation and unable to find the correct place in the script when the programme moves into the scripted, numbered shot sequence.

Scripted programmes

A production that has been precisely camera scripted would seem an easier option than continuously keeping up with unexpected dialogue and discussion, but this is not necessarily the case. The scripted shots and cutting points need to be proved with a rehearsal. Those that do not work need altering and in a very fast cutting sequence, each shot has to be taken at its appointed place otherwise everyone, from the PA calling shot numbers to the camera crew working precisely to their listed shots, lose their place. A tightly scripted production requires the vision mixer to clearly mark-up all the changes during the rehearsal, and to be satisfied that all the vision mixing requirements (e.g. DVEs, chroma key set-ups, etc.) can be achieved in the time available as the production progresses in the time scale of the event being covered.

To cut from this shot . . .   to this shot . . .

you need this shot to show change of direction.

Any subject covered by multi-cameras must follow standard basic space/time visual conventions if the resultant flow of images is to be intelligible to the viewer. These shot change conventions ensure that:

- shots are structured to allow the audience to understand the space, time and logic of the action
- each shot follows the line of action to maintain consistent screen direction so that the geography of the action is completely intelligible
- unobtrusive camera movement and shot change directs the audience to the content of the production rather than the mechanics of production
- continuity cutting creates the illusion that distinct, separate shots (possibly recorded out of sequence and at different times) form part of a continuous event being witnessed by the audience.

Vision mixing and video editing

See topics on editing, pages 138–169 for more detailed description of methods of shot transition, rearranging time and space, basic editing principles, types of edit, matching visual design between shots, matching spatial relationships between shots, matching temporal relationships between shot, cutting on dialogue, etc.

Opening and closing

Standard openings

The opening of a programme is often deliberately designed to be fast and engaging to hook the audience. It will often follow a standard pattern that establishes the programme's identity (e.g. the headlines of a news programmes). Often the director will rehearse the opening, even if the main part of the programme will be 'as-directed'. As a vision mixer, it is worth marking up your script in detail and snatching some time for yourself to go through all the effects, routine and desk set-ups that are needed. Do not rely on memory. Put it in writing on your script, even if you never read it. Make certain that you are technically clear on what you have to do and can cope with last minute changes if they happen. A common problems is the non-appearance of a contributor at an outside source who is to be featured in a scene-setter at the beginning of the programme. Anticipate that this may not happen and have a fall-back plan of what you will do if they fail to arrive.

It is particularly important to get the show off to a good start in order to grab the viewer's attention, and also because mistakes at the start can lead to a 'domino' effect that will ripple all around the production team and take time for everyone to return to competent operation.

Standard close

Many programmes also have a standard close. Three things often happen in quick succession. The presenter will wind-up the show, there may be a closing wide shot sometimes with a lighting change for closing graphics or credits to be supered over. The perennial problem with a live programme is time. If an interview precedes the close, the vision mixer will have been involved in a close and concentrated cutting sequence and may neither have anticipated nor set up the desk for the final sequence. At some time before the end you must anticipate what is required. A programme often crashes out because a contributor will not take a wind-up, and there is inadequate time remaining for the pre-timed music and end credits. Arranging for the credits and music to end together is the usual professional aim for the end of a show. Be prepared with the end sequence before it is required.

Customary technique

It is crucial in a fast ad lib spontaneous programme that the vision mixer and camera crew are on the same 'wavelength' as the director. This means everyone understands the customary technique for the programme and think in the same way. In practice, this means that when everyone anticipates a cut, it happens. Or when everyone anticipates a specific shot, it is taken. If a camera crew or vision mixer are puzzled by the cutting preferences of the director and it does not follow customary conventions then the director, in a fast moving ad lib production, will have to call every shot, and every cut, and this can be time consuming and inefficient. If everyone can keep in step, then the production team can up its work rate and still keep together.

For example, when a camera is 'on shot' on a interviewee and a neighbouring speaker out of shot starts to speak, the cameraman could pan in vision to the speaker, although this is usually not customary technique, or the mixer can cutaway to a quick reaction shot of the anchorman or group shot allowing the camera to quickly reposition ready for a cut back with hardly a word being lost on screen. When trust is built up between director, vision mixer, and camera crew many more shots are possible because repositions are faster. A cameraman may spot a person bursting to get into the debate and swing to them which usually prompts the speaker to speak. If the director wants to call every move and every cut and every shot they may miss a number of useful shots and, unless they are very lucky, be left several shots behind the flow of the discussion. Tying up several cameras solely as wide 'belt and braces' covering shots leads to a camera coverage that is too loose and does not engage and involve the viewer in the personalities of the debate.

183

Magazine format

In order for a topical daily magazine/news programme to be prepared, there is usually a well defined format with standard items and methods of presentation. Before working on such a programme, get to know the basic items which are going to appear on the daily running order and most importantly, understand the specific abbreviations or slang descriptions that are used by the programme production staff. Get someone to explain any jargon that is new to you because on transmission there will not be time to question what the implications of an unintelligible piece of information about changes to the running order that is thrown from the back of the control room to the director. You may be astute enough, for example, to work out that when the editor shouts out 'Kill the heads' that instead of going to presenter A on Camera 2 to read the closing headlines, the next shot will be presenter B on camera 1 who will then link to the weather report. The production team may have been working on the same programme format for many years and know instantly the rearrangement necessary when the headlines item is dropped. If it takes you five to ten seconds to decipher the insider jargon, you could be completely wrong footed and cut to the wrong camera. People who are in daily contact in the production of a programme have a habit of inventing shorthand descriptions of the daily items which only insiders are privy to.

The running order, although brief, is the key to what you as a vision mixer will need to know. Mark up any scripted links (which often arrive very late and sometimes while you are 'on-air') indicating camera and visual source in large letters (see Marking up a script, p. 198). Check the end words coming out of a recorded item as you will be listening for them to cut out of and back to the presenter. Some presenters will ad lib into an item and the cue to go the new item must be given by the director in order that both vision and sound can cut/mix at the same time. The director should always control any programme transition that requires coordination between sound and vision so that there is no misunderstanding causing sound or vision to lead or lag.

Keep up to date with changes, especially those last minute changes that occur in the last few seconds before transmission when everyone is checking sources, levels and setting the desk for the opening routine. Try to look ahead on transmission to any complicated set-ups that are upcoming such as chroma key weather set-ups (see Chroma key, page 190).

Name supers on recorded items need to be checked for accuracy and if there is sufficient time for the super to put up, read, and taken out before the shot changes. A timed list of supers and when they occur should be available from editing but be warned, if they have not been rehearsed the timings could be wrong.

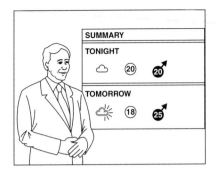

On air, watch out for the invariable jokey interchange between presenter and weatherman or specialist sports reporter. Watch your previews to check that you can cut back to a presenter after going to the weatherman if the repartee continues because sometimes a camera will clear immediately a link has finished. Check also that your desk set-up allows you to intercut between weatherman/chroma key background and presenter. This type of ad lib cutting can be visually very messy because of its spontaneous content and indecision about when it has ended.

Early morning and late night news bulletins

Local news inserts into a network programme or regional opt-outs can often be pre-rehearsed and accurately timed, but from a mixing point of view, there is often the need to be flexible and adapt to the time actually allocated. If a network programme is over-running the squeeze is often on the opt-out in order to catch up on the overall running time.

TV demonstration

A television demonstration can have as its subject anything from a DIY item to cooking a Christmas pudding. It is often conducted by a presenter and an 'expert' who will do the demonstration. The camera coverage will require shots of the two participants and close-ups of the demonstrated items. If the items can be positioned for clean CUs in rehearsal the demonstration will be that much more intelligible to the viewer. Be quick to cutaway from a small item that is held in big close-up and is being waved around by the participant. It is almost impossible to hold it in sharp focus and if it is waved around the viewer will not be able to understand the content of the shot. If tight close-ups are being picked up on a surface such as a table, be certain that the item is the one that is being referred to before cutting to it. Too often an interviewee will rest their hand on one item before discussing another item at the far end of the table. If in doubt, watch the two-shot on the preview monitor to check the direction of the eyeline.

Working in a production crew
Obviously the director/vision mixer wants the appropriate shot ready, in focus and steady when it is required, but for the cameraman there are a number of obstacles to achieving this. As a vision mixer, try to understand why the shot is not ready. It may be the cameraman's fault, but more likely there is a cable problem or scenery or a dozen other reasons why the shot is not steady, in focus and on the correct subject. The preview monitors are a useful communication tool in these situations, and an experienced camera crew will show what the problem is (e.g. the floor manager has lost talkback, etc.) if they are not otherwise engaged 'on-air'. Be consistent, on scripted shows, to cut as rehearsed as the cameraman may be relying on the rehearsed time to make a reposition or adjust framing. Likewise the cameraman must deliver the shot that was agreed and rehearsed to ensure the cutting is appropriate.

Last moment tweaks to the shot just as the mixer cuts
A recurring problem facing vision mixers is at the moment they are going to cut, the cameraman re-frames or makes a slight 'twitch' to the framing. There are a number of reason why this happens. The most common one is that the presenter/participant alters their body position before they speak forcing the cameraman to re-frame just when the cut is required. The vision mixer can only watch the preview monitor and think the same way as the cameraman and anticipate, for example, that he will recompose the shot when someone straightens up and hold the cut until the shot settles.

Audience show

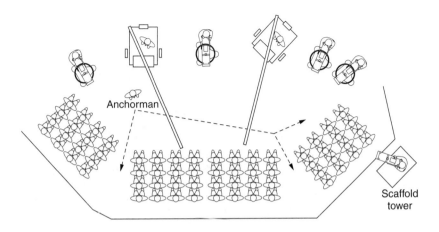

Anchorman

Scaffold
tower

Vision mixing on an audience show is similar to an enlarged interview. It helps if the anchor person is always on the same camera, and that there is a safety shot showing a wide shot of the audience. When a group of experts are gathered there may even be a seating plan with an order of speaking. Frequently however, an audience discussion is a free-for-all with a need for the camera crew to rapidly find the speaker or even anticipate who the next speaker will be. The director must coordinate and communicate when duplicate shots turn up. The usual guidelines for mixing an ad lib spontaneous event is to watch the previews, cutaway quickly to allow cameras to reposition, and trust that an experienced director and camera crew will provide the appropriate shot. Establish with the director the opening and closing routines and make certain the anchorman camera is released to go to the presenter for the wind-up.

Music coverage

Multi-camera music coverage on television includes a wide range of musical performances, production styles and visual preferences. At one end of the spectrum there are relays from concert halls of orchestral performances that are often tightly scripted and in general have an unobtrusive technique where the emphasis is on matching picture to content with the minimum of visual interpretation. In extreme contrast to this 'invisible' technique, there are multi-camera coverage of rock groups where an attempt is made to capture the atmosphere and excitement of a live event. Cutting rate and shots seek to reproduce the liveliness and frenzy of the rave.

Most of the following points are generalized and all are not applicable to the individual ways of presenting music on television within the wide range of production styles practised. They are an attempt to make the vision mixer new to multi-camera music coverage aware of some aspects of production technique that he/she should consider when working on a continuous musical event.

The different methods of covering music continuously with multi-cameras without recording breaks or post production are itemized in the text box opposite.

Cutting to music

It helps when cutting music to have a knowledge of music form, but the minimum skill that is required to be developed by a vision mixer is a feel for pace and tempo, and an understanding of bar structure. Most popular music is created around a 16 or 32 bar structure and the cutting rate and time of the cut happening will relate to this bar structure. Listen to a wide range of music and practise cutting on the beat.

Mixes are often used on slower tempo numbers. Remember that the cameraman will hold a static frame while the cue light is on. Sometimes the fader can be almost at its end stop with no hint of its image on the transmission monitor. The cue light will still be on, however, and the camera cannot clear until the fader is taken to the end stop and the cue light goes out. Match the speed of the mix to the music and attempt to imitate a sound technique which often uses a non-linear fade-up or fade-down. This technique fades the sound away so that the listener is not really aware when the music has gone. Something similar can be done with visual cross mixes and combination shots when images are brought in and taken out.

The different methods of covering music continuously with multi-cameras without recording breaks or post production can be grouped under the following headings:

- **Pre-scripted:** The whole performance is structured and shots assigned to each camera using a score or a break down of the number (e.g. concerts or production numbers in variety shows). With complex music (e.g. an orchestral piece) the director, vision mixer and PA will be following the score with the PA calling shot numbers and bar numbers to allow camera moves such as pans, zooms and tracks to be precisely timed. This complex event is usually well outside the experience of a technical operator.

- **Camera scripted during rehearsal:** After looking on camera at the performance, shots are structured by the director and each shot numbered. This shot sequence is then exactly reproduced on the recording or transmission.

- **Top and tail:** The start and end of a musical piece is decided, leaving the middle section to be as directed.

- **Assigned roles:** Each camera is assigned one or two performers or instruments and offers a variety of shots connected with them. This gives the director a guaranteed appropriate shot at any time.

- **As directed:** No shot structure is assigned and each cameraman is directed and/or offers a variety of shots, checking that the shot they are offering is an alternative to the shot currently cut to line.

Chroma key

Invisible keying of one image into another requires the application of a perfect electronic switch obtained by appropriate lighting of foreground and background, correct setting up and operation of the keying equipment, a match between foreground and background mood and atmosphere which is achieved by lighting and design, appropriate costume and make-up of foreground artistes, a match between foreground artiste's size, position and movement and background perspective achieved by camera position, lens and staging.

The control that selects the precise point where the colour key will operate is often situated on the vision mixing panel. This clip level control needs to be adjusted so that there is a clean switch between foreground and background images. Small detail in the foreground subject such as hair, can 'confuse' the keying equipment so that there is not a clean switch between foreground and background. This usually appears in the combined image as fringing around the hair. The clip level control needs to be adjusted to provide a perfect key. Problems also arise when clothing or other items closely match the background keying colour or there is colour spill onto the foreground subject from the background chroma key area. Smoke or glass items are difficult to chroma key with standard colour switching but linear keying eliminates the problems connected with transparency. It does not switch between foreground and background but suppresses the unwanted colour of the foreground (e.g. blue), and turns on the background image in proportion (linearly) to the brightness of the blue of the foreground image. Shadows cast by foreground objects can therefore be semi-transparent rather than black silhouettes.

Chroma key technique

A simple application would involve an artiste appearing against a blue background on one camera and a second camera looking at a picture or slide of a street scene. When these two pictures are used with chroma key the artiste will appear on the screen as if he is in a street. The blue background can be produced by either blue painted scenery or a blue lighted cyclorama. In a long shot within a studio, the blue backing is usually insufficiently wide or high enough. A box wipe can be set-up on the mixer with the background scene outside the box and the combination of foreground/background through chroma key, inside the box. To provide the illusion of artistes appearing behind objects which are in the picture into which the artiste is to be inserted, objects or flats painted in the keying colour are placed in front of the artiste to coincide with the foreground objects' position in the picture. All cameras must be locked-off and alignment is performed by using a mixed feed viewfinder on the camera which shows both pictures. There are technological methods of allowing cameras to move in synchronization.

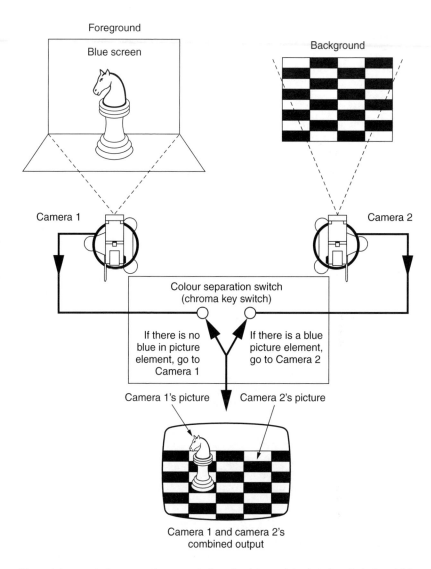

Foreground

Blue screen

Background

Camera 1

Camera 2

Colour separation switch
(chroma key switch)

If there is no
blue in picture
element, go to
Camera 1

If there is a blue
picture element,
go to Camera 2

Camera 1's picture

Camera 2's picture

Camera 1 and camera 2's
combined output

Chroma key technique requires a switch to be inserted in the signal chain which will electronically select the appropriate image. Blue is commonly chosen as the colour to be used as the separation key but other colours can be employed. When the chroma key switch is in use, any blue in the selected image (foreground) is switched out and that part of the frame which contained a blue object is blanked. The black holes left in the shot are now used as a stencil to cut out the corresponding portions in the frame of the background image. The parts of the background image that are within this template are inserted (as a perfect fit) back into the blank areas of the foreground image.

Mixer facilities

Picture manipulation

One method of inserting one image into another is via the digital video effects bank on the mixing panel. The inserted image is reduced to the required size and then positioned by joystick control. The position can then be memorized and recalled during recording or transmission. Remember that some adjustment may be necessary of the memorized position because although the electronic memory is infallible, the camera operator has to rely on shot box setting (if available), a marked position for the camera mounting on the studio floor and perfect visual memory of what the combined shot looked like at rehearsal. Computers are better than people in repeating perfect positioning within the frame. The same problem can exist with combinations of computer graphics and camera shots.

The split screen

A spilt screen is another method of combining two images. Although the term is often applied to the method of combining two images separated by a vertical or horizontal wipe, it can also be applied to a composite involving box, circle, shapes, etc.

Caption key

A caption key facility provides for sharper separation between lettering and background image. This improvement in legibility can be enhanced by a black edge generator. A colour synthesizer can be used to colour captions or backgrounds for captions.

Wipes

The speed of a wipe that moves across the screen between the outgoing image and the incoming Image can be controlled manually or programmed to move at a specified speed. Check with the director during rehearsal when setting up and memorizing the speed that is required.

Floor monitors

Frequently floor monitor feeds are switched at the vision mixing panel. A typical production requirement is for an 'in-vision' monitor to be switched at a specific point in the production. The monitor, for example, may be displaying a contributor for an outside location who will be interviewed by the studio presenter. When the interview is finished, the monitor, if it is still in vision, will require to be switched to possibly the programme logo or a similar graphic.

Floor monitors may also require switching during the production of programme formats such as game shows or slung monitors for audience, etc.

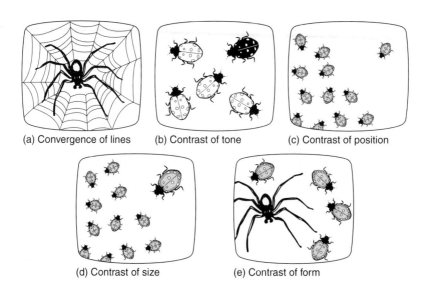

(a) Convergence of lines   (b) Contrast of tone   (c) Contrast of position

(d) Contrast of size   (e) Contrast of form

Good visual communication is:

- simple – unnecessary detail is eliminated with not more than three or four competing subjects for attention
- accessible – the main subject/topic is quickly understood as the message may be on the screen for a limited time
- clear – television screens vary in size, technical quality and viewing conditions therefore the message must be legible even in imperfect viewing conditions
- impactful – a visually dynamic design to compete, but not conflict, with surrounding visuals
- unambiguous – the observer's eye must be guided with unmistakable certainty to the principal message displayed.

193

Frame store

In its original basic form, a still store was a digital piece of equipment that allowed a frame of video to be stored and accessed when required. One frame of video in a standard 625/50 picture includes 720 pixel groups, each made up of full resolution luminance pixel plus two half-resolution colour difference pixels – a total of 829,440 pixels. Sampled at 8-bit resolution, this creates over 6.6 million bits of data (6.6 Mb). Each uncompressed stored frame therefore requires 6.6 Mb of memory.

As the cost of memory has plunged, there has been a huge increase in the storage and computing ability of still stores, allowing many more programme production techniques to be executed to augment the original function of storage and retrieval of television images.

Dedicated (and open architecture) still stores can provide:

- a high capacity of still images (e.g. up to 56 minutes of uncompressed video)
- file management using data bases that classify each image by title, category, original acquisition date, keyword, etc., for rapid search, sort and fast selection. As each picture is recorded it is given a number and can easily be recalled
- manipulation of the image size and position on screen for over-the-shoulder use
- arrangement and storing of selected images into stacks to match the running order of the production
- forming images into stacks for animation
- preview facilities to check the next image to be accessed on air
- acquisition of visual material from dedicated graphics machines, and input graphic files from many different computer formats
- frame grabs from moving images with the ability to process and eliminate interfield flicker, etc., on the image
- duplicate outputs to allow more than one 'client' to have access to the stored material and facilities
- remote control of access (e.g. an operational panel in a production studio or OB control room), plus the ability to network to many different users
- on-air control providing speed, accuracy and reliability
- drag and drop selection of required image
- a range of DVEs including wipes, transition and dissolves
- storing and replaying video clips
- keying signals to allow on-air semi-transparent graphics
- and many more facilities, depending on equipment design.

Storing picture information digitally allows individual images to be recorded from many sources such as graphics machine, still store, or character generator one at a time. Material can be built up, adding elements from a number of different sources until the sequences of images form an animated clip when played-out. Individual frames can easily be edited into a new order and the playback speed can be altered or made into a loop.

Dedicated frame store equipment has developed to overlap the function of computer graphics, vision mixing, video editing, animation etc., but the ability to acquire, store, index and replay a still, or a sequence of images, remains integral to most productions.

Character generators

A character generator originally began as a facility that allowed text to be entered via a keyboard. Various visual manipulations could then be carried out on the text and it could be stored, ready to be accessed when required. The main requirement was speed and reliability for on-air work. As the cost of digital computing power decreased, many more facilities were added and character generators can now include:

■ a vast range of font styles and size with the ability to incorporate new and unique typefaces. Text can be set in any colour with effects like a drop shadow, surround, or strap line added to make the type more legible against its background

■ manipulation of the text in its on-screen presentation such as real time dynamic titling effects, dissolve, roll, crawl, zipping, reveal in or out, etc., and flying text in 3D space. Three standard text movements are *zipping* (words or phrases appear on the screen letter by letter), *roll* (the text runs up the screen to a preset time, often matched to music in an end credit sequence), and *crawl* (a horizontal movement of text often from right to left)

■ as well as text, CGs can also generate shapes and areas of colour such as backings, charts, straplines, boxes, etc. and manage the design and storage of symbols or logos that can be recalled and positioned with text

■ a built-in still store

■ painting with pen and tablet

■ video capture and video clip management to import external video clips to incorporate with captions or graphics, and allow shrinking, repositioning, and zooming the external clip. A typical use is to squeeze down video clips and play them in the corner of the screen to promote up-coming items

■ dual/multi channel output

■ removable hard disks so that specific programmes' stings and animated graphics can be instantly available when loaded

■ spell checker plus the capability of importing from a PC a text file which can be formatted into the current production style template of appropriate font, size etc., plus the ability to integrate with newsroom workstation systems so that graphics can be created at the same time as a news script is compiled. The potential to move files from different production areas avoids retyping, allowing the production team to directly compile lists of credits, titles, and name-super graphics.

A prime function of a CG is still to prepare text for the screen, but the expansion of facilities allows a greatly enhanced range of graphic treatment. For example, an animated programme logo can be added to each name super in the 'house' style of the specific programme. At a time of ever increasing programme outlets, programme identification is becoming more and more important in the quest for audiences. Many productions have created their own typeface to continually remind the audience of the identity of the programme.

Different types of graphics

Graphics are used in a number of different ways in television production. Each format has its individual technique and conventions:

- **Straplines:** A strapline is a line of text supered over live action usually at the bottom of the frame. It can be static or crawled across the frame (see text opposite). It can be used to reinforce the main image and audio, or it can be used to add completely new information with the risk (and sometimes the intention) of conflicting with the background information. Name supers are frequently designed with the programme logo included.

- **Supered text:** Any text that is required to be supered over moving images should be checked for legibility. If the background image varies in contrast and tone, a grey toned strap or edge enhancement can make the text more distinct.

- **Stacks, maps and charts:** Specially designed maps are frequently used in news bulletins to show the location of the story. If it is a story about an unfamiliar country or city, a common convention is to establish neighbouring countries (or even continent), before focusing in on the designated area. Maps are designed to be easily read with the minimum amount of geographical information, cities, and towns, that are required by the story.

- **Words or pictures:** Full frame graphics can be made up of text, pictures, symbols, or any combination of these. The information can be animated by building up the complete frame using a background image, and movement appropriate to the subject. The graphic presentation should be simple and uncluttered to allow the viewer to understand the main points being communicated.

- **Headings:** Sometimes a story or a documentary uses a stand-alone graphic to identify a new subject or theme. These can be accompanied by musical 'stings' (a short musical phrase), all repeated in a similar style.

- **Quotes:** Graphical text that is displayed to reinforce a voice-over should usually be identical to the words spoken. The viewer will read along with the spoken words and any difference between what is read and what is heard can be obtrusive and jarring.

- **Insets and over-the-shoulders:** Most news bulletins use a chroma key window or DVE window sharing the news reader's frame. The graphic displayed in the window can either be a generic logo (e.g. a football image for match reports), or a specific graphic to match the subject of the story (e.g. a politician image). Many programmes other than news and current affairs use over-the-shoulder graphics to support a piece to camera.

- **Outline points:** With news stories, such as proposed new legislation, budget proposals, etc., the main points of the report are frequently built up, point by point, in the frame to form a summary of the changes. If each point is to be synchronized with voice-over replication make certain that the text is identical to the text read out or, if the summary is a 'headline' list, the spoken text enlarges on the keyword.

In rehearsal

Marking up a script

Vision mixing information on the script needs to be read at speed during transmission/recording. The size of the typescript is often inadequate to accurately check the next visual change when quickly looking between panel, monitor bank and script. The usual method of improving this is to write in large letters the camera number, instructions to cut, mix or fade and any other mixer facility to be used (chroma key, etc.). Identify key dialogue connected with visual transitions (e.g. changing graphic material in vision to match spoken commentary) or 'in' or 'out' words on insert material.

Why have a rehearsal?

Multi-camera television production is a group activity. A live transmission requires the coordination and contribution of many different crafts and skills, each perfecting their input into the production at the precise time that it is required. A recorded item may have the luxury of retakes to eliminate imperfections if the programme content is under the control of the director (e.g. it is not an actuality event that cannot be repeated). To ensure that everyone is clear about their contribution to a transmission, the director/producer/editor must either brief each individual or arrange to run the item before transmission. A rehearsal provides the opportunity for everyone involved to check that the planned structure and detail of the programme is practical and achievable.

What a vision mixer needs from the rehearsal

As we have discussed, a camera scripted programme needs to be run in its actual running time to establish the feasibility of the planning. It is usual to block the shots, altering and adjusting the shots and cuts as necessary. Because this is a stop/start activity it is very easy to overlook the time available to carry out complex mixer set-ups or cameras to readjust the frame. A non-stop run of each complete section establishes the true time scale of the production. Make certain that you keep up-to-date with any changes and pay particular attention to fast cutting sequences to ensure that you, and the camera crew, have sufficient time to provide the shots and cuts on time. If you are working from a running order, the director should try to ensure that everyone has at least a look at each set-up and sequence, even if the shots are rehearsed with the floor manger standing in for absent presenters or interviewees. The running order should indicate visual and audio source, duration and any scripted intros or pieces to camera.

Talkback discipline

Remember that a number of people are on talkback, with some wearing headsets for the whole of the rehearsal and transmission period. Avoid chattering on talkback about topics unconnected with the production.

Pre-rehearsal checks

There are a number of checks the vision mixer should carry out prior to rehearsal:

- Check the script or running order and establish the origin of all visual sources and where they will appear on the mixer, and on what preview monitor.
- Check source identification for incoming lines, and check if there are sufficient previews and sources on the mixer without the need to switch during transmission/recording.
- Make certain you have a method of identifying and a written record of the origin of a source on the matrix if switching is required.
- Check over the mixer and set up the facilities that will be required by the production.
- Check that you understand how to rapidly use all the facilities available.
- If it is the job function of the vision mixer, line-up the monitors with a test signal (e.g. PLUGE) if available and check for consistency in brightness, contrast, colour rendering and sharpness between previews and transmission monitors.
- Check the cue lights on preview and transmission monitors, and with the camera crew/vision control, check the camera cue lights. If you are unfamiliar with the mixing panel check that cue lights still function when using the DVE facility.

22.   Cam 3 *3*
MS presenter holding newspaper

mix to 4

(MIX to Cam 4 – newspaper detail)

199

Working with the director

At some time during the rehearsal, if you have not worked with the director previously, check on what cut decisions will be called and which mixing decision you should take from the script or programme content. The rehearsal period is also the time for you to assess the form of words with which the director will instruct you when he/she requires the edit points. It is not being pedantic to require good clear communication from the director to avoid, in the heat of a live production, misunderstandings and confusion. Someone snapping their fingers in front of your face is not clear communication unless they have preceded the signal with words such as 'coming to 1. Cut to 1.'

Previewing
Many experienced vision mixers display the next visual source on the preview monitor. This may be impossible in an ad lib sequence but it does indicate to the director the upcoming shot. It is necessary for the director to be as brief as possible on transmission, but not to the point of unintelligibility. Shouting one word 'cut' when there may be choice of cameras to go to can only lead the vision mixer to assume the preview source is being referred to. This may not always be the director's intention. There is a need for the director to stand the vision mixer and camera operator by before the instruction. This can be as simple as preceding the instruction with 'coming to'. With experience, a vision mixer can react very quickly to content and the director's instructions if there is some warning of their intention before the command is made. It helps if the director precedes an instruction, for example, 'Camera 2. Give me a two-shot'. For a vision mixer, 'Coming to 2. Cut' or 'Mix to four next . . . (pause) . . . and mix'. Be careful, when new to vision mixing, that you do not confuse a direction to a camera operator with a command to cut to that camera. This can easily happen if the director does not choose the instruction carefully.

On recording or on transmission there is no need for the director to call everything. The camera rehearsal period should have established the main structure of the show and the vision mixer should be confident of the flow of shots. On a fast cutting, scripted section, the less the director says the better. The director must however coordinate those transitions as, for example, coming out of a video insert, when both the vision mixer and sound need the command to make the cut coincide. The director should cue the artists so that by the time the cut happens, the artist is animated. The usual command is 'cue and cut'. Mixing to a presenter takes longer than a cut and it is usual to use the command 'mix and cue' to allow the mix to be fully complete by the time the artist starts to talk. By the end of the rehearsal the vision mixer should know as much about the shot sequence and cutting points as the director. The director's instructions during transmission or recording are merely an indication of when to do something.

Solving problems

A rehearsal exists to solve problems. What was a paper planning exercise has now to be converted into a three-dimensional activity for everyone concerned, all working against the hardest task master – the clock. Problems will arise, and sometimes sitting in your vision mixing chair you will feel you have the perfect solution. Depending on the moment, you can offer your suggestion, but make certain you have thought through all the implications and are not creating new problems elsewhere. Be cautious that one successful suggestion does not lead to a second and a third and so on. This is a diplomatic way of advising against trying to direct the show. There is only one director and all production communication should flow through the director's chair.

It is a slippery slope to anarchy once everyone starts offering their viewpoint, and, as in the famous committee that set out to design a horse, your production team could end up transmitting a camel.

VT clock

One final item to check on rehearsal for a recorded programme is the source of the ident clock and who is responsible for programming the correct details of the production. Make yourself aware of local custom and practice as to when you should fade to black before the top of the clock is reached.

201

Transmission

Transmission/recording procedure

With a good rehearsal, by the time transmission or recording begins, the vision mixer should be fairly confident of what is their contribution to the production. Unfortunately the unpredictable nature of television is such that most experienced practitioners subscribe to the belief that a good rehearsal often presages a chaotic transmission. This pessimism is frequently unfounded and you should always attempt to get as much information about your production role before you go 'on air'. If you are not told, ask, as the process of briefing everyone on the production crew can sometimes be less than perfect.

Anticipate the unexpected

Television programme production is unpredictable, but its unpredictability often falls within a pattern. With experience, you can anticipate the unexpected and make appropriate alternative arrangements. Anticipation allows you to find time to do what is required. Being suddenly faced with a set of unrehearsed events without pre-thought eliminates any time to sort out the desk and make the correct operational decisions. Part of your preparation for the show is to mentally plan what you will do if the rehearsed sequences are changed. Set up complex effects before they are needed to make time for yourself. Keep with the flow of the production but constantly look ahead to what is upcoming.

Problems during the show

No live or 'recorded as live' programme will be without its problems or unexpected emergencies. Artistes missing their marks or cameras prevented from getting to a prearranged position will require instant adjustment to the shot structure. Watch the previews for alternative shots. If you miss a shot or cut to a wrong camera, forget about it and make certain the next shot is there. Too often, the number of operational errors escalate because people spend time agonizing over their mistakes. If a shot is not ready and the director is unaware, bring it to their attention so that action can be quickly taken. If there is a production mistake on transmission, never spend time deciding on the cause. Get on with the next item and leave the post mortems until after the programme has finished. Remember to follow up equipment malfunction that affected your work and check that it will not occur next time.

Everyone makes mistakes, including the director. Sometimes he or she will call for a cut to a shot that is obviously wrong. The vision mixer in such circumstances will have to use their own individual initiative and a knowledge of the production to either cut to the right shot or if they feel this will cause greater confusion, go to the directed shot.

Summary of vision mixing operational technique

Preparation

- know how the mixer operates
- check over all the facilities and sources that are required
- check and mark up the script
- find out how the director will communicate with you

Concentration

- keep your attention on the transmitted content even if every one else around you in the control room is concerned with items yet to arrive or which are unobtainable
- do not try to do other people's jobs (such as directing)

Anticipation

- look ahead
- anticipate what can go wrong
- have a mental plan of what to do when it does go wrong

TV journalism

Video news journalism covers a wide spectrum of visual/sound reports which use a number of camerawork conventions. A loose classification separates hard news stories, which aim to transmit an objective, detached account of an event (e.g. a plane crash), from those soft news stories which incline more towards accounts of lifestyle, personality interviews and consumer reports. Acceptable camera technique and style of shooting will depend on content and the aim of the report. For example, a politician arriving to make a policy statement at a conference will be shot in a fairly straightforward camera style with the intention of simply 'showing the facts'. An item about a fashion show could use any of the styles of feature film presentation (e.g. wide angle distortion, subjective camerawork, canted camera etc.). The political item has to be presented in an objective manner to avoid colouring the viewer's response. The fashion item can be more interpretative in technique and presentation in an attempt to entertain, engage and visually tease the audience. A basic skill of news/magazine camerawork is matching the appropriate camerawork style to the story content. The main points to consider are:

- producing a technically acceptable picture (see Section 6, Working on location)
- an understanding of news values and matching camerawork style to the aims of objective news coverage
- structuring the story for news editing and the requirements of news bulletins/magazine programmes
- getting access to the story and getting the story back to base.

What makes a story news?
There is no universally acceptable definition of news. A wide diversity of stories can be seen every day as the front page lead in newspapers. There appears to be little consensus as to what is the main news story of the day. The only generalization that can be made in television is that news is usually considered to be those topical events that need to be transmitted in the next immediate news broadcast. Access, rapid working methods, a good appreciation of news values and the ability to get the material back, edited and on the air are the main ingredients of 'hard news' camerawork. There is no specific agreed technique in camera/recorder news coverage although there are a number of conventions that are widely accepted. People almost always take precedence over scenery as the principal subject of news stories. Faces make good television if they are seen in context with the crisis. Where to position the camera to get the shot that will summarize the event is a product of experience and luck, although good news technique will often provide its own opportunities. A news story can quickly lose the interest of its potential audience if it does not, at some point in the report, feature a person.

Access

One crucial requirement for news coverage is to get to where the story is. This relies on contacts and the determination to get where the action is. Civil emergencies and crises are the mainstay of hard news. Floods, air/sea rescue, transport crashes, riots, fire and crime are news events that arise at any time and just as quickly die away. They require a rapid response by the cameraman who has to be at the scene and begin recording immediately before events move on. Equipment must be ready for instantaneous use and the cameraman must work swiftly to keep up with a developing story.

In some countries or regions, access may be denied unless you are in possession of a certified police pass, press pass and in the case of some civil disasters the appropriate safety clothing. Inform the police and/or the appropriate authority for all day use of a street or public place for location recording. Security clearance is almost always required in order to enter military, naval and other restricted access sites.

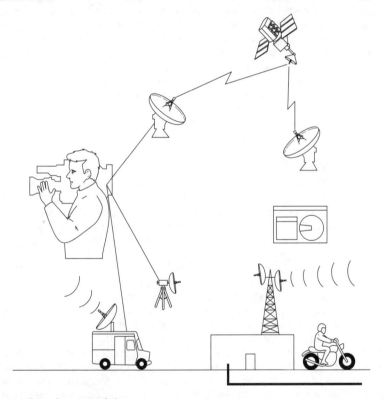

Returning the material

Getting the news material back to base can be by transport, land line, terrestrial or satellite link or foldaway SNG equipment. The important thing is to get the material to base fast with supporting information (if a reporter is not at the location) in a form (the cassette clearly marked) that can be rapidly edited. Use a separate tape for the reporter's voice-over and a 5-minute tape for cutaways to speed up editing. Use a new tape for each story so that the stories can be cut independently if required.

Objectivity

Record or interpretation

One basic convention is the distinction between news camerawork as a record of an event and camerawork as an interpretation of an event.

- **The record of an event:** Information shots are specific. They refer to a unique event – the wreckage of a car crash, someone scoring a goal, a political speech. They are often non-repeatable. The crashed car is towed away, the politician moves on. They are the guts of a news story and if the crucial shot is missing, the story will lose impact and significance. The item will deteriorate into an account of what has happened, but can no longer be seen.

- **Interpretative shots**: Interpretative or decorative shots are non-specific. They are often shot simply to give visual padding to the story. A typical example is a shot of an interviewee walking in a location before an interview. This shot allows the dubbed voice-over to identify who the interviewee is and possibly their attitude to the subject. The shot needs to be long enough to allow information that is not featured in the interview to be added as a voice over. The interviewee leaves frame at the end of the shot to provide a cutting point to the interview. Have the interviewee medium-close-up facing in the same direction as the preceding walk to the interview.

There is a basic dilemma in news bulletins between objectivity and the need to engage and hold the attention of the audience. As the popularity of cinema films has shown, an audience enjoys a strong story that involves them in suspense and moves them through the action by wanting to know 'what happens next'? This is often incompatible with the need for news to be objective and factual. The production techniques used for shooting and cutting fiction and factual material are almost the same. These visual story telling techniques have been learned by the audience from a life time of watching fictional accounts of life. The twin aims of communication and engaging the attention of the audience apply to news as they do to entertainment programmes.

A television news report has an obligation to separate fact from opinion, to be objective in its reporting, and by selection, to emphasize that which is significant to its potential audience. These considerations therefore needed to be borne in mind by a potential news cameraman as well as the standard camera technique associated with visual story telling. Although news aims to be objective and free from the entertainment values of standard television story telling (e.g. suspense, excitement etc.), it must also aim to engage the audience's attention and keep them watching. The trade-off between the need to visually hold the attention of the audience and the need to be objective when covering news centres on structure and shot selection.

Communication and audience involvement

- Communicate in an objective style without unduly 'colouring' the item.
- Identify the main 'teaching points' the audience should understand, i.e. What is this item about? What is the crucial point (or points) the audience should grasp?
- Find the appropriate method of presentation (shots, structure, narrative) to hold the audience's attention.
- Involve the viewer by pace, brevity (e.g. no redundant footage) and relevance (e.g. How does it affect me? Can I empathize with this situation?).
- Capture the attention by arresting images supported by lucid and appropriate narration and exposition.
- Although news is often an unplanned, impromptu shoot, the transmitted item should end up as a seamless flow of relevant shots spliced together to meet the standard conventions of continuity editing.
- Balance the shooting ratio (too much footage, and it cannot be edited in the time scale available) against sufficient coverage to proved flexibility as the story develops over time, to allow the editor to cut the item down to the required running time.

What increases subjectivity?

Subjectivity is increased by restaging the event to serve the needs of television (e.g. re-enacting significant action which occurred before the camera arrived), and by selecting only 'action' events to record. For example, violent demonstrations as opposed to discussion about the subject, or a police car chase rather than routine police work of computer checks through a data base. Also the use of standard 'invisible' technique editing can distort an objective report (e.g. the compression of time, selecting only action aspects of the story).

Editing is selection and can produce a partial account of an event. For example, a football match can be cut down to a 30-second 'highlights' report of the match and make it a great deal more exciting than the match witnessed by the crowd at the stadium.

Although there is an attempt to avoid these 'entertainment' aspects of story telling in news reportage, they are often unavoidable due to the nature of the news item or the demands of attracting viewers.

Magazine items

Like news, magazine items often attempt to capture spontaneous action and present an event objectively. But whereas news is generally topical information of the day, shot on the day, magazine themes and issues are shot over a period of time. A news item may have a duration of less than thirty seconds while a 'feature' report can run for three to five minutes. All these factors have a bearing on the camera techniques that are used on the different genres.

News attempts to emphasize fact rather than opinion, although journalistic values cannot escape subjective judgements. Feature items can use fact, feeling and atmosphere, argument, opinion, dramatic reconstruction and subjective impressions which can be very similar to standard feature film story telling. Non-topical items can be filmed and edited, and often shelved as stand-by or they can be used to balance the programme when required. Without the immediate pressure to transmit, they can have more considered post production (e.g. the addition of music and effects).

Diary events

Many topics that are featured in news and magazine programmes are known about a long time before the event occurs. These 'diary' events allow forward planning and efficient allocation of people and time. They also provide the opportunity for advanced research and a location shoot can be structured and more considered.

Even if a 'diary' item is considered to be predictable and straightforward, be flexible on the day and be prepared for the unexpected (e.g. an unexpected demonstration by protesters in the middle of a VIP tour).

Abstract items

Many issues dealt with by factual programmes are often of an abstract nature which at first thought have little or no obvious visual equivalent. Images to illustrate such topics as inflation can be difficult to find when searching for visual representations. Often the solution, with the above example, is to fall back on clichéd shots of shoppers and cash tills with a great deal of voice-over narration providing the explanations.

Whatever the nature of a news story, there must be an on-screen image, and whatever is chosen, that picture will be invested by the viewer with significance. That significance may not match the main thrust of the item and may lead the viewer away from the topic. For example, a story about rising house prices may feature a couple looking at a house for sale. To the viewer, the couple can easily, inadvertently, become the subject of the story. Consider the relevance of all details in the shot, and have a clear idea of the shape of the item, its structure, and what it is communicating.

Some news items are abstract topics that have no concrete image. Appropriate visual 'wallpaper' needs to be shot to support voice-over information. For example, shots of high street shoppers to accompany a news story about inflation.

Condensing time

A news bulletin has a limited transmission time to present the news of the day. There is always constant pressure, to reduce the running time of a topic. This should be borne in mind when shooting an item. Provide cutaway shots to allow the journalist/editor to compress the actual time of an item to fit the duration allocated in the programme (see Section 8, Editing).

The editor only has a certain amount of time to cut the item. The cameraman can help by remembering:

- to shoot with editing in mind and for hard news, keep shooting ratios low for a fast turnaround in the edit suite.
- it is important to be brief and provide only significant shots for news as tape has to be reviewed in real time before being cut
- with a hard news story, help to reduce the amount of shuttling the editor will be involved in and where ever possible, shoot in sequence and shoot interviews on one tape and cutaways on a second tape
- record each story on a separate tape to allow a separate editor (if required) to work on each story
- record only those shots that are significant and best sum up the essence of the story. Each shot must serve a purpose in telling the story
- the viewer will require a longer on-screen time to assimilate the information in a long shot than the detail in a close shot. Provide more detail than geography shots or scene setting
- avoid long panning or zooming shots. News stories are cut down to the essentials and need the flexibility of editing at any point in the shot
- it is more difficult to edit moving shots than static shots
- provide a higher proportion of static shots to camera movement. It is difficult to cut between pans and zooms until they steady to a static frame and hold
- use short pans (no more than 2 seconds long) to inject pace into story
- moving shots require more perceptual effort to understand than static shots; therefore include more close, static shots than ones with camera movement
- use the 5 second module for news which is:
    - 10 second hold at the start of the pan or zoom
    - 5/10 second camera movement
    - 5/10 second hold at the end of the pan or zoom

this provides the editor with three different shots.

- Check continuity and avoid shooting interviews against a moving background which could 'jump' when edited (e.g. a background to a 10-minute interview of a crowd leaving a stadium after a match which when edited may use comment from the start and the end of the interview and produce a mismatch with a background).
- A substantial change in shot size or camera angle/camera position are needed for shots intending to be intercut.
- Provide relevant but non-specific shots so that voice-over information (to set the scene or the report) can be dubbed on after the script has been prepared.
- Remember to provide adequate run-up time before significant action to allow for a stable shot/syncs for editing.
- Use 'record run' time code rather than 'time-of-day' wherever possible.
- Provide accurate information on cassette or add v/o on tape to identify specific people or events (e.g. on a courtroom exit, identify any significant people in the shot).
- Remember that a casual title given to the item at the morning editorial meeting may change by transmission. Provide a brief description of content on the cassette.
- Have in mind a structure for the shots you provide to allow the editor to create pace, shot variety and fluid continuity.

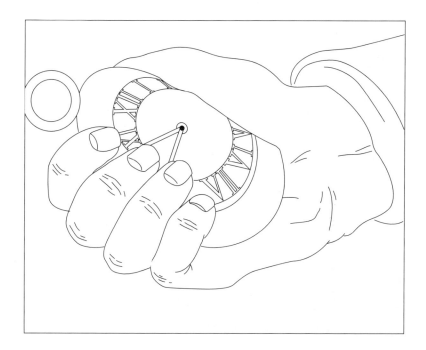

Structure

Hard news by its nature is seldom, if ever, pre-scripted and therefore material is recorded without a written plan. The cameraman with the journalist, needs to shoot with editing in mind and think in terms of a structure for the shots provided. A series of shots have to be meaningfully edited together and this relies on the cameraman anticipating edit points. As it has been emphasized, nothing is more time consuming than an attempt to edit a pile of cassettes of ill-considered footage into some intelligent and intelligible form. To avoid this, the editor requires from the cameraman maximum flexibility with the material supplied, and the nucleus of a structure.

Every shot is recorded for a purpose; that purpose should fit the outline of a possible structure. No shot can exist in isolation. A shot must have a connection with the aim of the item and its surrounding shots. It must be shot with editing in mind. This purpose could be related to the item's brief, script, outline, or decided at the location. It could follow on from an interview comment or reference. It could be shot to help condense time or it could be offered as a 'safety' shot to allow flexibility in cutting the material.

Definition of structure
Structure is arranging the building blocks – the individual unconnected shots, into a stream of small visual messages that combine into a coherent whole. Before a shot is recorded three basic questions need (approximate) answers:

1 The proposed running time of the item in the programme.
2 When will it be broadcast (i.e. how much time is available for shooting, returning the material to base, and then editing/sound dub)?
3 How many locations can be realistically used?

Most news items will not be scripted. There may be a rough treatment outlined by the presenter or a written brief on what the item should cover but an interview may open up new aspects of the story. Without preplanning or a shot list, the shots provided will often revert to tried and trusted formulas. A safe rule-of-thumb is to move from the general to the particular – from wide shot to close up. Offer a general view (GV) to show relationships and to set the scene and then make the important points with the detail of close-ups. The cameraman has to provide a diversity of material to provide a cutting point. Lastly, the structure of a television magazine item is often unplanned, but a location shoot for a two-minute item that results in ten twenty-minute cassettes with no thought to its eventual structure other than a misguided belief that it can all be sorted out in editing will usually mean that the time saved on location avoiding structuring the treatment will be more than quadrupled and lost when the editor attempts to bring order to the chaos he/she is presented with.

A useful shot

An appropriate shot will fulfil one of the following functions in the structure of the piece:

- It emphasizes the essence of the principal subject.
- It provides variation in shot size.
- It gives added prominence to the selected subject.
- It provides more information about the subject.
- It provides for a change of angle/size of shot to allow unobtrusive intercutting.
- It allows for variety of shot and shot emphasis.
- It allows variety of pace by camera or artiste movement.

Unusable shots

Many shots are immediately eliminated because:

- they are not relevant to the story
- they are too short
- significant action has begun before recording is stable
- camera movement is too slow resulting in the duration of the shot becoming too long for the news item (see the 5-second module for news on page 210, Condensing time)
- the speed of the camera movement conflicts with the pace of the story
- continuity mismatch
- size mismatch
- technical imperfections
- out of focus
- shaky
- badly framed
- conflicts with background
- difficulty with time code (e.g. edit controller using 'time-of-day' time code cannot find anticipated code on a rollback for a run-up to an edit – see Assemble edit, p. 142)

Engaging the audience

As we have emphasized, the strongest way of engaging the audience's attention is to tell them a story. Structuring a report is determining what to tell the audience, and when. Cause and effect or question and answer are convenient ways of holding the viewer's interest over time. A factual story can be created by building up a series of details rather than broad generalizations. The crucial decision by the journalist and the cameraman is to determine which visual details are chosen to best illustrate the main theme.

Visual communication and structure

Creating a structure out of the available material will tell a story, present an argument or provide a factual account of an event (or all three). It starts with a series of unconnected shots which are built into small sequences. These are then grouped into a pattern which logically advances the account either to persuade or to provide sufficient information leaving the viewer to draw their own conclusion. Usually the competing point-of-views are underlined by the voice-over but a sequence of strong images will make a greater impact than words. A necessary element to link the selected details is some kind of thread or motif which is easily followed and guides the viewer through the sequence of shots. For example, an item on the widespread colonization of the English countryside by Japanese knotweed, could be structured by walking the reporter and 'expert' along the bank of an infested stream. The walk could be shot starting at a point with a clear stretch of stream, then passing a stretch of weed, and then ending on remedial work being done to clear the stream. Each stage of the walk could be accompanied by actuality sound or voice-over dubbed in editing plus the required cut-in to close-ups relating to the interview comments. The walk is the thread that links the item together. Although this a fairly straightforward treatment, it does need some thought and preparation by the cameraman when constructing the shots (i.e. shoot with a structure in mind), so that normal continuity editing technique can be applied. To inject interest, and to avoid a predictable pattern to an item, not all structures need to lay the events of a story out in simple chronological order.

Any activity must be filmed to provide a sufficient variety of shots that are able to be cut together following standard editing conventions (e.g. avoidance of jump cuts, etc.) and to ensure that there is enough variety of shot to allow some flexibility in editing. Just as no shot can be considered in isolation (what precedes and what follows always has an effect), every sequence must be considered in context with the overall aims of the production.

Piece to camera

Probably the most frequent location shot in news, magazine and other topical programmes is the journalist/presenter speaking straight to camera. It is usually staged so that the keynote image of the item (Houses of Parliament, White House etc.) is the background to the shot.

If it is shot during the day, then care must be taken to find a camera position that allows the reporter to speak to the camera comfortably whilst allowing an exposure balanced between face and background 'topic'. This can often be achieved with the sun at the three quarter back position doubling as backlight and 'side kicker' to the face to provide some modelling. A reflector may be needed to lift the unlit side of the face depending on the intensity of the sun

At night the exposure balance is between the background floodlit building and the foreground presenter. A battery light needs to be filtered or the camera distance adjusted so that a good overall exposure is achieved between face and building.

The other point to consider is background traffic noise and, in a public place, freedom from the occasional eccentric passer-by who decides to stand in the background and divert attention from the presenter. With most public buildings, there is usually one favoured viewpoint marked out by 'tripod marks' from countless camera crews that have been there before.

Interviews

The interview is an essential element of news and magazine reporting. It provides for a factual testimony from a participant or witness to an event. Interviews can be shot in a location that reinforces the story and possibly gives more information to the viewer about the speaker (e.g. office, kitchen, garden, etc.).

Exterior interviews are easier to stage when there is a continuity of lighting conditions such as an overcast day or where there is consistent sunshine. The natural lighting will have to cater for three shots and possibly three camera positions – an MCU of the interviewee, a similar sized shot of the interviewer and some kind of two-shot or 'establishing' shot of them both. If it is decided to shoot the interview in direct sunlight, then the interview needs to be positioned with the sun lighting both 'upstage' faces (i.e. the camera is looking at the shaded side of the face) using a reflector to bounce light into the unlit side of the face. The position of the participants can be 'cheated' for their individual close shots to allow a good position for modelling of the face by the sun. Because of the intensity of sunlight and sometimes because of its inconsistency, it is often preferable to shoot the interview in shade avoiding backgrounds which are in the full brightness of the sun.

Staging an interview

An interview is usually shot using a combination of basic shots which are:

- an MS, MCU or CU of the interviewee
- a matched shot of the interviewer asking questions or reacting to the answers (usually shot after the interview has ended)
- a two-shot which establishes location and relationship between the participants or an over-the-shoulder two shot looking from interviewer to interviewee.

After the interview has been shot, there is often the need to pick up shots of points raised in the interview (e.g. references to objects, places or activity, etc.). In order for normal 'invisible' editing to be applied, the shots should match in size and lens angle between interviewee and interviewer. Sometimes it is necessary for the cameraman, who may be first on the scene of a civil disaster, to get eyewitness statements if a journalist has yet to arrive and there is the possibility that people may leave the scene of the incident. People respond and give more information if they are asked an 'open' question. This is usually an invitation to give an account or description of an event or what happened to them. It can be in the form of 'Tell us what happened to you' or 'What did you see?'. Some questions such as 'Did you see the crash?' can be answered in a single word, 'Yes' or 'No'. These are called 'closed' questions. They close down possible responses from the interviewee. Look for questions that will provoke the fullest response from the witness or participant.

Interview technique

- Agree with the journalist that he/she will start the interview when cued (or take a count of 5) when the camera is up to speed.
- It is useful for editing purposes to precede the interview with details of name and title of the interviewee.
- Remind the reporter and interviewee not speak over the end of an answer.
- Do not allow interviewee to speak over a question.
- Change shot size on question if needed.
- Do cutaways immediately after interview to avoid changes in light level.
- Always provide cutaways to avoid jump cuts when shortening answers.
- Watch that the background to an establishing two-shot is from a different angle to any cutaway shot of the subject. For example, a wide shot of the ruins of a fire is not used later for the background to an interview about the fire. This causes a continuity 'jump' if they are cut together.
- Think about sound as well as picture, e.g. avoid wind noise, ticking clock or repetitive mechanical sound, etc., in background.
- Depending on the custom and practice of the commissioning organization that cut the material, use track 1 for v/o and interview, and use track 2 for effects.
- Iindicate audio track arrangements on the cassette and put your name/story title on the tape.

Going live

The ability to broadcast live considerably increases the usefulness of the camera/recorder format. As well as providing recorded news coverage of an event, a single camera unit with portable links can provide live 'updates' from the location. As the camera will be non-synchronous with the studio production, its incoming signal will pass through a digital field and frame synchronizer and the reconstituted signal timed to the station's sync pulse generator. One advantage of this digital conversion is that any loss of signal from the location produces a freeze frame from the frame store of the last usable picture rather than picture break-up.

Equipment

Cameras with a dockable VTR can attach a portable transmitter/receiver powered by the camera battery in place of the VTR. The camera output is transmitted 'line of sight' to a base antenna (up to 1000 m) which relays the signal on by land line, RF link or by a satellite up-link. Other portable 'line of sight' transmitters are designed to be carried by a second operator connected to the camera by cable.

When feeding into an OB scanner on site, the camera/recorder operator can receive a return feed of talkback and cue lights, whilst control of its picture can be remoted to the OB control truck to allow vision control matching to other cameras. It can therefore be used as an additional camera to an outside broadcast unit. In this mode of operation it can supply recorded inserts from remote parts of the location prior to transmission. During transmission the camera reverts to being part of a multi-camera shoot. Unless there is very rapid and/or continuous repositioning, mount the camera on a tripod.

Communications

Good communications are essential for a single camera operator feeding a live insert into a programme. Information prior to transmission is required of 'in and out' times, of duration of item and when to cue a 'front of camera' presenter. A small battery-driven 'off air' portable receiver is usually a valuable addition to the standard camera/recorder unit plus a mobile phone.

SNG

Satellite news gathering (SNG) consists of a camera/recorder feeding into a small portable dish aerial transmitting a signal up to a satellite in geosynchronous orbit which relays the signal back to a base station. This allows live coverage of events from locations inaccessible to normal land line or terrestrial links equipment.

Ku-band and C-band

Whilst C-band satellite uplinks and downlinks share frequency bands allocated to common carrier microwave systems, Ku-band satellite systems have exclusive use of their allocated frequency band, and therefore are not restricted by sharing considerations. C-band satellites are limited to lower, downlink power levels to avoid interference with terrestrial microwave systems. Ku-band satellites have no such limitation and can operate at higher power within the limitations of the power source of the satellite. This generally permits the use of smaller downlink antennas in the Ku-band although Ku-band signal transmissions are subject to degradation from heavy rainfall, particularly in the tropics; C-band transmissions, however, suffer negligible attenuation when passing through belts of high rainfall.

Elevation angle

The elevation of the path to the satellite above the horizontal (the look angle), is critical to establishing an SNG link. A low elevation angle of the satellite just above the horizon can cause problems (see orbital arcs opposite). Careful site selection is therefore important to ensure a clear line-of-sight to the designated satellite. The antenna requires protection against strong winds which could shift the antenna's precise alignment to the satellite.

SNG set-up

The process involved in establishing an SNG link from location to a base station involves aligning the antenna onto the correct satellite using compass and azimuth bearings and if available, the transmitted beacon identification. Polarization is checked and the correct vision transmission frequency and communication transmission frequency is selected. The antenna signal radiation can damage electronic equipment (including camera/recorders!) and people, if they are in direct line of sight of the beam. Check for clearance before switching on the high-powered amplifier (HPA) to warm-up and then to stand-by. Contact the satellite operation centre (SOC) to confirm channel and booked time and seek permission to 'come-up' for line-up. Permission is given to transmit a clean carrier followed by a gradual increase in transmission power of colour bars and identification. Instant full power can damage the satellite transponder. Finally, check with base station that it is receiving a good strength signal.

Geosynchronous orbit

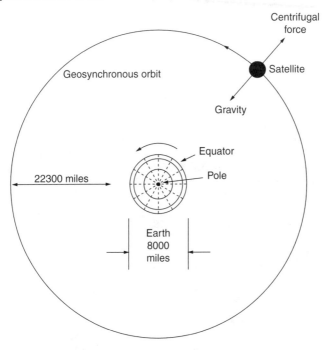

In order that an SNG unit can continuously transmit an unbroken signal without constantly realigning its dish aerial, the satellite must be placed in an orbit stationary above the earth. This is achieved by placing the satellite in an orbit 22,300 miles from the earth where it is held in place by the balance between the opposing force of the gravity pull of earth against the centrifugal force pulling it out into space. Geosynchronous orbit (GEO) satellites revolve at the same rotational speed as the earth and appear stationary from the earth's surface. Signals can be transmitted to and from them with highly directional antennas pointed in a fixed direction. It is the satellites' fixed position in relation to earth that has allowed the growth of small, portable dish transmitters.

Orbital arcs

The number and position of the satellites located in this orbital arc 23,300 miles above the earth, are regulated by a number of world-wide authorities. The satellites are positioned, after the initial launch, by a gas thruster which ensures they keep their position 2° from adjacent satellites. Frequencies used for communications transmission are grouped into Ku-band (10.7–18 GHz) and C-band (3.7–4.2 GHz). The Ku-band is almost universally used for portable SNG service because the antennas are smaller for a given beam width due to the shorter wavelength, and the freedom from interference to and from microwave systems.

There are problems with transmission paths to satellites positioned close to the horizon and therefore some orbital slots are more favourable than others. A minimum elevation angle of 10° to 20° for Ku-band is required to avoid difficulty in clearing buildings, trees, and other terrestrial objects, atmospheric attenuation, and electrical noise generated by heat near the earth's surface.

Further reading

Multi-skilling

Ward, Peter, Bermingham, Alan and Wherry, Chris, *Multiskilling for Television Production*, Focal Press, Oxford, 2000.

Audio

Amyes, Tim, *Audio Post-production in Video and Film*, Focal Press, Oxford, 1996.

Nesbit, Alec, *The Use of Microphones*, Focal Press, Oxford, 1993.

Watkinson, John, *Introduction to Digital Audio*, Focal Press, Oxford, 1994.

Watkinson, John, *Audio for Television*, Focal Press, Oxford, 1997.

Rumsey, Francis, *MIDI Systems and Control*, Focal Press, Oxford, 1994.

Rumsey, Francis and Watkinson, John, *The Digital Interface Handbook*, Focal Press, Oxford, 1995.

Rumsey, Francis and McCormick, Tim, *Sound and Recording – An Introduction*, Focal Press, Oxford, 1997.

Camerawork

Dancyger, Ken, *The Technique of Film and Video Editing*, Focal Press, Oxford, 1997.

Broadcast Equipment Group, Canon Inc, *TV Optics 11*, 1992.

Hunt, Dr R.W.G., *The Reproduction of Colour in Photography, Printing and Television,* Fountain Press, 1989.

Ray, Sidney F., *Applied Photographic Optics*, Focal Press, Oxford, 1994.

Ward, Peter, *Composition for Film and TV*, Focal Press, Oxford, 1996.

Ward, Peter, *Multi-Camera Camerawork*, Focal Press, Oxford, 1997.

Ward, Peter, *Basic Betacam and DVCpro Camerawork*, Focal Press, Oxford, 1998.

Engineering

Bermingham, Alan, Talbot-Smith, Michael, Angold-Stephens, Ken and Boyce, Ed, *The Video Studio*, Focal Press, Oxford, 3rd edn, 1994.

Hodges, Peter, *An Introduction to Video Measurement*, Focal Press, Oxford, 1996.

Inglis, Andrew F. and Luther, Arch C. *Satellite Technology,* Focal Press, 1997.

Rumsey, Francis and Watkinson, John, *The Digital Interface Handbook*, Focal Press Oxford, 1995.

Steinberg, Victor, *Video Standards*, Snell & Willcox, 1994.

Watkinson, John, *An Introduction to Digital Video*, Focal Press, Oxford, 1994.

Watkinson, John, *Television Fundamentals*, Focal Press, Oxford, 1996.

White, Gordon, *Video Techniques*, Focal Press, Oxford, 1988.

Wood, James, *Satellite Communications*, Newnes/Butterworth-Heinemann, Oxford, 1994.

220

Lighting

Bermingham, Alan, *Colour Temperature Correction & Neutral Density Filter in TV Lighting,* The Society of TV Lighting Directors, 1989.

Carlson, V. and S.E. *Professional Lighting Handbook,* Focal Press, Oxford, 1991.

Fitt, B. and Thornley, J., *Lighting Technology,* Focal Press, Oxford, 1997.

Gregory, R.L., *Eye and the Brain. The Psychology of Seeing,* World University Library, London, 1967.

Huntington, John, *Control Systems for Live Entertainment,* Focal Press, Oxford.

Millerson, Gerald, *TV Lighting Methods,* Focal Press, Oxford, 1999.

Moody, James L., *Concert Lighting Techniques,* Focal Press, Oxford, 1998.

Box, Harry C. (edited by Brian Fitt), *The Gaffer's Handbook,* Focal Press, Oxford, 1999.

Sandstrom, Ulf, *Stage Lighting Controls,* Focal Press, Oxford, 1997.

Safety

Health & Safety Executive, *Camera Operations on Location (Safety),* Crown Copyright 1997.

Glossary

A/D conversion Converting an analogue signal into a digital signal.

AES/EBU (American Engineering Society/European Broadcasting Union) Standards organizations who, amongst other specifications, have both defined the interface to connect digital audio signals.

Actuality event Any event that is not specifically staged for television that exists in its own time scale.

Ad lib shooting Impromptu and unrehearsed camera coverage.

Alarm control Control of audible warning through speaker of camera/recorder of a fault condition in camera or VTR fault.

Aliasing Incorrect sampling due to input frequencies exceeding one-half of the sampling rate.

Amplitude Maximum height of a waveform or signal.

Analogue signal A varying voltage signal.

Angle of view The horizontal angle of view of a specific focal length lens. Angle of view varies with a zoom lens.

ASA (American Standards Association) A method of rating the speed of film. Replaced by International Standards Organization, ISO, or Exposure Index, EI.

As-directed Unrehearsed camera coverage controlled at any moment by the director.

Aspect ratio The proportion of the picture width to its height.

Aston A collective name for any text generator (e.g. 'hoover' for a vacuum cleaner, 'biro' for a ball point pen).

Assembly edit Recording process where the video, audio and time code are recorded, in sequence, to a blank tape.

Attenuation Reduction of signal level.

Auto-gain An electronic circuit which automatically adjusts audio recording level to keep within prescribed limits.

Auto iris Automatic adjustment of the iris depending on main subject luminance.

Azimuth The azimuth on an audio tape machine is correct when the record head is at a right angle to the tape.

Back focus See Flange-back.

Backlight Lamp used to separate subject from the background by rim lighting the subject from upstage.

Balance The relative level between sound sources or light sources.

Balanced line Connection of audio signals where the two signal paths are kept separate from earth.

Bandwidth The range of frequencies required for successful transmission of audio (20 kHz) or television (PAL, 5.5 MHz).

Barndoors Hinged metal flaps on the front of a lamp used to control the spread of light.

Bars see Colour bars.

Bass Lower end of the frequency spectrum.

Battery lamp Small battery powered lamp often mounted on top of the camera.

Bias High frequency signal added to the audio during the magnetic recording process.

Big close-up (BCU) A description of the size of a shot. When applied to the face, the frame only includes the point of the chin to mid-forehead.

Betacam format 12.5 mm tape cassette video format recording, on two adjacent video heads, the luminance signal (Y) and a chroma signal consisting of a compressed time division multiplex of the colour difference signals (R – Y and B – Y).

Bitstream A series of binary digits.

Bit A unit of binary code.

Black balance Automatic adjustment of the black level of the camera.

Black level The amplitude of the television video signal representing the darkest part of the picture.

Black wrap Black anodized aluminium foil used to control spill light or shaping a light beam.

Blonde A 2000 W portable lamp.

Bouncing A method of transferring audio from one track to another. Also a method of obtaining a soft light source from a hard source.

BNC A twist-lock cable connector often used on monitor video cables.

Breaker button Automatic cut-out of power supply to electronic equipment if overload is detected.

Brightness A term often incorrectly used to mean luminance. Brightness is a subjective effect, it is how bright we see an object.

Bus A connection point in a sound desk for a number of signals.

Butterfly A large frame to hold nets, silks or blacks measuring 6 × 6 ft, 12 × 12 ft or 20 × 20 ft.

C-mount Standard broadcast video lens mount.

C10 rate A slow charge of constant current equal to $\frac{1}{10}$ of the ampere-hour rating of the battery. A safe extended charge rate that will not produce a build up of oxygen.

Camera angle The position of the camera relative to the main subject in the shot.

Camera left Left of frame as opposed to the artiste's left when facing camera.

Camera right Right of frame as opposed to the artiste's right when facing camera.

Camera sensitivity Quoted in relation to a subject with peak white sensitivity, scene illuminance (lux), f-number of lens and signal-to-noise ratio for a stated signal.

Candela The unit of measurement of the luminous intensity of a lamp.

Canting the camera Angling the camera so that the horizon is not parallel to the bottom of the frame.

Caption generator Electronic equipment that allows text to be created and manipulated on screen via a keyboard.

CCD (charge-coupled device) Converts light into electrical impulses which are compiled into the TV picture format.

Chroma key An electronic process for inserting an artiste (foreground) into a background picture; also known as colour separation overlay (CSO) in the BBC.

223

Chroma Another name for saturation, a control usually found on monitors.

Clean feed An audio source providing a programme participant with all audio signals but excluding own audio contribution.

Clear or clearance The instruction to a cameraman to move to his next position.

Coaxial cable Cable with a central conductor surrounded by a sheath of screening.

Coincident pair Two microphones that are effectively in the same position.

Coloration Unpleasant effect where sound is repeated with a small time delay. This may occur where two microphones pick up the same sound.

Colour balance see White balance.

Colour bars A special test signal used in colour television.

Colour temperature A convenient way to describe the colour of a light source by relating it to a black body radiator, e.g. heated poker, measured in Kelvins (K) after Lord Kelvin (physicist).

Component The individual or difference signals from the red, blue and green channels and luminance signal.

Composite The colour signals encoded (combined) with the luminance signal. Also, old definition for luminance signal plus synchronizing pulses.

Compression The process of reducing the amount of signal data that is required to be passed through a finite channel whilst endeavouring to maintain the quality of the originating signal. Also a method of reducing the range of audio levels.

Condenser A type of microphone using charged plates to transfer sound pressure changes into electrical signals.

Convergence In a monitor, the ability to converge all three television rasters to make a single raster.

Cookie or cucoloris A perforated plate used in front of a luminaire to break up the light beam producing a dapple effect.

Console Audio mixing device with many inputs.

Contrast ratio The ratio between the brightest part of the subject and the darkest part.

Control track A regular pulse recorded on video tape to identify the position of the video signal and tape speed.

Cosine law A law which follows the cosine 0°–90°.

Crash zoom Either an intentionally maximum speed zoom or an 'emergency' fast zoom to recompose 'on-shot'.

Crib card Camera card attached to the side of the camera describing the planned shots and production information connected with that camera.

Crossing the line Moving the camera to the opposite side of an imaginary line drawn between two or more subjects after recording a shot of one of the subjects. This results in intercut faces looking out of the same side of frame and the impression that they are not in conversation with each other.

Cross talk Unwanted signal picked up between adjacent signal cables or from one audio track to another.

224

CSO (colour separation overlay) see Chroma key.

CTDM Compressed time division multiplexed chrominance recording; part of the Betacam method of recording.

Close-up (CU) Shot size. When applied to the face, the top of the frame rests on the top of the head and the bottom of the frame cuts at the position of a knotted tie if worn.

Cue A particular lighting condition or an indication for action to start, i.e. actor to start performing or lighting change to start.

Cursor A vertical or horizontal line that can be positioned by the cameraman in the viewfinder as a reminder of a precise frame position or to check a vertical or horizontal visual element.

Cut to line The video source selected as the output of the vision mixing panel.

Cutaway Cutting away from the main subject or master shot to a related shot.

Cutter As Flag but long and narrow, usually used to darken off the top of a set.

Cyclorama A general purpose background curtain, usually off-white.

DAT Digital audio tape.

DCC (dynamic contrast control) Compresses highlights of the picture to allow a greater contrast range to be recorded.

Decibels (dB) A logarithmic ratio of changes in sound intensity similar to the ear's logarithmic response to changes in sound intensity.

Density A measure of the light transmitted by a film or filter.

$$\text{Density} = \log_{10} \frac{1}{\text{Transmission}} = \log_{10} \text{Opacity}$$

Depth of field The zone of acceptable focus in the field of view.

Dichroic filter A mixture of glass layers with different refractive indices, designed to reflect one colour whilst passing other colours through. Commonly used on battery lamps to convert the colour temperature of tungsten to daylight, and in light splitting blocks.

Diffuser Material which scatters the light to create a softer light source.

Digital A data stream of individual binary numbers representing an unbroken variable value.

Digital injection (DI) A method of directly connecting an audio output from a musical instrument or other audio equipment to a balance audio input.

Digital manipulation Rearranging and recombining small elements (pixels) of an image.

Dimmer An electronic device for controlling the light output from a light source. Usually a thyristor or silicon controller rectifier (SCR), but recent developments have included the transistor dimmer.

Dingle Branches placed in front of a luminaire to create a dapple effect or in front of a lens to create a foreground feature.

Discharge light source Lamps which produce light by ionizing a gas contained in a bulb.

Display mode Selecting particular information about the camera to be displayed in the viewfinder.

Distortion Unwanted damage to an analogue signal that results in the output of a system being different from the original.

DMX 512 Digital multiplex system for sending dimmer/moving light information down one pair of wires.

Dolby A noise reduction process used in audio recording and playback.

Downlink The signal path between satellite and receiver.

Down stage Moving towards the camera or audience.

Dropout The short loss of a recorded signal due to faulty head-to-tape contact or tape imperfections.

Dry Describes the inability of a performer either to remember or to continue with their presentation.

Dynamic range The relationship of the highest value to the lowest value of sound intensity or picture brightness that can be reproduced.

EBU (European Broadcasting Union) Advisory and regulatory body for broadcasting in Europe.

E-E (electronics to electronics) A VTR facility switch which enables the signal to bypass the recording head.

Edited master The final version of edited material that will be seen by the viewer.

EDL Edit decision list created to define the in and out points of an edit sequence.

Effects (Fx) Visual or audio effects.

EFP (electronic field production) Term used to describe single camera location video programme making other than news.

Electronic shutter An electronic method of varying the length of exposure time of the CCD. Can be used to improve the slow motion reproduction of motion.

Encode The technique of combining colour information with a luminance (monochrome) signal.

ENG (electronic news gathering) The single camera video recording of news events.

Equalization Increase or decrease in the level of chosen audio frequencies.

Entropy The unpredictable part of a signal which has to be transmitted by a compression system if quality is not to be lost.

Establishing shot The master shot which gives the maximum information about the subject.

EVDS (enhanced vertical definition system) A method of reducing motion blur.

Extender An additional lens which can be switched internally in the zoom lens to extend the zoom range of focal lengths.

Eyeline The direction the subject is looking in the frame.

F-number A method of indicating how much light is being allowed to pass through the aperture of the lens.

Face tones Signal derived from face tones, typically (average European face) about 0.5 V.

Fader A control for varying the level of an audio or video signal.

Feed Either a video signal or the cable that carries the signal.

Field One top-to-bottom scanning of an image. Two fields interlaced make up one frame.

Field integration A technique connected with the read out of a CCD where adjacent lines are averaged.

Fill light A light source used to make shadows transparent, i.e. reduce the contrast.

Filter wheels Filter holders of colour correction, neutral density or effects filters that are arranged within the camera to allow for the quick selection, by rotating the wheel, of the required filter combination.

First generation The acquisition medium on which the video signal was first recorded.

Flag A piece of metal or card placed near the front of the luminaire to give a hard edge cut-off to the light beam.

Flange-back The distance from the flange surface of the lens mount to the image plane of the pick-up sensor commonly known as the back focus.

Flight kit A portable set of location lamps and stands able to be packed in a compact container for easy transportation.

Focal length of a compound lens The distance from the principal point of a compound lens (e.g. a zoom lens), to the point at which rays from an object at infinity form the most sharply defined image.

Focus pull Moving the zone of sharpest focus to another subject.

Foot candle Unit of illuminance in imperial units, 1 lumen/ft^2 = 1 foot candle.

Format The method of recording the image (e.g. DVCPRO; S-VHS; Betacam, etc.).

Frame One complete television picture comprising of two interlaced fields or a single film image.

Frame integration A technique connected with the read-out of a CCD where vertical resolution is improved at the expense of motion blur.

Frame interline transfer (FIT) A method of transferring the CCD charge to eliminate vertical smear.

Frame store An electronic device for storing individual video frames.

Frame transfer (FT) The method of transferring the charge vertically from the CCD pixels exposed to the subject, to a duplicate set of pixels.

Free run Frame identification by time code which is set to the actual time of day when the frame was recorded.

Frequency The number of complete cycles per second.

Frequency response The range of frequencies that a particular system can reproduce without distortion.

Fresnel Stepped lens used in the Fresnel spotlight.

Fundamental The original or lowest frequency of a complex signal.

Foldback A feed to allow artists to hear selected sound sources on loudspeakers or headphones.

Gain The amplification of a video or audio signal calibrated in dBs (e.g. +6 dB of video gain is the equivalent of opening the lens iris by 1 stop).

Gaffer The chief lighting electrician.

Gallery Production control room.

Gamma The law of the transfer characteristic of a system, i.e. relationship between input and output signals.

GEO Geosynchronous orbit satellite that revolves at the same rotational speed as the earth and appears stationary from the earth's surface.

Gobo Stainless steel stencil used in profile projectors to create effects, e.g. windows, abstract pattern, moon, etc.

Grads An abbreviation of graduated, applied to front-of-lens filters which progressively filter or colour the picture vertically.

Graticule Engraved calibration scale on the front of waveform monitors and vectorscopes.

Grid area The structure above a studio floor.

Grip Supporting equipment for lighting or camera equipment. Also the name of the technicians responsible for handling grip equipment, e.g. camera trucks and dollies.

GV (general view) This is a long shot of the subject.

HAD (hole accumulated diode) A CCD sensor which increases the proportion of the sensor that can collect light without decreasing resolution.

Hand-held Operating a portable camera without a camera mounting.

Hard light Any light source that casts a well defined shadow.

Harmonic A range of frequencies that are multiples of the fundamental that make up a complex waveform.

Hertz Unit of frequency, 1 Hertz = 1 cycle/second.

High angle Any lens height above eye height.

High key Picture with predominance of light tones and thin shadows.

HMI A discharge lamp producing light by ionizing a gas contained in the bulb.

Hot head A remotely controlled camera pan/tilt head often on the end of a jib arm.

Hue The dominant wavelength, colour describing what we see, e.g. red.

Hyper HAD Increasing the sensitivity of the HAD CCD by the use of a micro lens with each pixel.

Illuminance (illumination) (E) A unit of light measurement for incident light, lumens/m² = lux.

Image size The image formed by the lens on the face of the CCD.

Interlace A method of scanning separate parts of an image in two passes (fields) in order to reduce the bandwidth required for transmission.

Interline transfer (IT) A method of transferring a charge from the pixels exposed to the subject to an adjacent duplicate set of pixels.

Insert edit The adding of video, audio or time code, out of sequence, to a pre-recorded tape.

Insert point An input/output in a system allowing the connection of other equipment.

Inverse square law A fundamental law in lighting and sound where the intensity of light and sound falls off as the inverse of the distance squared.

Invisible technique Production method which emphasizes the content of the shot rather than the production technique.

ISDN (Integrated Services Digital Network) A system that allows the transfer of audio or other data via a telephone line.

Iris Variable circular aperture in the camera used to control exposure, calculated in f-stops.

Isoed Recording the (isolated) output of an individual camera or cameras in a multi-camera shoot in addition to the main recording.

JPEG (Joint Photographic Experts Group) Identifies a standard for the data compression of still pictures.

Kelvin (K) A unit measurement of heat used to describe colour temperature.

Keylight or key The main source of light illuminating the subject.

Key Mood of a picture, i.e. high key/low key.

Key Keying signal for chroma key operations.

Kicker Light used at eye-level from upstage, at eye level to 'kick' the side of the artiste's head.

Knee Modified part of the transfer characteristic of a camera designed to progressively compress highlights.

Ku-band The frequency spectrum between 10.7 GHz and 18 GHz.

Level The volume of an audio or video signal.

Line level A reference audio level measured at 1000 Hz.

Linear matrix Involves cross-coupling between R, G and B to help obtain the desirable analysis characteristics essential for faithful colour reproduction.

Live The transmission of an event as it takes place.

Locked-off Applying the locks on a pan and tilt head to ensure that the camera setting remains in a pre-selected position. Can also be applied to an unmanned camera.

Long lens A lens with a large focal length or using a zoom at or near its narrowest angle of view.

Look angle The angle of elevation of the signal path above the horizon to a satellite.

Low angle A lens height below eye height.

Low key Picture with a predominance of dark tones and strong shadows.

LS (long shot) A description of a shot when the full length human figure fills the frame.

LTC (longitudinal time code) Recorded with a fixed head on a desig-nated track on the tape.

Luminaire Name given for a complete lighting unit, i.e. light source or lamp plus its casing.

Lumen Unit of quantity of light flow per second, 'weighted' by the photopic curve.

Luminance (L) A measure of the light reflected from a surface. A total flux reflected of 1 lumen/m^2 has a luminance of 1 Apostilb. (Imperial measurement 1 lumen/ft^2 = 1 foot lambert).

Luminance signal That part of the video signal which represents the relative brightness points of an image.

Luminous intensity A measure of a lamp's ability to radiate light, measured in candelas (old term, candlepower).

Lux A unit for illuminance; 1 lumen/m^2 = 1 lux.

Macro A switchable facility on a lens that allows focusing on an object placed closer to the lens than the normal minimum object distance (see MOD).

Matrix Electrical circuit for deriving 'mixtures' of signals, e.g. colour difference signals and luminance signals from RGB signals.

Matte box A filter holder and bellows extension for the control of flare, fitted to the front of the lens.

Medium close-up (MCU) A shot description usually describing a framing of a person with the bottom of the frame cutting where a suit breast pocket would normally be.

Medium shot (MS) A description of shot size with the bottom of the frame cutting at the waist when applied to the human figure.

Megahertz (MHz) One million cycles per second.

Metal particle A video tape coating allowing a wider frequency response to be recorded and an improved signal-to-noise ratio compared to oxide tape coating.

Millisecond One thousandth of a second.

Mired Micro reciprocal degree value allows the relationship between a correction filter and the colour temperature shift to be calculated.

MOD Minimum object distance; the closest distance a subject in acceptable focus can be to the lens.

Modelling The action of light revealing contour and texture of a subject.

Monitor termination A switchable electronic 'load' (usually 75 ohms) on the back of a monitor inserted at the end of a video cable feed to prevent the signal 'bouncing back'. If several monitors are looped together, termination only occurs at the last monitor.

Monochrome Reproduction of a single colour such as a black and white image.

Movement blur The degradation of the image related to the speed of subject movement during the exposure time of a single picture.

MPEG2 (Moving Picture Experts Group 2) A series of benchmark values specifying different degrees of compression.

Multi-generation Numerous re-recordings of the original recording.

Neutral density filter A filter which reduces the amount of light transmitted without altering the colour temperature.

Ni-Cad Nickel-cadmium is the constituent of rechargeable batteries widely used to power broadcast camcorders and cameras.

Noddies Television jargon for cutaway shots recorded for editing purposes after an interview showing the interviewer listening and 'nodding' at the interviewee's comments.

Noise reduction A method of reducing the noise on recorded or transmitted analogue audio.

230

NTSC (National Television System Committee) Usually signifies an American method of encoding colour.

OB (Outside Broadcast) Usually a multi-camera production from a non-studio venue using a mobile control room.

Off-line editing Low quality images that are used to produce edit lists or a non-transmittable edited guide tape.

Off-shot describes the camera when its output is not selected at the vision mixing panel to be fed 'to line'.

On-line editing Any system that produces a final edited broadcast quality programme.

On-shot Describes the camera when its output is selected at the vision mixing panel to be fed 'to line'.

Opacity The reciprocal of transmission of light through a film or filter.

Oscillator Equipment to produce pure tone (sine wave) used for lining-up and calibrating systems.

Oscilloscope Cathode ray oscilloscope used to provide a visual display of video signals.

Oxide tape Tape coating used in the first generation of the beta format cameras.

Pad A circuit used to reduce or attenuate the signal level.

PAL (phase alternating line) A European development of the American NTSC system of encoding colour.

Pan-pot (panoramic potentiometer) Adjusts the apparent position of a sound source in a stereo image.

Pulse coded modulated (PCM) Digital transmission system.

Peak white Either 100% video signal level or 60% reflectance neutral grey surface.

Peak white clipper A 'gain limiting' circuit set to the same level in each colour channel of the camera that restricts any signal to a maximum level.

Ped (pedestal) A camera mounting.

Perspective The apparent position of closeness of sound in an image. Also the optical methods used to assess or construct image depth.

Phantom power The DC supply to some types of condenser microphone using the signal cable.

Phase A time delay between two signals. It is expressed in degrees as the actual time will vary with frequency.

Picture monitor Good quality viewing monitor, similar to a receiver but without RF and sound sections.

Pink noise A random signal that appears to the human ear to contain an equal level of frequencies.

Pistol grip Hand grip controlling zoom movement that may be attached to a lightweight lens when operating the camera 'hand-held' or attached to a pan bar.

Pixel (picture cell) A single point in an electronic image.

Planning meetings A meeting of some members of the production staff held for the exchange of information and planning decisions concerning a future programme.

Playback Replaying a recorded shot or sequence of shots or audio.

Point-of-view shot A shot from a lens position that seeks to duplicate the viewpoint of a subject depicted on screen.

PLUGE (Picture Line-up Generating Equipment) Test signal used for alignment of monitor contrast and brightness.

Polecat Adjustable spring loaded aluminium tubes with rubber feet that can be used vertically or horizontally to support lightweight luminaires.

Pole-operation System for remotely adjusting pan/tilt, spot/flood, etc., of luminaires from the studio floor using an operating pole.

Post production Editing and other work carried on pre-recorded material.

Peak programme meter (PPM) This measures sound by averaging the peaks of intensity over a specified period and rapidly responds to high level transients.

Practical An in-shot light source, e.g. wall light.

Prime lens A fixed focal length lens.

Print-through The transfer of magnetic information from one layer of tape to another when stored on a reel.

Production control rooms Production areas on outside broadcasts (see Scanner), or adjacent to studios used by production staff, lighting and audio.

Prompters A coated piece of glass positioned in front of the lens to reflect text displayed on a TV monitor below the lens.

PSC The production method of recording material on a portable single video camera.

Purity In a monitor, the ability of the red gun only to hit red phosphors, etc.

Quantize In a digital system, allocation of 'sample' level prior to coding.

Real time Time code which changes in step with the actual time of day.

Real time The actual running time of an event as opposed to 'screen time'; the compression of time achievable by editing.

Recces the inspection of a location by production staff to assess the practicalities involved in its use as a setting for a programme or programme insert.

Record run Time code which increases only when a recording is made. Record run only records a frame identification when the camera is recording.

Recorded-as-live A continuous recording with no recording breaks.

Redhead A 800 W portable lightweight lamp.

Redundancy When compressing a signal, the part which can be predicted from the signal already received and therefore need not be sent. It is redundant.

Reflector Any white or silvered surface that can be used to reflect a light source.

Reverse angle When applied to a standard two-person interview, a camera repositioned 180° to the immediate shot being recorded to provide a complementary shot of the opposite subject.

Reverberation The gradual decay of reflected sound.

RMS (root mean square) A method of calculating the effective value of an alternating voltage or current.

Robotic camera A camera with a remotely controlled camera head, e.g. pan/tilt, zoom and focus. May also include camera position and height.

Rocking focus Moving the focus zone in front of and behind the selected subject in order to determine sharpest focus.

Sampling rate The number of measurement points over time that describes a continuously variable voltage.

Saturation A measure of the purity of a colour, e.g. pale red or deep red.

Scanner The production control rooms of an outside broadcast production.

Scene file A removable data storage chip from the camera that contains memorized settings.

SECAM (Sequential Couleur à Memoire) A French-developed method of encoding colour.

Shooting off Including in the shot more than the planned setting or scenery.

Shot number A number assigned to a specific shot as detailed in a camera script or camera rehearsal.

Shuttling Rapidly reviewing video tape to determine content or edit point.

Signal to noise The level difference, in dB, between the wanted signal and the unwanted background system noise.

Simple PAL Monitor mode which enables the eye to average out colour errors, i.e. no delay line used. Also enables phase errors to be seen.

Single shot technique The single camera discontinuous recording of a number of shots that are later edited in post production.

Sitcom ('situation comedy') A mini-drama (usually of approximately thirty-minute duration) performed before an audience.

Slo-mo replay Replaying a pre-recording at a slower speed than normal transmission.

SNG (satellite news gathering) The technique of relaying video location news reports or news material via a satellite to a base station.

SOC (satellite operation centre) The control centre of the owner/operator of a satellite.

Soft light A light source that produces a soft-edged shadow.

S/PDIF A consumer version of the AES/EBU digital interface.

SPL Sound pressure level expressed in dB where the reference is the threshold of human hearing.

Spot effects Sounds that relate to short actions, usually in vision.

Star quad A four-core sound cable designed to reduce unwanted interference pick-up.

Station out The programme output being fed to a transmitter, satellite or for cable distribution.

Stereo Usually understood to mean a system of reproducing a wide sound image using two channels.

Stop Either the f-number the lens is set to or the unit change between two standard f-numbers.

Studio out The output of the vision mixing panel.

Switcher see Vision mixer. Note that job titles vary from country to country.

T-number Indicates the amount of light transmitted by a lens at a specific iris setting. Unlike f-numbers, identical T-numbers on lenses will transmit the same amount of light independent of lens design.

T-piece Small BNC connectors to allow teeing of video connectors, e.g. connect two video cables to one video socket.

Talkback Inter-communication by microphone and headset between a television control room and other operational areas and technicians.

Termination 75 Ω resistor included across the video cable at the end of a transmission chain. Inclusion of 75 Ω termination ensures no reflection of energy, and ensures the signal level is correct.

The narrow end of the lens The longest focal length of the zoom that can be selected.

Tight lens A long focal length primary lens or zoom lens setting.

Time code Enables every recorded frame of video to be numbered.

Transformer A device made with two coils wound around a magnetizable core to isolate a signal or to change its voltage.

Transient A fast changing signal.

Transient response The ability of equipment to follow fast changes in level.

Translucent Semi-transparent; usually some form of light diffuser.

Tungsten The filament material in a lamp producing light by heat.

Turtle Very low lighting stand for rigging luminaires at floor level.

Tweak Term used for small adjustments to lighting rig or operational settings, e.g. black level or iris setting.

Tx Abbreviation for transmission.

Uplink The signal path from an earth station to a satellite.

Upstage Moving further away from the camera or audience.

User-bit A programmable identification code compiled by the 'user' of the camera which is recorded as part of the time code on each video frame. User-bit allows up to nine numbers and an A to F code to be programmed into the code word which is recorded on every frame.

VCA Voltage controlled amplifier.

Vectorscope Special oscilloscope designed to display the chrominance information in an easily recognizable way, i.e. hue and saturation.

Video barrel A small in-line adaptor designed to connect two BNC video cables together.

Video contrast range The relationship between the brightest part of the scene and the darkest part.

Video wall A number of individual TV screens often stacked in a rectangle displaying multiple, individual or composite images.

Vignette The shading of the edges of the picture area.

Virtual reality System of chroma key where the background is computer generated. The size and positioning of the background is controlled by the foreground camera movements.

Vision control The person who adjusts camera exposure, colour, gamma, etc., in a multi-camera production. Also applied to the area where they perform this function.

Vision mixer The person who switches between video sources. Also applied to the equipment they use to perform this function.

VITC (vertical interval time code) These are time code numbers recorded in one or more of the unused lines in the TV signal and can be read when the tape is in still frame.

Voice over A commentary mixed with effects or music as part of a sound track.

Vox pops (vox populi) The voice of the people, usually consists of a series of impromptu interviews recorded in the street with members of the public.

VTR Video tape recorder.

VU meter Volume meter indicates average level of sound.

Waveform monitor Oscilloscope with appropriate time-base for displaying the television waveform. Usually includes a face-plate graticule to indicate sync level, black level, peak white and percentage signal level.

Wavelength The length between adjacent peaks of a signal.

White balance The electronic process of defining a reference white lit by a light source of a specific colour temperature.

White noise Random noise containing an equal level of the audio frequency spectrum.

Wide angle The horizontal field of view of a lens greater than approximately 40°.

Wide shot (WS) A description of shot size which includes objects greater than the size of the human figure.

Working behind the camera Operating the camera using remoted lens controls attached to pan bars and a non-monocular viewfinder.

Working-as-live Continuous recording with no opportunity for recording breaks or retakes.

Wow and flutter Variations in speed of a mechanical system, audible as frequency variations in an analogue recording.

Zebra exposure indicator A black and white striped pattern that appears in the viewfinder at points in the picture corresponding to a pre-set video level. Used as an aid to manual exposure.

Zero level voltage A standard reference audio signal of 0.775 V at 1000 Hz used for audio equipment line-up.

Zoom A variable focal length lens achieved by internally moving elements of the lens.

Zoom ratio The ratio of the longest focal length to the shortest focal length a specific zoom lens can achieve.

Zoom tracking A lens pre-focused on a distant subject will stay in a focus for the whole of its zoom movement towards (or away from) that subject, providing the back focus (flange back) has been correctly aligned.

Also available from Focal Press ...

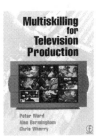

Multiskilling for Television Production
Peter Ward
Alan Bermingham
Chris Wherry

Multiskilling has become an integral part of television culture, requiring that new entrants are competent in a variety of specialist production skills.

Written by television trainers who run their own multiskilling courses, **Multiskilling for Television Production** offers a comprehensive introduction to the range of skills and technical knowledge needed for television production. Anyone baffled by the range and scope of skills to be mastered will find this book invaluable.

❏ A complete guide to the skills, techniques and operational procedures for today's television environment
❏ A quick and easy reference for on the job use
❏ Covers the latest digital technology

April 2000 • 368pp • 246 x 189mm • Paperback
ISBN 0 240 51557 9

To order your copy phone +44 (0)1865 888180 (UK)
Or +1 800 366 2665 (USA)
Or visit our website on **http://www.focalpress.com**

Focal Press

http://www.focalpress.com

Visit our web site for:

- ❏ The latest information on new and forthcoming Focal Press titles
- ❏ Technical articles from industry experts
- ❏ Special offers
- ❏ Our email news service

Join our Focal Press Bookbuyers' Club

As a member, you will enjoy the following benefits:

- ❏ Special discounts on new and best-selling titles
- ❏ Advance information on forthcoming Focal Press books
- ❏ A quarterly newsletter highlighting special offers
- ❏ A 30-day guarantee on purchased titles

Membership is FREE. To join, supply your name, company, address, phone/fax numbers and email address to:

USA
Christine Degon, Product Manager
Email: christine.degon@bhusa.com
Fax: +1 781 904 2620
Address: Focal Press,
225 Wildwood Ave, Woburn,
MA 01801, USA

Europe and rest of World
Elaine Hill, Promotions Controller
Email: elaine.hill@repp.co.uk
Fax: +44 (0)1865 314572
Address: Focal Press, Linacre House,
Jordan Hill, Oxford,
UK, OX2 8DP

Catalogue

For information on all Focal Press titles, we will be happy to send you a free copy of the Focal Press catalogue:

USA
Email: christine.degon@bhusa.com

Europe and rest of World
Email: carol.burgess@repp.co.uk
Tel: +1(0)1865 314693

Potential authors

If you have an idea for a book, please get in touch:

USA
Terri Jadick, Associate Editor
Email: terri.jadick@bhusa.com
Tel: +1 781 904 2646
Fax: +1 781 904 2640

Europe and rest of World
Beth Howard, Editorial Assistant
Email: beth.howard@repp.co.uk
Tel: +44 (0)1865 314365
Fax: +44 (0)1865 314572